Net Value

Other books by Stephen Neill and Peter J. Clark

The Value Mandate

Other books by Peter J. Clark

Beyond the Deal

Net Value

Valuing Dot-Com Companies—
Uncovering the Reality
behind the Hype

Peter J. Clark and Stephen Neill
www.vbm-consulting.com

AMACOM
American Management Association
New York • Atlanta • Boston • Chicago • Kansas City • San Francisco • Washington, D.C.
Brussels • Mexico City • Tokyo • Toronto

Library of Congress Cataloging-in-Publication Data

Clark, Peter J., 1950-
    Net Value: valuing dot-com companies: uncovering the reality behind the hype/ Peter J. Clark, Stephen Neill.
    p. cm.
Includes bibliographical references and index.
ISBN: 0-8144-0604-1
1. Corporations—Valuation. 2. Electronic commerce. 3. Internet industry—Finance. I. Neill, Stephen, 1963- II. Title.

HG4028.V3 C58 2000
658.15—dc21
                                     00-063941

Printing number

10 9 8 7 6 5 4 3 2 1

Dedicated to
Charles, Courtnay, Oliver, Kristen, Patrick, JCLG

Have you seen the new cloth?
It is extraordinary.
But fools cannot see it.

The Emperor's New Clothes

The market price is frequently out of line with true value;
there is an inherent tendency for these disparities to correct themselves.

Benjamin Graham, in the 1930s

CONTENTS

ACKNOWLEDGMENTS

We are grateful to the active participation of a wide range of people and organizations who made this book possible.

First, we would like to give thanks for the constructive insights and comments of senior management from past and present VBM Consulting client firms on specific topics in their areas of specialization.

Special thanks are extended to those who participated in interviews with one or both of the authors. Interviewees include (companies in parentheses): Mark Walsh (VerticalNet), Aram Fuchs (www.fertilemind.net), David Levin (Psion), Peter Pervere (Commerce One), Graham Sadd (Infobank), Paul Gibbs (JP Morgan), Jack Willoughby (*Barron's*), Henry A. Davis (HD Research), Philip Coggan (*Financial Times*), Jim Seymour (Seymour Group, also contributor to TheStreet.com), Jeff Bronchick (Reed, Conner & Birdwell, also TheStreet.com), Fred Barbach (*Washington Post*), Kambiz Foroohar (formerly TheStreet.com), Patrick Dorsey (Morningstar), Craig Karmin (*The Wall Street Journal*), Jesse Eisinger (*The Wall Street Journal*), Prof. Aswath Damodaran (Stern School, NYU), Joseph Beaulieu (Morningstar), Justin Lahart (TheStreet.com), Ryan Alexander (WitSoundView), and Jennifer Friedlin (TheStreet.com and *The New York Times*).

We also wish to thank Andy Ambraziejus and Ray O'Connell of Amacom Books, who almost make this work easy and certainly make it enjoyable. Also, David Seham, whose effective work under tight time schedule is greatly appreciated, and Stuart Crainer, who originally introduced us to that organization.

Mark Gooding and Jane Landells did yeoman work on this book, pulling them away from other VBM Consulting work. Consulting goddess Juliana Rowe did fantastic work in helping with the editing. Finally, we thank our families and friends and clients, who are always more reasonable that we have a right to expect in the case of an intensive exercise such as this.

LISTING OF EXHIBITS

Chapter 8: Aftermath

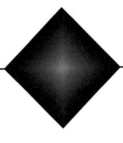

INTRODUCTION

NetPhase I: the Commercial Internet's wild, explosive, deliberately excessive buyer feeding-frenzy initial period.

Born 1996,
Died April 14, 2000

We're on the verge of . . . the biggest structural change in the economy in 50 to 70 years. Today e-commerce is only 2% of the (United States) economy. In five years, I think we'll see 20%. Last year was the first year of recognition of the whole [B2B] space, so now you're talking about only the second year of a bull market.

Alberto Vilar of Amerindo Investment Advisors,
in "The Best Is Yet to Come," July 3, 2000 [1]

This is not a book about bubbles.

This is a book about the Internet champion segments and companies poised to soar in netPhase II—our shorthand term for the imminent second major period of the Commercial Internet (netPhase I ended April 14, 2000). Phase II is when the Dot-Coms grow up. When the leaders of these companies move beyond just trying to achieve minimum profitability to fulfilling the complete promise of the Net.

Unlike netPhase I, where many Surfbuzz.coms and other e-Bankruptcy2001.coms were shoved through an overly accommodating IPO structure in the shortest possible time, the Phase II champion's path is directed to building No. 1 or No. 2 leaders in high value Internet segments. These are segments where 40/40 critical mass is achieved, which means 40+% penetration of the Net to total demand (we go beyond the Vilar quote, above), *plus* a 40% stake of the Net's segment controlled by that champion Dot-Com company.

The champion's path is directed at creation of the enduring Internet wealth, which means creating the new major Internet corporations of the 21st century through the combination of one, revitalized market-value propositions, two, accelerated internal growth, and three, active programs of industry consolidation.

NetPhase II Dot-Com corporations will be financed through new forms of syndicate-based, Dot-Com-directed secondary financing, yet to emerge. The syndicates will be led by people with the energy and insight to help build the dozen or so enduring major Net companies of the early 21st century.

These people will not be distracted by near-term anguish about whether the failure rate of hundreds of small B2C IPOs before January 1, 2002, is 70% or 85%.

You see, we believe that obituary notices for netPhase I and the Vilar quote at the beginning of this introduction are *not* in conflict. To the contrary, the frothy, consumer-myopic netPhase I had to stumble and crash in order to make the Real Net possible.

The important part of the southwestern Pennsylvania oil boom of the late 1800s was neither the dizzying surge nor the crushing collapse, *but the major industry that emerged later*. It was the same in the automobile industry, and the same in electric utilities. Five to seven years after it started, the irresistible, explosive first-growth spurt period imploded—just like netPhase I.

Is the Net a one-off phenomenon? In many ways, the Net is right on the curve of major product/service categories that change peoples' lives (see Figure 0.1). And the early extreme excess of netPhase I is just part of the stage-setting for what is to come: netPhase II, when the Dot-Coms grow up, when the major new corporations of the 21st century begin to be built, and when the new Internet champions soar.

Who Should Read This Book

You should. Unless you live in a cave someplace, the winding down of netPhase I and the winding up of its successor period affect every aspect of your work and parts of your life. Industry observers, investors, shareholders, and others who have endured both sides of the March 10, 2000, Nasdaq Composite peak are hungry to know about the imperatives and the opportunities that netPhase II promises. They will find that out, here.

More specifically, leaders of major Internet firms (and those who are driven to become leaders) can use this book to understand what has happened in the Net boom so far, why the best is still to come, and how to get there.

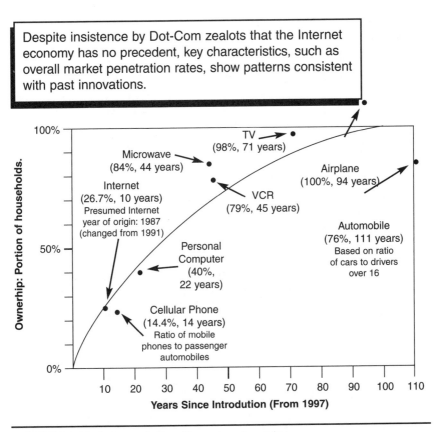

Despite insistence by Dot-Com zealots that the Internet economy has no precedent, key characteristics, such as overall market penetration rates, show patterns consistent with past innovations.

FIGURE I.1. Market penetration: Time since invention.

Financiers will find this book to be a resource for dealing with a wide range of situations and companies, from the living-dead Dot-Coms that cannot survive without continual infusions of cash that will probably never be repaid, to the pre-champion major Dot-Coms that require flexible multi-year financing, not just stop-gap patches, to soar. [2]

Chapters of This Book

Chapter 1 provides a broad and topical overview of a variety of Dot-Com valuation approaches, their uses, their misuses, and the motivation underlying those choices and approaches.

Chapters 2, 3, and 4 address different aspects of the Commercial Internet's first phase, as these developments directly impact conditions and realities faced today.

Chapter 5 looks at the shakeout itself: how, why, and how much further lower the re-valuation that is, of the Dot-Com tier must go. Chapter 6 looks at the key issues as the world moves to the Net's new second phase. Chapter 7 focuses on B2B, which we believe will be a source of several of the Net champion segments and firms in the second phase.

Chapter 8, the book's final chapter, looks at key issues going forward. One issue involves the case for what we refer to as the "super tech" 70 to 130 times P/E ranges. This record valuation reflects the Net's true value potential, and yet it has a lifeline to reality.

The best is yet to come. But only for those willing to glance backwards at the excesses and false valuations of netPhase I, and then apply the lessons from that period to excel in netPhase II.

Notes

1. John H. Christy, *Forbes Global*, 124. A slightly expanded version of the full Vilar quote is found at the beginning of the book's Chapter 5.
2. Acknowledgment to Perkins and Perkins and *Red Herring* (www.redherring.com) for the phrase "living dead." And of course, for the reference to "bubble" found at the beginning of this introduction.

Chapter 1

WHO IS THE DOT-COM COMPANY VALUATION?

The Miracle has already happened, and the Internet stocks are still priced as if Baby Jesus is about to be born.

Aram Fuchs, *Upside Today*[1]

To get at the answer of what the company is actually worth, it isn't particularly fruitful to look at the world the way security analysts do.

Jesse Eisinger, *The Wall Street Journal*[2]

To understand the netPhase I (1996 to spring 2000) valuation calamity accurately, you have first to single out the real problem. Then, to benefit from that understanding during the Net's second major phase—which started sometime in 2000—entrepreneurs, financiers, and management of key surviving Dot-Coms, investors, and shareholders must all be skilled at separating the cyber-wheat from the chaff.

The tougher, successor financing system now being constructed in fits and starts doesn't tolerate cyber-chaff. The new phase will be nothing like the first wild feeding frenzy phase of the Net, when e-Bankruptcy2001.com could easily be sold to the public for billions of dollars even though its chances of survival were less than three in ten.

So as the Meshkin brothers, Alex (19) and Brian (23), founders of our netPhase I poster-child company, Surfbuzz.com ("[Our business model] is borderline crazy"), might say, *Dude, all you had to do was look at the company's name. Like duh.*

Surfbuzz.com ceased operations on June 6, 2000.[3]

Why the Market Has Difficulty Valuing E-Bankruptcy2001.com

Or 2002.com. Or 2003.com. Or 2004.com.

Funny thing, the many kinds of valuation approaches (Figure 1.2) range from complex three-letter-acronym proprietary models carefully preened and buffed by their owners like vintage Jaguar XKEs, to homespun twaddle, with little or nothing to them, developed by pundits with little more than front and the correct sense that none of the other valuation methods are perfect.

Even if there might have been one overall best category in the past, based on pioneering research and empirical analysis by management consultants McKinsey & Co. (Figure 1.5), that doesn't necessarily mean anything now.

This is what it says right there in the small print of the prospectus of that Net turkey that you bought at $20/share in May 1999, only to see it soar to $90 in November 1999, and then plunge to $5/share now: *Past performance is not necessarily indicative of the results you can expect in the future.*

Seventy Percenters Brought to Market Too Early

Of course, there's no problem with the valuation of the most terrifying of companies, the Dot-Com pure start-ups with at *best* three chances out of ten of surviving a couple years, much less

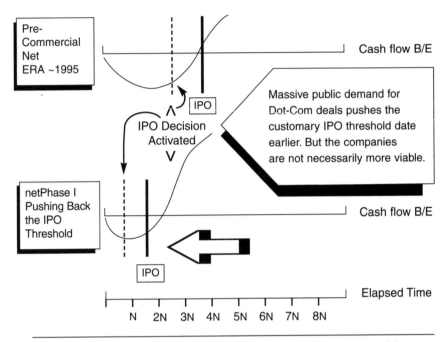

FIGURE 1.1. Bringing the non-investment-quality (NIQ) company public.

thriving. These are infant companies, far from being ready for the marketplace.

Don't worry. For good reason, these raw, unproven Boo.coms and Surfbuzzes and Toysmarts of the world remain cloistered within venture capital organizations, where they are valued at one dollar until there is rock-solid proof otherwise.

A 70+ % insolvency risk suggests that it would be irresponsible to do anything else. No one at Dot-Com Packagers wants to risk making their next URL www.Leavenworth.com.

And of course, those Not-Ready-for-Public-Market players are never, ever permitted to come to market prematurely, lest the valuation issue be forced on markets and companies before either is ready. After all, no one in his right mind can possibly imagine how to value a company with a 70% or higher chance of failure.

Figure 1.2. Dot-Com company valuation: WHO is the question.

Advocate Group	Valuation Methodology	Positives of Approach	Negatives	Implications
(A) Objective, Detached Observers	Discounted cash flow (DCF) of management's projected free cash flow, INCLUDING assumptions for defensible business and financial risk, primary analysis term	No contamination of input data to reach pre-determined goal Not an advocate Only method proven by correlation to changes in market value (MV)	Reduces flotations: reduces number of Non-Investment Quality (NIQ) Dot-Coms becoming IPOs Doesn't fully explain elevated market values for most of netPhase I 1997-Spring 2000	Stratospheric Dot-Com valuations perceived as extended abberation -Spring Break' 2000 seen as the beginning of a return towards more rational valuation structure
(B) Pre-IPO Packagers, I Investment Bankers, Some Venture Capitalists	Base structure of (A) DCF, methodology above, but with tough-to-defend components such as (1) 15-year periods of comparative advantage (t) for companies that only last three years in industries that only survive of five; (2), low risk assumptions grossly out-of-step with market realities	Enough surface resemblance to proven methodology, above, to ensure at least initial credibility Advocate is able to "price" (value) NIQ companies for IPO Fees	Radical swings in market value undermine credibility of "Contaminated DCF" Lowers quality standards for public market quality	Re-(that is, de-) valuation eventually forced by an unforgiving marketplace that eventually obtains enough information to function once again Radical "advocacy elements" discredited

Figure 1.2. Dot-Com company valuation: WHO is the question (continued).

Advocate Group	Valuation Methodology	Positives of Approach	Negatives	Implications
(C) Pre-IPO Packagers, II **Mostly Venture** **Some Angel Capitalists, Investors, All Pursuing Rich IPO Payout**	Mostly market value-to-revenue multiples, supported by some operations data, e.g., subscribers, hits, other volume indication	Ease of calculation Simplistic "rules of thumb" displace more complex (but also more systematic investigation) Fees	Very poor correlation of changes in EPS to changes in market value (Figure 1.5b) Operations surrogates underestimate churn, ease of competitor entry Revenue distortion, especially when revenue swaps with troubled Dot-Coms are involved	Advocates' objectives have little to do with Dot-Com company's worth Even greater risk of Non-Investment Quality (NIQ) companies making it to IPO as (B)
(D) "Reachers" **Various Parties Attempting to Justify the Case for Massive Short-term Price: Appreciation Guru Wannabes, Instant Investment Letters**	Bits or random data-bits laced together to create an apparent "Can't Miss" story	Even easier to calculate than (C)-largely emotional appeals uncluttered by substantive analysis Reputation defense in short term	High risk gambling —dealing with the most marginal parts of very long odds companies Possible liability: when is Dot-Com without viable business model fraud?	Close to con: Classic high-urgency pitches for companies, most won't be around a year
(E) Gamblers **Price Action Lemmings**	Momentum is misinterpreted as an alternative valuation structure, not by analysis but rather by default	Catching the wave: no need for any analysis whatsoever. Just react	Momentum is NOT alternative form of valuation Encourages anti-analysis approach in the business itself —flog a story, don't build a great company	Momentum-driven investing means major distortions and disruption in thin float markets characteristic of netPhase I Dangerous whipsaws in sideways markets

So there's no chance of a premature public offering for the company that can be justified simultaneously as worth $100 million or zero, depending on the valuator's methodology and agenda. Right?

Wrong. Companies that were valued at one dollar in the past (on the basis of success probability) were magically made into publicly traded vehicles, because the public tired of Lotto and demanded that it be allowed to dabble in the next sure thing it had been hearing all about: the paradigm change market of our generation.

Customary IPO timing is pushed backwards (Figure 1.1) to help fill up the Dot-Com start-up deal pipeline. Instead of being strengthened within some private organization, e-Bankruptcy2001.com is instead rushed to market years before it is ready—assuming that it will ever be qualified for the public trust.

So *of course* there is massive controversy about valuing these "seventy percenters." Before their true identities are known, the seventy percenters can and are "valued" (actually, it's more like a manipulated guess) anywhere between zero and infinity. It is only after tough-to-dispute data begins to reveal the seventy percenters' true identities that the valuation becomes rational. But note that non-investment quality (NIQ) companies don't lose their identity merely because they are publicly traded.

Massive Technological-Economic Revolution, with No Chance of Success for Naive Participants

The Internet *IS* everything that the starry-eyed hypsters promised: more than just a new market, a fundamentally different and additional source of value. If anything, the true potential of the Net economy is often *under*estimated, since people tend to focus primarily on converting those activities already familiar to them. But it is the hidden applications, the convergence that only a few can see, where the real future wealth resides.

While others were content to use oil for lamp lighting only, John D. Rockefeller came to understand and help develop the

extended applications for refined oil, which were invisible to nearly all others during the prospecting panic. And the applications of
the Net best known during the 1996-to-first-quarter-2000 buying
panic are not at all the same ones that will create wealth in
netPhase II and beyond.

The tidal wave of an economic-technological revolution changing everything would seem to be the greatest time to prosper. Or, in
the language of those stoking the flames of hope and money-lust at
such times, this is the time to "get in on the ground floor."

But instead, history teaches us that the first five-to-seven-year
buying period is the *worst* possible time for naive participation.
Great, solid business plans (not the stuff described in Chapter 4 of
this book) are *always* welcome. The well-thought-out approach
that combines comprehensive profit, critical share, and financing
plans always has a chance of success.

But naive participation is dead on arrival. Just showing up
with little more than a slick story never works. Those who ignored
the warnings in 1850 that the seam was thin at Sutter's Mill but
rushed ahead anyway found they were later too broke even to get
home. The same applies to some of their Dot-Com counterparts,
150 years later.

It may sound irrational, but enduring successful companies
don't necessarily emerge in that first wild stage of an irresistible
technological-economic revolution. On the contrary: history
suggests that five to seven years after the origin of the first wild
rush to great wealth, almost everything and everybody is ground
to dust.

Needed, Now: Ice Water in the Bloodstream

But give up on the Net dream when it's just now getting good? Not
a chance.

Far from signaling that the bubble has popped or that opportunities are limited, the cathartic action of the seventy percenters
being flushed from the corporate financing system following
"Spring Break 2000" signals that the best is yet to come.

Spring Break (that's *break*, as in broken hopes, not as in respite) is our phrase for Nasdaq Composite's decisive 34% break from March 10 to April 14, 2000, as illustrated in Figures 5.1 and 5.2). Survivors of the Net's first chaotic phase who can somehow stabilize and then expand, position themselves for the real wealth of the second phase, while everyone else is panicking about the system's collapse and the next addition to the dead Dot-Com lists.

In netPhase II, the leaders of the Internet will emerge and become major corporations, leaving some of the victims cited in Jack Willoughby's March 2000 *Barron's* "Burning Up!" article and others incinerated and out of the way.[4] The netPhase II champions will be the companies whose leaders and financiers have ice water in their veins and the guts to put netPhase I behind, except to pick up quickly the lessons learned. They will never, ever linger on the string of depressing news for week after week, as the seventy percenters work themselves out of the financial system and into oblivion.

The seventy percenters shouldn't have been there in the first place, so there are no positive benefits in staring too intently as the illusions disappear. JR is dead? No, it was all a dream. For four years.

Rockefeller. Bezos? Kriens? Walsh?[5]

The netPhase II champions will consolidate their segment into a few strong players, while the hangers-on just try to survive (even if they do, they won't last for long). The netPhase II champions will also concentrate on devising a workable Dot-Com secondaries marketplace for handling the multiple-year internal and external growth requirements of segment champions (see Chapters 6 and 8). Meanwhile, all the fast-disappearing seventy percenters will be hoping for a return of the venture capital-IPO financing model. But it isn't coming back.[6] This "cleaning out the hubris" view of getting rid of the non-investment quality companies that should not have gone public in the first place is clearly not what those companies want to hear these days.

So let's get moving forward. The good part's coming up next.

Dark Models, Black Holes, and Zero Valuations

The supposed problem with valuation of Dot-Com companies is that it is difficult if not sometimes borderline impossible to value accurately a company that has no profits today. However, the actual Dot-Com valuation problem for netPhase I (1996 to first quarter 2000) companies is that 70+ % will go broke, and that means close to zero value. Hiding that reality long enough to get the IPO out the door was a major challenge. But we can't let a minor detail such as shoveling pre-bankrupt dross to the public get in the way of earning financing and intermediary fees, can we? That tech companies that lost money in 1999 saw their market value (share price times shares outstanding) appreciate far more than profitable companies suggests that there weren't many problems with the *market's* valuation, at least.

That neat little soup ladle-shaped AA curve in Figure 1.3 is based on the earlier Figure 1.1. Roughly speaking, the soup ladle curve is the venture capitalists' Dot-Com ideal: a start-up that establishes a solid foundation in the early years through sizable but necessary investment spending, but which then uses that investment foundation as a launch pad to spectacular success.

It's pretty easy to see how insistence on Year 1 positive cash flow and profitability can actually destroy value. The bureaucrat thinks that he's doing a great job for the corporation by turning down all those Internet projects and separate business proposals that call for negative cash flow in the earliest years.

We can't have anything threaten the corporation's stellar string of EPS advances, he figures, even though that string has absolutely nothing to do with increasing shareholder value (Figure 1.5B). But the bean-counter proceeds anyway, giving competitors a free opportunity to grind his company into cyber-dust in the future as they act on the opportunities and value he missed.

But such self-inflicted value destruction is just one matter. Other Dot-Com value issues involve the classic upswing that will occur, or whether one of the two other valuation train wrecks shown in Figure 1.3 awaits the company.

Dark Model

The Dark Model (AB in Figure 1.3) is the stand-alone company or identifiable part of a bricks 'n clicks unit that *looks* to everyone as if it is on the classic AA venture capital success curve. The fact that AB initially traces the same path as AA gives everyone cause for optimism. Future revenue and profit forecasts are derived from the best available forecasts from that well-regarded "Rings O' Saturn Research" organization, and market penetration percentages applied to those big, big numbers are suitably modest.[7]

But at some point, say around Year n in Figure 1.3, the indicators begin to sour. At a minimum, it appears that profitability will not be achieved anywhere near the time that management expects. In the worst variant of this Dark Model case, profitability will never be achieved at all—although that potential is always expressed as imminent to justify extra infusions of cash. And investors may be afraid to jeopardize their major investment.

The spin may be intact for now, but the financial justification lies in ruins. With little or no prospect of future positive cash flow and profitability, red ink flows all over the financial spreadsheets—in private.

The spin to the outside always remains upbeat, such as: "We are experiencing a slightly longer period of necessary market investment, requiring a broadening of our original business concept. This is a very positive development. However, it does signal a slight lengthening of the time until we become profitable on an ongoing basis."

Watch out for those "howevers." No wonder that the CFO who can deliver such drivel—and with a straight face—is among the highest paid of all the company's specialist talents. But if *you* hear this particular explanation/apology, think of AB (Dark Model). And get ready to run for the exits.

But such dire circumstances only occur with grossly misjudged fad and/or commodity markets, such as the sliver of a margin merchandising business where there is never enough scale to pay for a switch to network-based merchandising, or the business with a threatened adverse swing in segment economics that could not have been foreseen, such as implosion of the down-loaded US music sector, right?

Yes, that's part of it. But the problem is that many companies and Dot-Com ventures are *already* profitless Dark Models—or headed that way with no indications that management understands the true plight, much less knows how to pull the company out of its death dive.

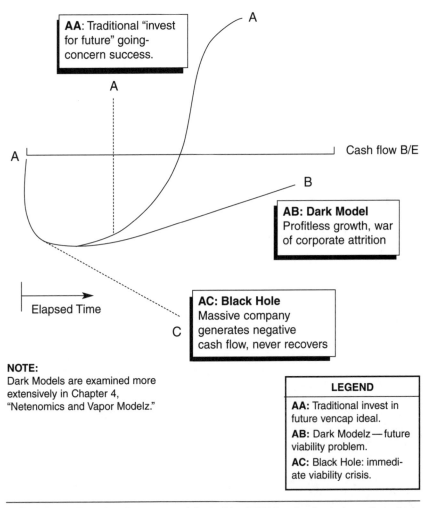

NOTE:
Dark Models are examined more extensively in Chapter 4, "Netenomics and Vapor Modelz."

FIGURE 1.3. Two situations not anticipated by DCF (contaminated or otherwise): "Black Hole," "Dark Model."

VBM RESOURCE CTR.
www.vbmresources.com

January 24, 1999

NET CONCEPT STOCKS DEJA VU
HAVE WE SEEN THIS PHENOMENON BEFORE?

Market observers watch the stratospheric prices of Internet concept stocks with equal parts of exhilaration and terror. Thin air will do that to you. We seem to have a vague sense of having seen this car crash before, but we can't remember when. We wonder if we walked away from the wreckage that time.

Companies in high tech industries boiling over with triple digit revenue growth but no earnings are nothing new. As one associated with one of the larger US venture capital firms in the early '70s, Heizer Corp., I saw such whiz bang phenoms all the time. Company founder Ned Heizer had a deliberately disturbing phrase to describe what we were doing: "investing in losses." No one knew which, if any, of the concept companies could endure three to five years of crushing losses and then still have enough customers and market edge to thrive.

There was no public market for such technology companies at the time, for good reason: risks were unreasonable for earth people. Only after (1) profits became clearly visible, and (2) it was confirmed that the company would be a survivor after the inevitable industry shakeout would the vencap concept be elevated to Initial Public Offering (IPO) candidate. But until and unless both critical issues could be resolved, the concepts were not ready for public markets. No matter how torrid or exotic the technology story.

Parallel high concept "less than investment quality" loss-generators exist today, of course: the Internet companies. But instead of being insulated from the public until the critical profit and shakeout questions are resolved, these latter-day vencap concepts instead go straight to IPO.

Oil drilling companies try to reinvent themselves as Net stocks. Merchants of yawn products such as books and groceries attempt to supercharge their P/Es by adapting their analyst pitches to a Net-hungry audience.

If there are any P/Es, that is. A price to earnings multiple (P/E) presumes positive earnings: if not today, in the foreseeable future—a minor impediment for the mega fee-earning Net stock packagers. They say, calculate the market valuation on revenues, or "eyeballs" (page hits), instead.

But one of two situations exists when investors are asked to ignore earnings and value a company on some lesser basis. The first is that future earnings are a sure thing, management just doesn't know when. The second is far more disturbing: there will never be any profits.

Bad news: the precedent of past venture capital "non-investment quality" grade companies and their stocks is that the second consequence is exactly what happens to the majority of phenom firms.

Management's projections don't reflect the true gravity of the situation, in large part because in nanosecond-change Dot-Com competitive markets, material changes that affect competitiveness, cash flow, and viability can and do regularly arise within 90 days of the IPO launch.

But the financial backers have *said* that they don't like surprises, and the investment community is even less forgiving. So even if the exception occurs and management is fully aware of its Dot-Com's slippage into Dark Model territory, it probably will say and do nothing. Disclosing the truth is likely to be misperceived as incompetence, although the exact opposite is true.

After all, how many etailers can you count on to both recognize the fast deteriorating situation and provide a warning, even at the cost of short-term grief? For example:

"Look, tear up all those old projections. Our high price spike back in 1999 effectively spoiled the market for all competitors, but then some figured they could enter this market and do just as well or better. Maybe the whole sector will eventually grow and benefit. But over the near term, it's a zero sum game. And if we don't win that game, our liquidity risks soar. And companies with

---

Such days of reckoning occur at the time of industry shakeout. Already, the Internet "industry" is rapidly consolidating towards three or four transnational backbone carriers, one quarter the number of Internet Service Providers (ISPs) that existed two years ago, and three major Internet equipment providers instead of twelve. Markets can only support a few portals, probably less than those seeking acquisition partners today.

When will the public investors who have bought venture capital concepts disguised as IPOs experience the shakeout in their stocks? Only one sure indication: when neither institutional nor individual investors can get out.

Note*: Previous was developed on January 24, 1999, by VBM Consulting's Peter J. Clark. Permission to Motley Fool's (www.fool.com) UK unit to display on Jan. 27, 1999 (www.fool.co.uk). Reappeared as VBM Consulting article (www.vbmresources.com) in Feb. 2000. (c) 1999-2000, VBM Consulting and Pondbridge Ltd., all rights reserved.*

serious liquidity risks cannot be valued—in other words, they're worth nothing."

You probably haven't heard that too often, although the evidence is strong and becoming stronger that numerous segments are becoming Dark Models. The ones we know about are generic dial-up narrowband Internet Services Providers (ISPs), electronic merchandisers online, and Me-Too search engines not affiliated with a major portal. Two segments emerging in the future are Web hosting and wholesale broadband access.

But what about the Dark Models that are not apparent? So long as they are invisible, funding justification models will presume the Figure 1.3 AA classic curve, rather than the AB reality. And that means massive errors in funding. It also means value

---

valueOUTPERFORMER
www.vbmresources.com

May 24, 2000

CASH.COM

Arguably, the ultimate fantasy valuation occurs when a company with nothing but cash and a business plan is valued at a huge multiple of that cash amount. On the appropriate date of April 1, 2000, Philip Coggan described the situation of Paradigm Media Investments (PAR, LSE), brought public without any investments at all as of that date, according to the *Financial Times* columnist. But here's the magic.

On flotation Coggan reports that cash was BPS 20.7 million, but that market value at close was BPS 134 million. Coggan refers to PAR as the stock market equivalent of "a perpetual motion machine. . . . Put a coin into the slot and hey, presto, it generates BPS 6.50." ("Price Today, Growth Tomorrow," *Financial Times,* Onlooker Col., April 1, 2000, WM, p. 3). "PAR closed at BPS 17.5 yesterday on May 23, 2000, compared to a high close of BPS 27.51."

Is such a situation limited to Western markets alone? Hardly. The Hong Kong GEM market could have made a sideline business selling places in line to buy the next hot-hot Internet company with nothing but cash and a business plan. At least until Spring Break broke the back of Dot-Com markets worldwide.

destruction. One hint to uncovering the Dark Models in hiding is to look for management particularly insistent that it has erected an impenetrable series of defenses against excess entry, including the mostly fictional First Mover Advantage.

Beyond signed long-term exclusive contracts or absolute standards, there are typically few barriers to actual Dot-Com entry. Which is why management of the newly endangered Dark Model company goes out of its way to explain its theoretical unique selling proposition. Spin is its only defense, but this doesn't always work. In many instances, the much-hyped exclusive advantage is only in company founders' and financiers' imaginations. To customers, most of the competitors look the same.

Black Hole

As this cheery name may suggest, Black Hole companies (AC in Figure 1.3) make the Dark Model seem like a stroll in the park.

Cash flow tends to be a more stable indicator of company performance than accounting after-tax profits, because cash flow reflects underlying operations before accounting and financial complications.

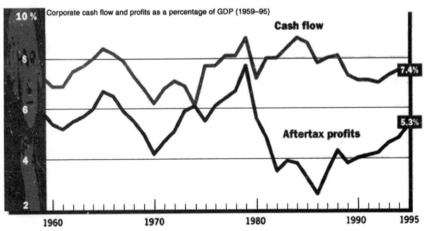

Source: National Bureau of Economic Research, cited in Peter Brimelow, "The Greed Myth," *Forbes*, June 3, 1996, p. 43. Research by Edwin S. Rubinstein, Right Data Associates.

"Cash flow" as defined in this figure equals total internal funds plus inventory gains.

FIGURE 1.4. The case for cash flow I.

valueOUTPERFORMER
www.vbmresources.com

May 30, 2000

UGH, TECHGLOMERATES

Start with detached portfolio management. Add a dogs 'n cats mix of a couple of Dot-Com winning companies plus many more Walking Dead e-victims permanently cut off from all future funds. Cut off ever since the netPhase I fantasy financing window closed after the devastating March 10–April 14, 2000 world Internet markets' plunge.

What do you have? The worst of of both worlds. Say hello to the techglomerate. The passive cyber-portfolio company that performs even worse than the sum of its parts because of classic, continuing conglomerate discounts. Discount one: Lotsa-Nets-R-Us has no comparables, thus no adequate analyst coverage on Wall Street or in the City. Discount two: at a time when hands-on corrective action is critical, the high profile 'multi-company' is notorious for putting spin ahead of fact, propaganda before progress.

In the aftermath of "Spring Break 2000" those separate Net companies REALLY want to survive and thrive learn the hard way that they must concentrate on transforming their powder puff elevator presentations into real, grown-up business & value approaches. Achievable steps that work in unforgiving marketplaces. This is quite a stretch, and is impossible for many. But add to that difficulty the yoke of posturing and non-direction from a corporate center hundreds of miles away, and the chances for viability decrease still more.

FINANCIAL TIMES

AN EVEN DOTTIER DOT-COM
Simon London

May 12, 2000

Dear Fellow Investor,

It is my pleasure to be able to report admirable progress in the evolution of Dotty.com.

Since I wrote to you in February, the company has consolidated its position as one of the UK's least profitable commercial ventures. Moreover, your response to our Readers' Subscription offer was overwhelming. With your money, and the continued support of Shortsight Capital Partners, our private equity backers, Dotty.com is well placed to implement the next stage of its strategy.

In the current investment environment, the adoption of mobile Internet and broadband technologies is essential to maintain the overvaluation of any e-commerce venture. Dotty.com is no exception. With this in mind, an Unproven Technologies team, comprising 10 overrated professionals, has been assembled. A director of Unproven Technologies will be appointed as soon as we can identify an executive search firm dumb enough to take shares in lieu of cash.

While moving ahead with the adoption of new technologies, however, the directors feel it is important to maintain a fluid approach to product development. Companies that pin their hopes on any particular product or service are inviting competition. In the new economy, barriers to entry are low: customers are competitors. We will continue to manage the business according to this creed.

Turning to current trading, it is the opinion of the directors that the application of normal accounting principles is inappropriate in an e-commerce environment. The worth of your company cannot be judged on crude "old economy" measures such as profits, earnings or hard cash. Our preferred yardstick is based on the idealized discounting of obscure transfers (IDIOT), a methodology devised by teenagers at Goldberg Lunch, our investment banking advisers. Dotty.com continues to make exceptional progress on this measure.

At the end of the first quarter, Dotty.com's IDIOT value was approximately £500m. It is the opinion of Goldberg Lunch that this figure could easily double if some of the underlying assumptions were changed. The directors will continue to pay unscrupulous attention to the valuation of your company on this basis.

It is worth pointing out that global population growth has increased the size of Dotty.com's potential market by some 230m persons since the start of this year. Further strong growth is anticipated. Even when judged by conventional accounting standards, Dotty.com is making its mark. It is with some pride that I note that we are now losing money at a faster rate than the flagship of the new economy, Lastminute.com.

Indeed, I am pleased to report that, at the current rate of cash burn, Dotty.com will need to raise additional monies within six months — sooner if the expenses incurred by the board accelerate into the holiday season. But while your business has been destroying shareholder value at a rate faster than we dared hope, I am sad to report that our plans for a stock market listing have been put on hold.

It is the opinion of Goldberg Lunch that conditions in world equity markets are no longer conducive to the wholly opportunistic strategy outlined in my last letter.

We recognize that the decision to postpone the flotation is of the upmost seriousness for investors who hoped to crystallize their stake in the business at the first opportunity, including Shortsight Capital Partners. However, I have received personal assurances from Shortsight's chairman, Mr. Stig Fastbuck, that we will continue to receive his full backing until such time as the battery runs down in his Palm Pilot.

The recent resignation of your chairman has also been taken into account in the reformulation of our flotation plans. Whatever you may read in the press, however, I would like to make clear that the chairman never intended to mislead, defraud or otherwise fleece investors in Dotty.com.

Any losses sustained by shareholders arose solely from his naivete, avarice and naked ambition — qualities without which your company would not be in the unenviable position it is in today.

The Black Hole Dot-Com start-up/unit/division/project/part of a clicks 'n mortar hybrid starts its life cycle the same way as both of its cousins with appropriately massive front-end investment for future benefit.

By far, the best valuation method — regardless of industry or company — is that based on discounted free cash flow, with a critical caveat: analysis must be based on defensible input data, including assumptions for risk, growth, and term.

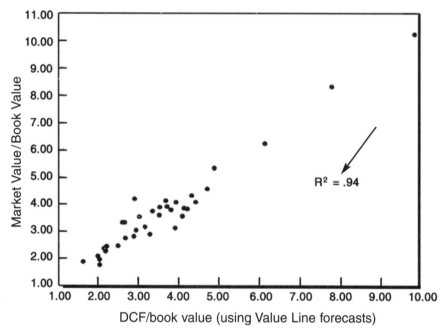

DCF/book value (using Value Line forecasts)

Source: Tom Copeland, Tim Koller, and Jack Murrin, *Valuation: Measuring and Managing the Value of Companies*, 2d ed. p. 85, Exhibit 3.7. Copyright © John Wiley & Sons. Reprinted by permission. New York: Wiley and McKinsey & Co., 1985.

This graph shows what workable valuation is not. Despite the simplicity and extensive use of price-to-earnings multiples, a study cited in the *Independent* (London, February 8, 1997, p. 28) and elsewhere indicates an extraordinarily poor connection between P/E ratios and EPS growth over four years for sample companies.

The most important aspect of this figure is that $R^2 = .94$, indicating as close a correlation of market value/book value to DCF/book value as practical.

FIGURE 1.5A. The valuation case for discounted cash flow.

But Black Hole keeps going down. It is apparent to all that something is very, very wrong, that the business is not taking hold the way it should, the way management had projected.

Sometimes a non-starter Dot-Com marketing concept that would be laughed out of the room in a terrestrial business is to blame, such as a vague plan for creating some generalist free information portal that will excel because of a torrent of advertising

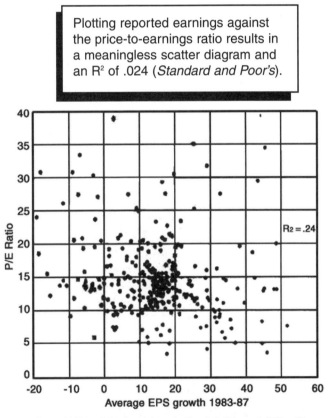

Plotting reported earnings against the price-to-earnings ratio results in a meaningless scatter diagram and an R^2 of .024 (*Standard and Poor's*).

Source: McKinsey & Co., from *Independent* (London), February 8, 1997, p. 27.

EPS: earnings per share
P/E: price-to-earnings multiple

FIGURE 1.5B. Pursuing the wrong measure: Absence of correlation between report earnings growth market value.

revenues from undefined firms. But in the netPhase I's heyday, numerous sites such as this were rushed to market with only that much information and sometimes a good deal less.

More often, the original business plan seriously underestimated some material operations aspect of the business, due diligence may have missed the problem, or there was insufficient ongoing due diligence, so as not to crowd management.

You don't hear any more about "push marketing" for good reason. The hard-disk-crashing software was such a calamity that not only did the phrase drop from trendy bromide to dust in half the time of most other management consultants' parables, but the market was destroyed.

Like the network computer (another Black Hole disaster), what goes around comes around, and the basic business concept may some day be reincarnated in the marketplace, but with an all-new name and positioning to prevent any linkage to the past.

The Dot-Com slipping toward Black Hole and the resulting commercial market damage means that management can't pretend that everything is OK, that the business is really on the AA track. The outward signs are all around, such as inferno-level burn rate, key high-value middle management exodus, or huge rows over basic concepts presumed to have been finalized months earlier. Which is why the best spin available to management is that the company is in low-probability Dark Model mode, not no-probability Black Hole mode.

Some spin. Both Dark Model and Black Hole are eventually *non-viable*, so what's the difference?

Discounted Free Cash Flow in Crisis: Confronting the Going Concern Problem

Embraced by most before 1994, discarded by some by 1998, valuation based on discounted free cash flows (DCF) is backed by a considerable body of empirical evidence as the single best methodology for determining corporate value. And there is no second place.

valueOUTPERFORMER
www.vbmresources.com

April 26, 2000

Adapted from
VALUE AND THE SHAREHOLDER HIERARCHY

Continuous providers of major sources of permanent capital. Long-term shareholders. Interim holders. Near term speculators. Daytrader gamblers. What does each of these very different category of company owner share? The designation "shareholder."

CEO pledges to pursue "maximum shareholder value." But to WHICH shareholder group is he directing his proclamation? To which radically different definition of the word "maximum"? Is he directing his pledge to the lowest life form on the company ownership spectrum, the daytrader with affectations of being a professional speculator who spends his day down at Stocks-R-Us? To him, maximum means the widest and wildest trading range for the day. Next tier up is the short-term trader-investor. He believes that watching financial TV every day gives him a trading edge rather than encouraging overtrading. Next higher is the Holder, to whom the phrase "long-term capital gains" actually means something.

At the top of the Strong Hands investor Darwinian scale is the Foundation Investor. This Strong Hands may shares to secure board representation. He tends to believe the CEO's first two value underperformance excuses but can run out of patience.

The group interpreting the Dot-Com value according to its own self-interest is important. So are the actual owners of the firm, who judge whether "maximum" is just a hollow phrase or not when it comes to value in the firm.

TheStreet.com's James Cramer speaks of strong shareholders, as does Jim Seymour. But can there be any "strong" holders at all in a Dot-Com characterized by a managed, paper-thin float and daily stock gyrations driven by the most fickle of daytraders?

The Valuation Approach Works

That's no typo in Exhibit 3.7 of Copeland/Koller/Murrin's *Valuation* (which is also shown in Figure 1.5A). The correlation between market value/book value and DCF/book value was based *Value Line* on corporate data forecasts and is 0.94 (1.00 is the unreachable perfect).

FINANCIAL TIMES
www.ft.com

April 23, 2000

STRETCHING THE FIGURES
Calculating Accurate Values for Companies in the New Economy Takes
More than a Grasp of Mathematics (excerpts)

by John Kay

Do the math. The slogan favored by Jim Clark, creator of Silicon Graphics, Netscape, and Healtheon, has become the mantra of a generation of consultants and investment bankers. The new economy, they claim, requires new principles of valuation.

C.com is one of the most exciting prospects in business-to-business commerce. It is the world leader in a growing market—annual sales by 2010 are likely to be $500,000bn. If C.com can maintain a 5 per cent share and earn only 1 per cent net margin, its prospective annual earnings will be $250bn.

If we assume that market growth after 2010 is 5 per cent and discount future revenues is 10 per cent, the prospective value of C.com is $5,000bn—about 10 times the recent market capitalization of Microsoft, Cisco, or General Electric.

You don't have to wait for the IPO. You can buy shares in C.com right now for less than 5 per cent of that value. C.com is called Citigroup and in addition to its foreign exchange trading, which is the business I have described, you get its other wholesale, retail, and investment banking activities and a leading insurance company thrown in.

Of course, nobody would be so stupid as to value Citigroup in this way. Yet I have followed more or less exactly the methodology recommended in the latest McKinsey quarterly for the valuation of new era companies.[1] They use precisely analogous calculations to arrive at a valuation of $37bn for Amazon.com. Paul Gibbs, head of merger and acquisition research at J.P. Morgan (London), recently used similar principles to confirm that assessment of Amazon. He then performed the same calculation for Internet service provider Freeserve.

Assume that UK retail sales grow at 5 per cent a year, that 25 per cent of sales take place on the net, that portals capture 50 per cent of these, that Freeserve gets 30 per cent of the portal share and maintains an 8 per cent commission on sales. Multiply these together and you establish that in 2017 Freeserve will make profits of £2bn ($3.2bn). This, he argues, justifies a value today of £6.50 per share.

1. Driek Desmet, Tracy Francis, Alice Hu, Timothy Koller, and George Reidel "Valuing Dot-Coms," *McKinsey Quarterly*, 2000, No. 1.

That 35-company research has since been confirmed by numerous other analyses. The problem is that the second edition of *Valuation* by Copeland et al. (tom_copeland@monitor.com) missed the height of the Commercial Internet mega-boom by about a year. Discounted cash flow analyses struggle with the problem of valuing companies with soaring share prices but unstable (and probably very short) life spans, two very different popular hypotheses trickled up.[8]

The first path was that the DCF analyses simply "didn't work." The Dot-Coms represent a new paradigm, and the old valuation tools must be discarded. The second path was that DCF valuation was not the problem, but rather, it was how best to force-fit the analysis to a pre-set "solution"—whatever nosebleed price happened to be affixed to e-Bankruptcy2001.com's share price on that particular day.

Second things first. Defended by assumptions of rational, efficient markets (explored more extensively in Chapter 3), apologist-analysts apparently figured that it was OK to justify Dot-Com market valuations backward using interrelated manipulations, all legal if not always reasonable.

The reason the Citibank calculation is nonsense is simple, but fundamental. The margins Citibank makes on its forex business vary widely. If you buy small quantities of notes from a bank, the spread is much wider than 1 per cent. If you are a large corporation trading major currencies, the margin is wafer thin. Entry and competition force prices down to the related costs.

In Mr. Gibbs's model, Freeserve earns profits of £2bn, about equal to the current profits of Tesco, J. Sainsbury, and Marks and Spencer together. And it earns these on revenues of only £2.5bn, so that profits are 80 per cent of the value of its sales. No established business earns margins of that size.

The idea that profit is a return on capital invested still has some role in new economy valuation, at the level of the overall market. There is a key formula in the new math. The required yield on a security is equal to the difference between the rate of return demanded from that class of securities and its expected rate of growth. So, if you expect a return of 5.5 per cent from a share whose dividends will grow at 5 per cent, calculations show that the dividend yield should be 0.5 per cent.

"Alex" reprinted with permission by www.telegraph.co.uk alex-cartoon@etgate.co.uk.

These devices are described in this and other chapters of this book but are already known to almost anyone who has not been stuck on Mars since 1995. By itself, each separate element of legal manipulation is insufficient to sustain the enigma of nosebleed faux-valuations for companies possibly reeling toward collapse.

On their own, each of the five devices—(1) short float, (2) thin daily trading volume, (3) IPO price explosions to ensure perpetual public buying frenzy, (4) "price objective" cheerleader-analysts crowding out fundamentalists, or (5) extra margin dollars to fuel retailer buying binges — tend to not exert much impact.

But together they are another matter. Put them together and the frothy five help sustain the valuation hallucination. The Net's first commercial period began to sputter, slow, and unwind far before the climatic Spring Break 2000, March 10 to April 17 period. As investment bank cheerleader-analysts moved on to cover the next wave of initial public offerings in 1999, the wave of earlier launches failed to receive the promotional hype necessary to sustain buy-at-any-price fervor. Any expiring lockouts or trading restrictions on shares held by founders or others (items 1 and 2) spoil the ideal conditions of carefully calibrated supply of shares to keep share prices buoyant.

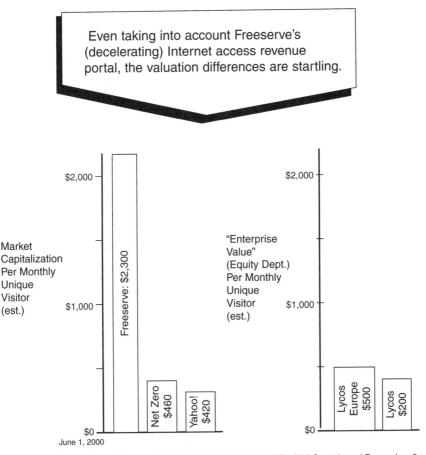

Even taking into account Freeserve's (decelerating) Internet access revenue portal, the valuation differences are startling.

Source: Jesse Eisinger, "Value of Freeserve Might as Well Be Its Sales Price." *The Wall Street Journal Europe*, June 2, 2000, pp. 13, 16. Copyright © 2000 by Dow Jones & Co., Inc. Reprinted with permission.

FIGURE 1.6. Debunking the exotics: "Monthly unique users."

But more on that later. Back to DCF and its struggles in trying to closing that awkward gap between nosebleed faux-valuations in the market now (thanks to management by the frothy five) and the far lower valuations that result when Planet Earth assumptions are used exclusively in key parts of the equations. Real-world, justifiable assumptions such as risk and company lives which are consistent with what anyone can see, every day (see John Kay *FT* article, included in this chapter).

But if the mindset is that the market is always right—even if that market price is manipulated—then the problem is not bringing Disneyesque numbers down to reason. For the Dot-Com company founder or financier obsessed with sustaining the valuation hype at any cost, the problem is instead, how to pump enough hot air into a defensible valuation scheme to make today's stock price credible to most of the people, most of the time.

Apparently the logic is that when everyone is dressed in a clown outfit, then the first clown doesn't look so preposterous. The opposing view is that they all look ridiculous.

Backward-Cram, Illusory Valuation

Start with the "answer"—in this case whatever nosebleed valuation quickens pulses on Wall Street and Threadneedle Street today.

There are a half dozen DCF valuation model components preconceived that can be tweaked to help force-fit the analysis methodology to this "answer," if so desired. Your junior analyst can quickly confirm that formula elements such as analysis term (t), financial and business risk (r), and the combination of revenue growth and cash flow/revenue margin can be particularly useful in such illusions.[9]

The kindest thing that might be said for the junior number-crunchers who try to force-fit is that this deliberate shell game is not always their idea. They are just following orders of bosses scrambling to somehow create the illusion of value where there is none. We surmise as much in eyes that communicate (at least to us): *Hey, I know this is total nonsense, but I have to defend the official company line or pay the consequences.*

"Burn rate" per se is irrelevant—what's important is outflow versus both inflow from operations and external financing. Out-of-favor business-to-consumer (B-C) Dot-Coms find themselves at a severe disadvantage in attracting NetPhase II financing because of fierce competition (see Chapter 6).

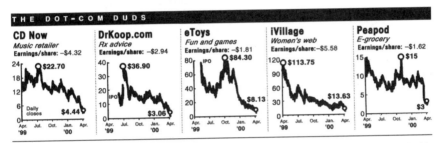

THE DOT-COM DUDS

Source: *Time*, April 7, 2000. Copyright © 2000 by Time-Life Syndication. Reprinted with permission.

(No comment regarding future financial and/or operational viability of any company depicted here or elsewhere in this book is made by authors, book owner or publisher, express or implied).

FIGURE 1.7. Value Armageddon "Spring Break" 2000.

According to Professor Kent Womack at the Tuck School, analysts who issue sell recommendations often find themselves "exploring new personal opportunities." We suspect that the researcher who came up with the unwelcome but sound analysis that shows that the seventy percenter is not a going concern and thus is worth nothing, faces that same "opportunity."

This holds true especially if that company is a client of the investment bank's corporate finance unit, if the seventy percenter's IPO was just three weeks ago, and if the stock price pattern is a negative.

You see, the market is described as efficient by the tethered house economists only if the resulting prices are full. When the prices are lower, such as post-Spring Break 2000, that's not an efficient market. No, *that's* undervaluation.

A

Before netPhase I:

All discounted cash flow valuation methods (DCF) assume a link between market-value share price and the analysis method, with both reflecting signals about current and future worth contained in company information and outside interpretations. The method has two distinct elements: the valuation formula and input assumption set.

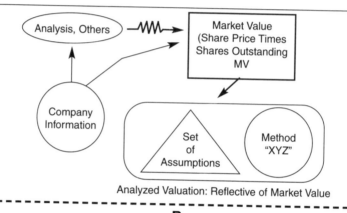

Analyzed Valuation: Reflective of Market Value

B

netPhase I:

Suppose that there is no company information. The publicly traded company must have some valuation, but with no reliable data to determine whether this is one of the "70 per-centers" (70 + percentage of companies to fail by 2002) or a survivor, other factors influence MV: managed float, company "informercials" in place of real data. But conventional, conservative valuation fails to support the fiction, so new, contaminated inputs replace defensible ones.

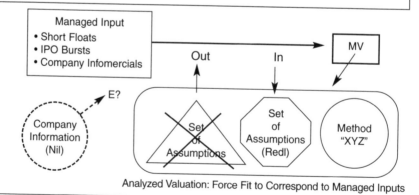

Analyzed Valuation: Force Fit to Correspond to Managed Inputs

FIGURE 1.8. How the illusion was sustained: "Contaminated DCF" faux-value manufactured from thin air.

Method	(+) Strengths	(−) Weaknesses	Examples
Valuation by Conversion to "harder asset"	Links the Dot-Com to companies with core consistent value	Very, very few Dot-Com-to-terrestrial combinations	AOL-Time Warner
Replacement cost	Objective analysis	Underestimation only applies to companies with proven demand	—
Private market value	Comparison of public financing with private-deal terms sometime later	Subjectivity	eToys PIPE financing, June 2000 (see Chapter 6)
Post-IPO discount	Comparison of IPO launch "value" with market valuation around one year later (ratio)\n\nReadily Available data	Comparison gives appearance of capital thrown away	Dot-Com Dead, 2000 (RIP)

FIGURE 1.9. Other valuation alternatives.

Mandated Valuation Based on Investment: Or, When *Pricing* Is Confused with *Valuation*

The theory underlying this tortured valuation approach is that a Dot-Com company's value is based on the sum of total investment as grossed up to achieve an ever-increasing return on investment.

Obviously, is this just another form of dubious backwards analysis. There is no direct causal relationship between amount of investment and the value of the business. If there were such a linkage, then salespersons would travel to client calls in gold-plated

Rolls Royces, confident not only that the additional investment would be covered, but that the extra spending would *increase* the prospects of success.

Of course, the exact opposite is more likely to be true. The subject company's basic business changes at an evolutionary pace. The basic attributes of the business that influence its value — technology, customer base, level of market dominance, growth rates, and cash flow-to-revenue margins—all tend to change gradually. It matters little that investment levels in Month 4 are, say, double that of Month 1. The key value-relevant characteristics of the corporation are effectively unchanged. Which means a lower return, and thus lower rather than higher value.

Admittedly, in the intelligence void of the Dot-Com heyday, this and similar twists of logic almost seemed to make sense in 1996-99. Notice that we use the word *intelligence*, not information. There are acres of pseudo-data in the earliest Dot-Com periods, when it seemed that the Internet business could be worth whatever anyone said it was worth. Not because that self-serving guess was particularly accurate, but rather, just because there was nothing else.

Graham Anderson of Euclid Partners claims that Dot-Com "valuations" increased in 1999 in step with record investment. According to Anderson, citing numbers from *Venture One*, venture capital investment in the Net in 1999 was more than in previous years of the Net boom combined. Not only was each level of financing in the daisy chain growing, but also the number of layers expanded, multiplying the investment effect.[10]

Which leads to the curious presumption that Dot-Com "valuation" goes up, as more and more financing middlemen get involved as well. The quotes around "valuation" are deliberate: the word that Mr. Anderson and his colleagues probably means is actually just "pricing"—what the financier hopes the value is, whether or not such fiction is defensible.

The pipe dream of every financial middleman is to earn a full return on every dollar invested. But if that happens easily, waste is rewarded. The company with comparatively high unit costs is imagined to be worth far more than a more efficient competitor, as the tortured "analysis" model churns out the desired number. Welcome to number-cruncher fantasy land.

The ultimate customer—the end user who actually buys the product or services—pays based on his or her perception of what the product being sold is worth. Details about the costs are an irrelevant detail to the customer, no matter how important the issue is to the venture capitalist or the angel with funds on the line.

The Exotics: A Peg Down

Contaminated DCF at least makes a pretence of being loosely connected with an existing creditable valuation backed with empirical substance. Never mind that for the moment contaminated DCF represents a masquerade.

But what we refer to as "exotics" here have little or no connection to proven effective valuation methodologies. Exotics are

---

valueOUTPERFORMER
www.vbmresources.com

May 9, 2000

Adapted from
BOILER ROOM

Gartner Group predicts an 85% failure rate for Asian pure play Dot-Com companies. Others' predictions (including our own) call for failures in the US to exceed 70%, with Europe in step.

So how high does the expected future failure rate have to reach before someone is liable for bringing some e-Bankruptcy2001.com to the public market? No matter how complete the language in the prospectus, few disagree with the statement that those bringing the company public face considerable possible exposure when the failure rate is 100%. When the milk is poisoned, the dairy can't count on ducking responsibility merely by placing huge warning labels on the carton. So if 100% means danger, how much LOWER must the failure rate drop before principals and intermediaries can feel safe again? 90%? 85%? "Only" 70%? The thought balloons rise from The Street and The City: *How absurd. Only bring those Dot-Com companies public with a better that 50/50 chance of survival? How will we eat?*

---

valueOUTPERFORMER
www.vbmresources.com

May 22, 2000

DOT-COM VALUATION COMPONENTS. YAHOO!

Yahoo! is petitioning the US Securities and Exchange Commission for exemption from the Commission's tough reporting and operating requirements for mutual funds, which the portal technically is because of the extent of its investment in other firms, almost all Dot-Coms. The business reasoning behind Yahoo's petitioning is clear. Management insists that it is an Internet company and is not in the business of investing or trading in securities.

But other factors may contribute to the Yahoo! petition. Companies holding share positions in other Internet companies create a particularly vexing valuation challenge, as recent in market valuations of Softbank, Internet Capital Group, and Durlacher suggest. If the holding companies are merely passive investors and financing sources, that corporate investor has limited ability to influence forward strategy and implementation in what may become yet another imploding Dot-Com. And then there's the thin float problem.

Closed-end investment companies typically suffer from an additional 10-15% value valuation reduction from the combined net asset value of the component investments, reflecting the combination of conversion costs plus negative synergy from interfering central management. Thin floats potentially exaggerate this discount still further, as concerns emerge about the ability of the investor to liquidate large positions if necessary.

Some facts from: Judith Burns, "Yahoo! Seeks Exemption from Mutual-Fund Rules," *The Wall Street Journal*, May 22, 2000, 16. Copyright © 2000 by Dow Jones & Co., Inc. Reprinted with permission.

---

homespun, make-it-up-as-you-go guesses at what changes shareholder value. If there is massive empirical evidence proving conclusively that the number of, say, web site hits determines company worth, then by all means, let us know.

Most of the exotics are based on operational data, plus a couple of apples and oranges combinations of some financial numbers. To our knowledge, Steve Harmon's article "The Metrics for Evaluating Internet Companies" is one of the best examples of this approach to Dot-Com quasi-valuation. We admit to being firmly oriented to more subtantive valuation approaches. Web site hits don't neccesarily equate to Dot-Com company value (see *Alex* cartoon, p. 24).

The Venture Capitalists' Favorite Valuator

"I am a huge fan of Steve Harmon's analysis," Kleiner Perkins' John Doerr is quoted as saying in the addendum to Harmon's article. The meat tends to be in the back of Harmon's analysis, with the front end a diatribe against conventional valuation perspectives that appear to be the polar opposite of *Barron's* Alan Abelson's views in the late 1990s. Contends Harmon, "Old-line thinking prevents value from being identified, evaluated, and realized or perceived."

Harmon's ratios, such as "lifetime value of an e-buyer" and "market cap/Websteader" and others, rate a look, even with the lack of a clear causal link to shareholder value, the ultimate purpose of every corporation.

Several of the indicators are particularly useful as interim performance measures. The one involving customer acquisition cost is especially useful as an advance indicator of deterioration.[11]

Unconstrained by limitations imposed by the more traditional valuation approaches, many IPO packagers can probably find at least some quasi-official sounding justification in hybrid metrics such as these, thus permitting more daring mandated valuations. But the market ultimately assesses the worth of all value theories, including whichever ones were used for the companies shown in Figure 1.7.

Price/Earnings to Growth: PEG

Among the quasi-valuation ratios, PEG (price/earnings as multiple to the annual company revenue growth rate) deserves special mention—if only because this becomes one of the few valuation fall-backs for the analyst covering the huge Net company selling at P/Es well over 100 times. Such stratospheric multiples are "full" by any estimation.

The theory is reasonable enough. Investor-shareholders should be willing to pay an extra premium for extraordinarily high revenue growth. So if that particular analyst's reasonable threshold is, say, 2:1, that means that a 100 times P/E might actually be described as reasonable if the annual revenue growth rate is more than 50%.

The logic flaw in PEG is double-counting for growth. Market price *already* reflects all factors relating to that company's worth, including the future expected rate of revenue growth and the probability that the expectation can be achieved.

So the notion of explaining away a very top-heavy P/E by saying that the company has a very high rate of annualized revenue growth is a bit like saying, *We really like the revenue growth pace of this company, so we've made sure that this factor is fully reflected in the company's stock price. In fact, we like the revenue growth aspect so much that we'll add an additional factor for it.*

The data is already in the P/E. Compare the 110 times P/E company in the sector with its mere 70 times laggard, and you won't just find margins as the only difference. Revenue growth is already embedded in both valuations.

The reality of course is that the securities analyst who fails to justify the present share price may be branded as not being a team player within that investment bank.

Is use of a homespun ratio with little defense worth retaining good relations with the boys upstairs who brought HappyBang.com public two months ago? Sure.

Notes

1. "This Market's Done For," *Upside Today* (www.upside.com), June 13, 2000.
2. "Value of Freeserve Might Just as Well Be Its Sale Price," *The Wall Street Journal Europe* (www.wsj.com), June 2, 2000, 13.
3. "The Dotcom Graveyard," *Upside Today* (www.upside.com), June 7, 2000.
4. To our knowledge, *The Industry Standard* (www.thestandard.com), *Fortune* magazine (www.fortune.com), and zd.net joined *Upside* in actively tracking Dot-Com victim companies in mid-2000, which means that there are probably several we missed. Willoughby is Jack Willoughby (jack.willoughby@barrons.com), senior editor of *Barron's* and author of the highly controversial March 20, 2000 (www.barrons.com), article

"Burning Up!" which just happened to be published ten days into the five-week Spring Break 2000 period.

5. Kriens refers to Scott Kriens, CEO of Juniper Networks (also, Chapter 6). Walsh refers to Mark Walsh, chairman, VerticalNet (Chapter 8).

6. Figure 6.1 in Chapter 6 shows our view of the breakdown of the base Venture Capital-IPO financing assembly line in 2000's second quarter.

7. "Rings O' Saturn" (ROS) is a fictional research organization, used only for purposes of illustration here. Funny thing, ROS's multi-trillion Year 2004 market projections remain the same month after month, despite material changes in marketplace conditions and application of emerging technologies each quarter. These issues are visited again in Chapters 6 and 7.

8. Copeland, Koller, Murrin, McKinsey & Co., *Valuation, Measuring and Managing the Value of Companies*, 2nd ed. (New York: Wiley, 1996), 85. Tom Copeland (tom_copeland@ monitor.com) informs us that *Valuation*'s third edition came out in summer 2000. That third edition is listed in the short reference section in the back of this book.

9. John Kay, "Stretching the Figures," *Financial Times*, April 23, 2000, www.ft.com; Also as featured here: Emily Bell, "Any Model You Like—Still Won't Work," *The Observer* (London), May 7, 2000, Business, 3.

10. At IBF Private Equity Internet Investment Conference, April 11, 2000, New York.

11. Steve Harmon, "The Metrics for Evaluating Internet Companies," February 23, 1999, from *The Internet Stock Report* (www.internetstockreport.com), May 16, 2000.

Chapter 2

NOTHING SUCCEEDS LIKE NET EXCESS

There comes a point when the absurdity is obvious to everyone. . . . You can't assume that the company should trade today on what the fundamentals might be 10 years from now.

Dalton Chandler, Needham & Co.
analyst on the Internet stock excess [1]

Yahoo! is selling at 583 times next year's earnings. I like doing that. We should continue doing that.

CNBC's David Faber,
December 22, 1999

It's $150 million worth of nothing right now. But if they get even one company to market, then wahoo.

David Lile, Haymarket Securities,
Vancouver, describing the prospects
of ecubator NetValue Holdings
(no relation—Figure 2.3) [2]

The rewards of creating something from nothing are not to be underestimated. In Manhattan, veteran journalist Duncan Hughes tells of one hard-working crew that "has been searching for better ways to profit from the boom in stocks by setting up companies and learning how to earn millions for selling stocks that were virtually worthless."[3]

Oops. Our mistake. That quote above does not refer to Wall Street's finest, as they introduce the public to the joys of ownership of "seventy percenters" (Chapter 1—the percentage of those netPhase I B2Cs who won't be around as independent entities by 1/1/02).

Because to our knowledge, at least, few of the larger brokerages have employees named "Vinnie the Pork" in their employ, but maybe we missed something.

Easy mistake to make. The quote above refers instead to the FBI's massive arrest of alleged boiler room operators in June 2000, when 120 people—thought to include members of all five New York organized crime families—were put under arrest following a prolonged period of audio and visual surveillance.

The indictments alleged sales of worthless equities, mostly on the volatile micro-cap exchanges. Naw, can't be our friends. Most of the companies *they* brought to market skipped the micro cap level and went straight to the grown-up Nasdaq.

THE GOOD NET / BAD COMPANY PREDICAMENT

The fundamental logic disconnect underlying the Dot-Com companies hype-boom since late 1996 has two parts and goes something like this. One: Internet is the irresistible path to future corporate performance and maximizing shareholder value. Two: Therefore, companies that seize early advantage today are poised to become tomorrow's high value champion firms of the Net age.

Not a particularly outlandish boast. You've heard far more incendiary promises from boiler room stack salesmen calling at home, late at night.

Problem is, even the most benign combination of those two statements doesn't often work. Look at Statement 1, that the Internet is the path to the future. No problem there. Those Old

Economy curmudgeons who insisted that the Net was nothing but smoke and mirrors were listened to intently in 1997. They were tolerated in 1998. By 1999, no one listened anymore.

And it is impossible to disregard fundamental productivity and value-creating mechanisms offered by the core infrastructure and B2B leadership companies. It is shortsighted and just plain wrong to miss the hard dollar savings that companies can and do achieve with the right programs in the right parts of their organization.

But while a compelling case can readily be made for the Net in general, that doesn't mean that individual participating companies prosper. Particularly during the Net revolution's explosive five- to seven-year first phase, when there are only untested theories about what works.

It now becomes clear that three factors — excess competition, confusing market-defined true needs with mere wants, and implementation problems — all contribute to the gap between expectations and results. But it is the expectations that drive funding, advertising outlays while setting the general market temperament.

During Netboom's roller coaster initial five to seven years, the unspoken attitude is that anything is possible unless proven otherwise. Experiences are all new, so everyone from homespun instant valuators to business experts to financiers can all foist their theories, confident there's nothing from Net experience to contradict them.

It is only after the shock and retrenchment of a major market break that phrases such as "Net experience teaches us that . . ." might be applied. But not applied until later, during the Net's far less exciting, but far more prosperous second phase (Chapter 6).

THE DISRUPTIONS OF NET EXCESS

Other major paradigm change watershed markets have exhibited their own excesses in that first, memorable cowboy phase. That's when everyone thinks that the only direction is up.

When even undercapitalized, poorly planned and organized participants believe, sincerely, they can do as well as anyone else. Or even better.

Time becomes the most precious commodity because that's all that stands between the individual and the promise. The unspoken slogan for this frontier mentality is there are no rules — we'll make 'em up as we go along.

Those Early Explosions, Necessary to Get the Revolution Started

Early oil patch prospectors in southwestern Pennsylvania discovered that some pools of oil were so close to the surface (sometimes on the surface) that they could scoop them up with their hats and into barrels. Some of the Midwest's retail clothing and hardware chains were established just to outfit speculators prospecting for gold in California, more than a thousand miles away.

Four-digit price/earnings multiples (P/E) were sustained by market enthusiasm during netPhase I (Figure 2.1). If there is no "E" (net earnings), then revenues are used, with price to revenue (PTRs) in the high hundreds. Shares of companies that lose money outperform shares of firms with earnings. *Red Herring's* Peter Henig explains that:

> According to the PricewaterhouseCoopers' *MoneyTree* survey of venture-backed deals for 1999, venture capital deals last year reached $35.6 billion, a rise of 150 percent over 1998. Internet related investments rose nearly 500 per cent, from $3.4 billion in 1998 to $19.9 billion in 1999, and constituted 56 percent of total investments.[4]

Explosive IPOs. B2B leader VerticalNet ended 1999 with an astonishing 1,950 percent gain from the time of its February 1999 IPO to December 31, 1999. That's a number three ranking based on change to end of the 1999 calendar year as calculated by Thomson Financial Securities Data and shown in Figure 2.1.[5]

Triple-digit price-earnings multiples for Cisco systems? That's chump change compared with some of Nasdaq's real "valuation" stars.

Company	P/E	Business	'99 revenues (millions)
SonicWall (SNWL)	8.675	Internet security	$21.0
Aurora Bio. (ABSC)	8.400	Drug discovery	50.3
VeriSign (VRSN)	7.454	Internet security	85.0
Koplin (kopn)	2.992	Semiconductor	38.6
Hummingbird (HUMC)	2.250	Business software	166.0

NOTE: Based on prices as of February 22, 2000. Price-earnings multiples based on trailing (1999) earnings.

Source: "Word on the Street," *Money*, April, 2000, 1:46. Copyright © 2000 by Time-Life Syndication. Reprinted with permission.

FIGURE 2.1. High P/Es for Cisco? You ain't seen nothing yet.

In the Net's first phase boom, Philip Katz, hero of computer culture, creates the new international standard for compression software for use on the World Wide Web, "PKZip," before succumbing in a tragedy reminiscent of other victims of their own success in earlier revolutions.[6]

Commenting on whether the business-to-consumer B2C "etailing" warranted a 12 to 14 multiple on revenues as suggested in a J.P. Morgan "E-tailing" report, CNBC's David Faber describes the reasons for his concerns: "If a company is earning $10 today, and selling at $100, and there is no increase in earnings, then that means that it would take that company 10 years to pay for its price. But if the market price is $100 and the earnings are just one dollar, then that means 100 years to pay back."[7]

American e-tailers spent more than $3 billion on advertising in 1999. And for what advantage? CDNow, once expected to be the leading online music retailer, was one of the earliest of the *Barron's* March 20, 2000 "Burning Up!" companies.[8]

Early, Conspicuous Excess
Is Necessary to Dislodge Inertia

Conventional wisdom holds that there's no real harm in going off the rails in this first period. To the contrary, without that initial explosion, there's good reason to believe that nothing will happen.

Inertia, after all, is the *real* dominant force in business. All markets are supply-demand driven, and without that initial dream of astonishing—many times unreasonable—profits, there are doubts as to whether capital is drawn to the new sector. Or whether corporations will change strategies enough to create something new where nothing existed before. Without the peer pressure that raises fears of being left behind, the "learning from others' mistakes" mindset becomes a justification for inaction.

We had a client named GTE Internet in the mid-1980s. The strategy at that time was to try to slowly but surely increase the packet switching business of the unit, an afterthought of a unit within the huge Stamford, CT, firm (recently merged with Bell Atlantic). While some scientists there and at Net pioneer BBN (later acquired by GTE) insisted that there were far more exciting applications for this packet technology (the foundation of today's Commercial Internet), no one but they saw it at the time.

No spark, no capital, no change. Only after the creation of browsers and the World Wide Web were the pieces in place to transform a business already around for years (Figure 0.1, Introduction) to something far greater.

Arguably, as the spark plug is necessary to get the internal combustion engine going, early excess is necessary to get the key market revolution of the 21st century under way at nanosecond speed.

But NIQs Come to Market, Too

So everything associated with Net excess is positive? Not quite. There's that minor detail of financiers, packagers, intermediaries, and their fellow travelers dumping hundreds of companies on the public that will fail and in some cases are failing already.

The key distortion caused by Net excess was a tsunami of non-investment quality (NIQ) companies rushed to market to meet runaway demand. And other NIQs that were brought to IPO that shouldn't have been candidates at all. *Wired's* Po Bronson warns that " . . . of every 1,000 business plans sent to venture capitalists, 6 are accepted. Of those 6 companies, 4 will go bankrupt. Only one will go public."[9]

If Bronson's numbers are even remotely close to reflecting the real Dot-Com e-wheat versus chaff crisis, then failure rates of 70% appear to be blissfully optimistic. Gartner Group predicts a failure rate up to 95% for Asian netPhase I B2C start-ups.

TRIPLE DIGIT P/E? THAT'S NOTHING

In his controversial May 8, 2000, article, Thomas G. Donlan refers to Cisco System's approximate share price of $67. The *Barron's* writer points out that at that price, the Internet infrastructure leader sells at a rather full 190 times trailing year (July 31) earnings per share. Or, 130 times Street estimates for FY 2000.[10]

Even with a robust, positive quarterly earnings announcement shortly after the Donlan article, the magnitude of triple digit P/Es tends to be tough to shake from one's mind. Pre-Internet age, superrich tech company P/E multiples above 40-65 times were subject to continuous, excruciating scrutiny as to whether such a prize valuation was deserved.

Now, with the March 10-April 14 Spring Break having broken the back of the Net's hazy, crazy initial explosion phase (1996-2000), a new question emerges: How much more of a premium beyond traditional high tech P/E levels do Net Blue Chips such as Cisco deserve?

Merely asking a Dot-Com valuation question in this bottom-up fashion is a shattering change for the momentum traders who have ruled the Internet up to now. Under momentum trading Dot-Com "logic," the unspoken instruction is to forget about all that P/E and discounted cash flow blather. The only thing that matters

Twenty-five initial public offerings of 1999, ranked by percentage gain through year-end.

ISSUER	SYMBOL	IPO SIZE (SM)	IPO DATE	% CHANGE AS OF 12/31
1. Commerce One	CMRC	69.3	7/99	2,707.1
2. PurchasePro.com	PPRO	48.0	9/99	2,478.1
3. Verticalnet	VERT	56.0	2/99	1,950.0
4. Brocade Comm. Sys.	BRCD	61.8	5/99	1,763.2
5. Vignette	VIGN	76.0	2/99	1,615.8
6. Liberate Technologies	LBRT	100.0	7/99	1,506.3
7. Redback Networks	RBAK	57.5	5/99	1,443.5
8. Ariba	ARBA	115.0	6/99	1,442.4
9. Red Hat	RHAT	84.0	8/99	1,408.9
10. Vitria Technology	VITR	48.0	9/99	1,362.5
11. Phone.com	PHCM	64.0	6/99	1,349.2
12. Epiphany	EPNY	66.4	9/99	1,294.5
13. Kana Comm.	KANA	49.5	9/99	1,226.7
14. Akamai Technologies	AKAM	234.0	10/99	1,160.1
15. Foundry Networks	FDRY	125.0	9/99	1,106.8
16. F5 Networks	FFIV	30.0	6/99	1,040.0
17. Silknet Software	SILK	45.0	5/99	1,005.0
18. Art Technology Group	ARTG	60.0	5/99	967.7
19. Agile Software	AGIL	63.0	8/99	934.5
20. Braun Consulting	BRNC	28.0	8/99	921.4
21. Tibco Software	TIBX	109.5	7/99	920.0
22. Juniper Networks	JNPR	163.2	6/99	900.0
23. Proxicam	PXCM	58.5	4/99	856.3
24. Digital Island	ISLD	60.0	6/99	851.3
25. MyPoints.com	MYPT	40.0	8/99	825.0

Source: Joanna Pearlstein, "The Top IPOs of 1999," (June 2000) *Going Public 2000*, A supplement to *Red Herring*, pp. 10-11. Copyright © 2000 *Red Herring* magazine. Reprinted with permission.

FIGURE 2.2. Nothing succeeds like . . . a breakaway IPO in 1999.

is price action. So as long as there is a continuous flow of positive news to juice the market—and as long as you and other smart fellas like you ride the stock up, hey, then don't spoil the party.

At some point, of course, this fractured non-thinking implodes with a whoosh! The *real* smart fellas confirm that they never believed any of those ionosphere valuations in the first place. They were just following a rule even more important than any valuation rule in Chapter 1. That mandate: Don't fight the tape.

But if triple digit P/Es for top echelon Internet stars of the future cause indigestion at the peak of netPhase I in late February-early March 2000, just wait until those P/Es crash. Ulcer time.

The heading in the April edition of *Money* magazine sounds like a show on Fox: "America's Nuttiest Companies." Based on February 22, 2000, prices (a couple of weeks before the Nasdaq Composite exhaustion gap peak on March 10), Figure 2.1 shows some trailing year P/Es that make Cisco's triple digit numbers look like chump change.

SonicWall (SNWL) receives the questionable distinction of an 8,675 P/E times trailing FY99 earnings per share. SonicWall sells online securities devices and made $147,000 in profits in 1999. Far behind is Internet security company VeriSign (VRSN) at 7,454 times, and mere business software company Hummingbird (HUMC) is far behind at 2,250 times.[11]

It gets better. These were only the companies that made *profits*. The trailing year P/E for a Black Hole Dot-Com that is profitless now and possibly forever is either infinite or zero, depending on how high you can count.

EXCESS, THEN CRASH: NETSPEED BRANDING

In the United States, Dot-Com advertising on national television soared from an estimated $240 million in 1998 to a whopping $1.16 billion in 1999 (source: CNN *Moneyline*, May 11, 2000). But now that ad spending chart threatens to resemble the share price chart of your favorite Dot-Com over the Spring Break bloodletting.

A Curious Theory
That Spreads Like Wildfire

NetSpeed branding arose in the latter half of netPhase I, 1996-Q1 2000. Simply stated, this is the brainstorm that throwing billions of other peoples' dollars at N-minus one and two past generation media is the best way to ensure a robust Dot-Com brand capable of making prevailing nosebleed valuations seem slightly more justifiable. And presumably, somewhat better insulated against imminent collapse.

The billions spent by Dot-Coms on this type of advertising in 1999 set up the terrestrial advertising industry for a withdrawal jolt in 2000 as vapor ad budgets were abruptly cancelled, sometimes along with the companies themselves. This caused double-ulcers at those ad agencies where management erred by mistaking a fluke for a long-term trendline.

Ah, but aren't such misjudgments the essence of the ultimate game of roulette, playing the momentum market? Hundreds of Braniac Dot-Com marketeers all seemed to come up with the same brilliant notion at about the same time. With that much talent all leaning in the same direction, how could the idea be anything less than stellar?

As Virtual Bob, the VP in charge of painting a word picture of cyber marketing success, explains the situation:

> *The best way to build an online, franchise-level nameplate is through a blitzkrieg of ephemeral images on TV and billboards. Images that will only be remembered for seconds afterwards, if at all. Then, we reduce those ads' effectiveness still further with distracting graphics and cutesy ego-trip touches. One-upmanship is essential. This isn't a business we're talking about here, it's a matter of personal creativity. So our latest idea combines the best of both.*

But What If Everyone Else Is ALSO Catapulting Porcupines on Super Bowl Spots

B2C competition more than doubled in 1999, which meant that ad budgets had to double or more just to keep pace. There was no extra value for these outlays of course, just industry-wide value reduction as everyone paid more and more in order to be heard over the increasing din.

What, you say that lightweight TV and media ads almost never work in building franchise-caliber brand strength? That it takes years of careful positioning, as H.J. Heinz learned under Tony O'Reilly's leadership when the company first retrenched and then added back its ongoing foundation brand spending in the late 1980s to mid 1990s. Boring man, we have to develop a household name nameplate in a fraction of the time because we only have two years cash, max.

Just because we're a publicly traded company, don't make the mistake of thinking that we are financially or operationally viable for more than eighteen months.

Ah, But Who Pays?

Fool someone once and they'll be foolish for a day. But teach someone to fool themselves, and they'll be foolish for a lifetime.

RJ to Vern, *Over the Hedge* cartoon

Hey, don't worry, dude. Bubba GreaterFool is picking up this bill. You don't think we'd be stupid enough to pay for this stuff out of our own pocket, do you? Oh, and we'll continue to cite examples of Yahoo! as the one time that scattergun media saturation approaches worked in creating a major Net brand worth hundreds of millions in its own right. We'll stick to that cover story until forced to file for bankruptcy.

What we won't remind you of (and what we hope you don't remember) is that Yahoo! was a one-off phenomenon never to be repeated because of the absence of any comparable Web offerings at that time in the Netboom.

Dozens of Yahoo! wannabee portals — ISPs-community sites (hey, one of 'em has to make some money) have of course learned that Yahoo! one-off lesson the hard way. But it's not so hard for us, after all. GreaterFool pays, always.

And now, our greatest victory. We've actually fooled Bubba into mislabeling throwaway marketing outlays as core investment in the future. So the worse we do, the more he thinks we're adding to the foundation for future success.

"DOING A BLODGET"

Another conspicuous example of Net excess arises as the explosive growth of the Internet market occasionally comes to be viewed as a vehicle for career enhancement.

Setting the Price

Merrill Lynch's Henry Blodget is one of the Dot-Com Big Three analysts, along with Mary Meeker and Abby Joseph Cohen. They have names that are not just recognized on lower Broadway in Manhattan but also on Broadway in Los Angeles and Dallas, anywhere that amazon.com, Cisco, Yahoo!, and Qualcomm are monitored daily.

The articulate Mr. Blodget's visibility and compensation surged after he "priced" amazon.com at a high target level in early netPhase I, only to have that target beaten far more and far sooner than expected. Thus are Dot-Com super-analyst reputations made.

So "Doing a Blodget" is our term for a career enhancing price-setting recommendation. A target set in the future. Babe Ruth pointing to right field before his Series home run (we don't care if in the real event against the Cubs it didn't happen that way. Blodget has only heard that story a million times by now).

Must Get the Timing Right

One caveat, though: if you're going to set a future high price objective, make sure it's during a clear upsurge market. Because even if the individual company/stock languishes, there's always a chance that the rising tide effect of an overall market surge may bail you by raising all valuations, including your company's.

However, the opposite can happen in turbulent markets. And there were few more turbulent markets than on April 6, 2000, the fourth week in the five-week Spring Break period that saw the Merrill Lynch B2B Internet Holders Trust drop by 68.6%.[12]

On April 6, 2000, *The Wall Street Journal*'s Steve Frank interviewed QXL.com chairman Jonathan Bulkeley on CNBC's daily

Internet Investor segment. QXL is listed on both the Nasdaq and in London. The topic in the interview was the company's 123+% share price rise that day following what can only be characterized as an incendiary report issued by SG Cowen analyst Tom Bock, based in London. The analyst set a "price objective" of $25 billion in two years for the European online auction site, according to CNBC and Mr. Frank at the time.

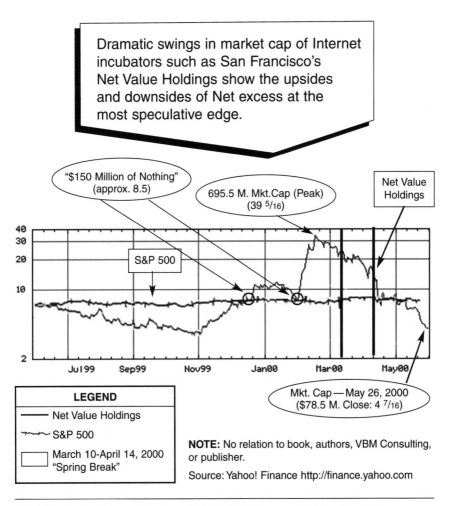

FIGURE 2.3. NetValue-Holdings (NETV.OB): One year to May 26, 2000.

Obviously, such an ambitious target issued during a watershed period of major market transition was based only on the most exhaustive analysis. SG Cowen has a well-earned reputation as a research leader, and that first echelon standing wasn't built by pulling numbers out of the air.

Of course, such an aggressive call leaned heavily on exacting discounted free cash flow (DCF) analysis, as changes in DCF correlate almost perfectly with market value and thus have emerged as the only consistently credible methodology for more than two decades (Figure 1.5, Chapter 1). Right?

Not quite. Mr. Bock's methodology, interpreted by Frank, was to say—in effect— that since EBay achieved a market "valuation" of $25 billion at some point in the past, then QXL.com could also reach that same level within a couple years.

Why the Ruthian guess? We suspect that the continuing rise of the Merrill Lynch Internet star analyst lingers in the minds of many other capable but lesser-known securities analysts. And of course it is just coincidental that the European edition of *The Wall Street Journal* ran articles the week before about the absence of European Internet gurus able to steer markets in the same manner as the US Dot-Com Big Three of Meeker, Cohen, and Blodget.

NET EXCESS POSTER CHILD

1999's Dream Share Price Progression

But if we had to choose one company, one stock that best epitomizes excess in the Commercial Internet's first phase, our vote would go to Qualcomm, Inc. (Figure 2.4). Why is Qualcomm our choice for illustration here? Because of a share price progression in netPhase I's final full year, 1999, that looks as if it was drawn by a market angel. Relentlessly upward, blasting right through the April 1999 quasi-correction.

Most charts on QCOM must be done using a log scale, as the share price surge in 1999 was so astonishing. We've deliberately shown an arithmetic scale just so you can fully appreciate what happens when a momentum market clicks just right and fundamentals seem to support the price movement.

"Mo" (Chapter 3) is a self-fulfilling prophecy, and in the case of QCOM, a simultaneous look at both the price action AND volume through that year, and you can almost sense the momentum building up through each of the four quarters. The 200-day moving average was first broken back at the beginning of the year, and although the dollar share gains were modest, the increases on a percentage basis caught traders' attention with the result that the company was designated as a breakaway candidate in March.

Blessed with that gravity-defying designation and with massive daily volume spikes in March and April 1999, QCOM was off to the races. QCOM bulled through the April mini-correction that stalled some Dot-Coms and that was described at the time as the most serious threat to the Net up to that time. With a predictable sawtooth price pattern in place, backward justification takes over. Hey, these recommendations to buy Internets (in general) and Qualcomm (specifically) actually work.[13]

---

valueOUTPERFORMER
www.vbmresources.com

May 24, 2000

SIX INDICATIONS THAT YOUR DOT-COM'S BURN RATE IS EXCESSIVE

6.) Madonna calls the Dot-Com to inquire about becoming media spokesperson.

5.) Abba's "Money, money, money" is played to callers put on hold in place of Muzak.

4.) Electronic transmission of the company's monthly check detail causes a crash.

3.) Betting shops in London agree to take odds on when the company's cash will dry up.

2.) ALL employees who don't work out are made vice chairmen in charge of business development.

1.) Jack Willoughby, author of *Barron's* "Burning Up!" article of March 20, 2000, is waiting at the front door with notebook in hand one morning.

Morphing into Whatever
Is the Hot Net Sector at the Time

Another characteristic making Qualcomm the 1999 Net excess poster child is the capability to adapt to whatever the hot sector is.

In the third and fourth quarter of 1998, some disquieting rumbles began to emerge about the shaky business-to-consumer (B2C) sector. Some spoilsports suggested that the broadly held B2C concept that markets could grow fastest by reducing price and making up the difference was fatally flawed, a vapor model (more on this in Chapter 4).

By the first quarter of 1999, the business-to-consumer story was beginning to get a little frayed, especially for those late entrants who spoke of having to go on an ad blitz to make up for their timing disadvantage and too many competitors. Slowly but surely, the Dot-Com world shifted to a new mode: find the winning sector.

Qualcomm? Momentum has a funny way of making the arguments all fall into place. When B2C was seen as the true promise of the Net at its fastest, most explosive best, Qualcomm technology was described as critical for growth of "smart" cellular systems directed at today's increasing number of mobile consumers. And when that momentum swung to B2B in the second half of the year (that is, away from B2C), well Qualcomm was also described as essential to next-generation business-to-business wireless communications, both within firms and between customers and their suppliers.

Individual Investor Favorite

NetPhase I was all about the online individual investor acting with the confidence that they were smart money. And about institutional investors smart enough to let that story ride, in return for setting up a built-in shock absorber for if/when markets turned south (handy, as it turned out).

QCOM was one of Bubba GreaterFool's absolute favorites, treated for practical purposes as Dot-Com (because of its third-generation, Net-enabled phone aspect) but with positive earnings, unlike many of the other Nasdaq Internet and Net-related blue chips. 1999 was still young when that compelling upward saw-tooth pattern first manifested itself.

It's just like they say in those "experts" sheets. Buy Internets on every dip. Look at the dips and the volume simultaneously, and you can almost see all those "idea" light bulbs go off, all at once.

The other aspect of Qualcomm that was right for the time was that volume was deep enough to support that single stock player pouncing on quarters and halves (hopefully not on eighths), making the brokerage, along for the ride, rich. Thin floats that exaggerate movement? Far less of a factor here than with most of the other Dot-Coms.

Return to Fundamentals, But Only after Mo is Winged

We also chose Qualcomm as the "poster child" here for reasons beyond the classic 1999 super-boom price pattern. Another consideration was the *nature* of enthusiasm for the San Diego-based company.

Although CDMA is understandably pushed as a technology miracle by CEO Irwin Jacobs, some regard CDMA somewhat differently, as one of several alternative cellular technologies battling for the Net future. And with marketing and alliances probably being as important as the technology in growing that platform as a standard.[14]

NET EXCESS: IMPLICATIONS FOR NET PHASE II

Internet excess during the 1997 to spring 2000 first phase was spectacular. On macro and a micro basis, the Net earned full scores for the explosion of new financing, valuations that defied sanity. And even a set up for a spectacular post-IPOs crash.

The excess is hardly less on a micro basis, as Alex (19) and Meshkin (23) form a lifestyle online community, Surfbuzz.com,

Qualcomm (QCOM)'s unrelenting 1999
momentum market surge capped netPhase I's
last full year. But on the downside, QCOM also
shows what happens when there is no
"Mo" (momentum).

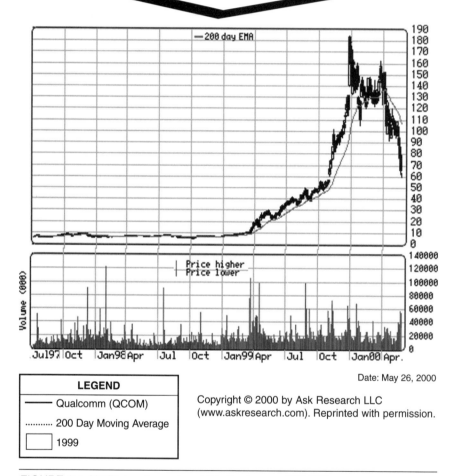

LEGEND
—— Qualcomm (QCOM)
·········· 200 Day Moving Average
▢ 1999

Date: May 26, 2000

FIGURE 2.4. NetPhase I's poster child, Qualcomm (QCOM).

complete with self-assessment of a compelling business proposition that is possibly lunatic.

And there's the interestingly named Boo.com, where founders that looked like they came from central casting spent more than $120 million over a year or so and then blamed financiers for not giving them more money.

In the 1849 California gold rush, there were stirring stories about kids cleaning up the saloons becoming tycoons as they collected gold dust that made its way under the floor boards to the ground below. Massively valuable natural gas was routinely burned as worthless at the southwestern Pennsylvania and Spindletop (Texas) oil strikes, demonstrating massive waste.

Seems that every time that exotic excess explodes and sometimes even consumes many early participants, there's always someone eager to proclaim that the economic world is coming to an end. But it isn't. This excess is the foundation that makes future periods of Dot-Com success possible.

THE WALL STREET JOURNAL
www.wsj.com

February 1, 2000

Excerpt from
SUPER BOWL VIEWERS SUFFER
FROM DOT-COM OVERLOAD

by John Dodge

On Super Bowl Sunday, 17 dot-coms, a half-dozen of them complete unknowns, entertained viewers with everything from cowboys herding cats for EDS (my favorite) to one sponsor proudly airing the "worst ad" by flashing single lines of type on the screen against a bilious yellow background. That was LifeMinders.com Inc. (www.lifeminders.com), and its ad lived up to the hype: It was bad.

A year ago, Cyberian Outpost Inc. (www.outpost.com) set the tone for dot-com advertising, simulating the cannon firing of a gerbil into a wall. For the rest of 1999, viewers were barraged with humorous, freakish ads aimed purely at attention-getting. Problem was, viewers found the ads memorable and the sponsors forgettable.

Notes

1. Joe Lauris, "Technology Stocks under Pressure as Frenzy Ends," *The Sunday Times* (London), January 9, 2000, Business 3/9.

2. "Stocks to Watch," *Red Herring* (www.redherring.com), March 2000, 416.

3. Duncan Hughes, "For the Mafia, It's Not Crime, It's Just Business," *Sunday Business* (London), June 18, 2000, 20.

4. "Living Dead," *Red Herring* (www.redherring.com), June 2000, 226.

5. *Going Public in 2000, Red Herring* (www.redherring.com), June 2000, 11.

6. Matt Murray and Jeffrey A. Tannenbaum, "Anatomy of a Crash: From Software Star to Hotel Corpse," *The Wall Street Journal*, June 20, 2000, 1.

7. *CNBC Market Watch*, December 9, 1999.

8. "Burning Up!" by Jack Willoughby. Statistic from: Alexander, Garth, "Dotcon Burnout," April 9, 2000, *The Sunday Times* (London), 3.5.

9. As told to Bronson by a would-be Internet start-up entrepreneur, from *The Nudist on the Late Shift and Other Tales of Silicon Valley* (New York, Random House, 1999), 29.

10. "Cisco Bids," 31.

11. "Word on the Street," 45–46.

12. Bob Tedeschi, "How Killer B-to-B's Slid to Endangered List," *The New York Times* (www.nytimes.com), May 7, 2000. Also Figure 5.1, Chapter 5.

13. "Stocks to Watch," *Red Herring* (www.redherring.com), March 2000, 416.

14. "Free Value: Qualcomm's Dr. Strangelove," *The Economist*, June 17, 2000, 96.

EFFICIENT MO

"Technical trading strategies (became) self-validating" says Professor W. Brian Arthur, economist at the Santa Fe Institute in New Mexico. "Ripples of change in expectations avalanche their way through the market in domino effect."

> Ip, Greg, Browning, E.S.,
> "Unprecedented Nasdaq Swings
> Don't Leave Investors Shaky,"
> *The Wall Street Journal,*
> May 12, 2000, 6

Remember momentum? It was a widely touted style back when the market's "mo" was one way—up. They loved aggressive growth stocks—i.e., technology. If momentum investors wanted to take a stock up, they did. They impaled short sellers. They defied value investors.

> Brett D. Fromson,
> "Woe Is Mo: A Struggling Momentum
> Manager Waits for Tech's Moment,"
> www.TheStreet.com, May 30, 2000

Homespun valuations, sometimes based on contortions of respected techniques, opened the door to IPOs for the seventy percenters: the non-investment quality (NIQ) firms with less than a 50/50 chance to survive, much less thrive.

Momentum let all the netPhase I Dot-Coms soar, both deserving firms and NIQs. For a while.

Globe.com was the IPO that started it all, surging in a torrid first day IPO that helped set the precedent for later netPhase I deals. Not that the momentum continued forever. Globe was 94% off its all-time highs as of mid-June, 2000.

But that's the dark side of the Dot-Com market implosion in Spring 2000. Before that time of reckoning, the illusion was maintained that even though many of the Dot-Coms were losing massive amounts of money, overall they deserved nosebleed valuations. A couple might become future stars. You could never tell whether a Dot-Com you owned was a star or a dog. In optimistic times, that can mean that many assume that a star is born, regardless of the facts.

For the netPhase I valuation manipulator, the key was to somehow, some way, extend temporary enthusiasm. With enough people believing that the Efficient Market means that the company is worth whatever the market says, the stage is set for a circular self delusion: the Dot-Com company is worth a nosebleed valuation because of the market valuation, which in turn reflects the valuation of the Dot-Com company.

Keep that loop spinning fast enough so that the common sense questions stop, and Mo—the momentum market—is established. Seemingly with a stamp of compliance if not approval from Efficient Market and the related Rational Theory.

WHEN THE RATIONAL MODEL IS IRRATIONAL

The idea that the unpredictability of returns means that markets are efficient is one of the most remarkable errors in the history of economic thought.

Professor Robert J. Shiller, author,
Irrational Exuberance (2000)[1]

All but the most extreme Efficient Market zealots admit that there are some situations when the Efficient Market just doesn't work. The issue is how long that situation persists, and how severe the distortion becomes.

The short-term breakdown means an investment opportunity to the opportunistic "value" investor. *The market should be reacting in this manner based on all the information known or suspected, but it isn't, so I'll take advantage.* But the belief is that these are aberrations, and that as soon as all available information is fully assimilated by the marketplace, all inefficiencies, all disparities disappear. Along with any chance to take advantage.

Extended Periods of Exuberance Versus Market Efficiency

The applause (if you agree with his key arguments)/controversy (if you don't) generated by Professor Shiller's book *Irrational Exuberance* reopens the Efficient Market issue, with some new aspects. Rather than viewing the market's departures from Efficient Market as very limited short-term windows of primary interest to the act-now-ask-questions-later opportunist investor, Shiller describes extended periods of market "exuberance." That's the polite word for "craziness."

Shiller argues today, as Charles Mackay did almost 160 years earlier in *Extraordinary Popular Delusions and the Madness of Crowds*, that underlying these apparently irrational market periods are mass emotional states.[2] Reactions that cause a believable illusion of an alternative reality. Some even suggest that this is a form of mass hypnosis.

For when the mania is at full effect, the momentum market mesmerized participants all believe they are acting perfectly normally—at least based on the new rules in effect in the new era. So, yesteryear's Dutch tulip bulbs, phantom property rights in the French Louisiana Purchase, property in Tokyo's downtown Ginza district in the late 1980s, and Qualcomm in the fourth quarter of 1999 all take on fantasy values that seem high at the time, yet still rational.

When I Snap My Fingers You Will Awaken and Feel Wonderfully Refreshed

At certain extreme points, both Mackay and Shiller hint that even the deepest mass hypnosis spells unwind.

A ravenous sailor in Holland devours a tulip bulb thinking it is a sweet onion and is presented with a bill for many years' salary. As described in Mackay: "Little did he dream that he had been eating a breakfast whose cost might have regaled a whole ship's crew for a twelve month."[3] Property in Tokyo's Ginza in 1990 had to be quoted in terms of square inches because there were too many zeros to express the price.

Of course, these are modern times and none of these past excesses have anything at all to do with the Dot-Com surge economy, right? Small fuzzy mammals shot through the air for millions in millennium TV ads to "build core brand awareness" of Dot-Com companies is reasonable. Right.

A Dot-Com travel and reservation service with infinite competitors and alternatives, online and otherwise, creates instant paper millionaires. Investment advisory sites combining financial news found in a dozen newspapers are initially valued in the tens of millions of dollars.

Snap Back

Shiller argues that when such extremes become too great, the result can be a shock return back to more customary conditions, often an abrupt change that shatters markets and prosperity at the same time. The Great Depression and economic downturns following market peaks in 1901 and the late 1960s support that general argument.

Many believe that *Barron's* March 20 cover story "Burning Up!" by Jack Willoughby was a trigger to the March to April 2000 Nasdaq initial collapse, as described later in this chapter. Willoughby warns that the vacuum caused by imploding Dot-Com markets could slam sentiment in the opposite direction, with investors forced to dump any and all remaining assets for "salvage."[4]

Efficient Market purists argue that all such behavioral factors are sidebar considerations. That everything that anyone ever needs to know about the market is contained solely in the price and volume data. By contrast, supporters of "behavioral finance" contend that the numbers reflect the emotions of the era.

Viewed in this way, some of the actions and assumptions that were laughable in spring 2000 seem almost reasonable, at least some of the time.

As with any brainwashing, the first requirement is said to be to detach the subject from any reference point. The military interrogator applies darkness, fear, and pain to achieve this detachment. In 1996 to 1999, the device is the mind-boggling 13-figure (yes, that's *trillions*) projections that bubble up in venerable "Rings O' Saturn" Research Company (etc.).

Trillion. Such a figure defies imagination and paints a magical world where just showing up and somehow managing even a sliver of a whisper of market penetration assures astonishing success.

But it's all an illusion. There are no markets anywhere where participation alone is enough, as the fourth Internet Services Provider in a field consolidating to two discovers, painfully, as Year 2000 progresses. Along with the seventh online search engine in a field headed for three (the Dot-Com consolidation imperative is examined in Chapter 6).

The Message

The Internet marketplace is the new paradigm. The old rules no longer apply. Profits are irrelevant to future success, at least in the early stages. The key is Netspeed.

Even when such messages are patently absurd, enough reinforcement means that the big lie might become as conventional wisdom. Psychologists have experimented with subjects being presented with absolutely absurd statements by peers on a continuing basis. In one such instance, about a third of the subjects started chanting the same nonsense as the babblers.

In the case of the netPhase I (1996 to spring 2000), part of the Dot-Com boom, the most powerful reinforcements were prices themselves. What better way to argue that a new order exists than to see market values soar far past the levels of industrial leaders of

past decades? In 1999, no one *cared* that Qualcomm's CDMA technology was only applicable to part of the world's total future cellular phones—key was the share price action. *Did you see Qualcomm's share price suge today? They must really be on to something great!*

Trader mentality helps speed the process of self-hypnosis, accepting momentum illusions as real. *Never fight the tape* might alternatively be translated as *Don't think about it too much.* Don't over-intellectualize what is essentially an observe-and-react game.

If the reward for suspending belief that the world is round is riches, the trader says be careful when you travel around the world you don't fall off the edge of the Earth.

The danger comes when price action reinforces the irrationality. Jimmy Ling's "redeployment" was laughable in the early 1970s, but then the share price of LTV increased and hallucination and reality swapped places. For a while. Everyone in the world is going to buy their own CDMA cellular phone from Qualcomm some day, anyway.

CASH INFLOWS GENERATE MOMENTUM

> *The Federal Reserve blew up the money supply in 1999, which is why the tech stock prices soared.*
>
> Courtney Smith, Courtney Smith & Co.,
> CNN *Moneyline*, May 19, 2000

Money makes the world go round. And excess money causes surge valuations. Market cash flow in the form of M3 (in Figure 3.1) cash flow in the form of inflows to Internet-intensive mutual funds.

Monetary Policy and the Dot-Coms

Each month without fail, a circus surrounds that month's new speculation about imminent changes in the Federal Reserve Board's interest rate policy. Will Greenspan change the overnight funds rate? By how much? And what will the Fed's bias be for future actions?

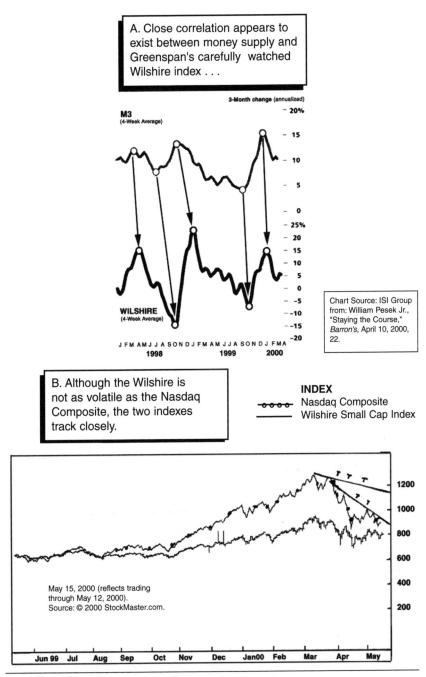

FIGURE 3.1. Dot-Com momentum and money supply.

But those questions all involve *fiscal* policy. Figure 3.1 points to the linkage between monetary policy and the tech/Dot-Com indices. The Wilshire Index has been identified as one of the Fed chairman's key reference points for assessing market conditions. The Wilshire is not the same as the Net-rich Nasdaq Composite, but the two indexes generally track together (Figure 3.1, B).

Implications? While all the focus is on the next interest rate action, the Fed has shown itself to be willing to err on the side of ensuring liquidity rather than risk a recession. The surge in the four-week average for M3 in late 1999 just happens to mirror the hockey stick upswing in share prices of your favorite business-to-business company in those months, such as VerticalNet or Commerce One.

Of course, this is all just a coincidence. It just happens that B2B was the favored Net sector at that time, attracting funds investment from institutions and individuals "buying" the B2B overall master business model, hook, line, and sinker.

Cash Flows into Mutual Funds

Cash inflows to US mutual funds slowed to a trickle in April 2000, to a reported $2.4 billion. No surprise, considering the aftershocks of the Spring Break 2000 shakeout. But where is that money going? Part goes to pay off debts, some under the mattress.

But a significant amount is also going into direct purchase of shares, as investors try to outdo boring market returns projected by Abby Joseph Cohen and others.

In March 2000, the Goldman Sachs star analyst announced that she anticipated an annual increase in the S&P 500 of less than 9% per annum. Cohen's projection may seem impressive compared to single-digit Fed funds rates, but that's chump change for investors accustomed to thinking of a 20% annual return as a disappointment.

In arguing that individual investors should place their funds in a mutual fund calling for diversified investment and reduced risk, *The Wall Street Journal*'s Jonathan Clements may have instead revealed why many such investors often do the exact opposite.

In attempting to make his case for lower risk, greater return through mutual fund ownership, Clements nonetheless admits that "most of the huge gains in recent years have been achieved by a mere handful of companies."

Bubba GreaterFool compares the performance value-investing mutual fund versus his handful of blue chip Dot-Coms and sees that he can triple his return by gambling on a few net stars.[5]

---

valueOUTPERFORMER
www.vbmresources.com

March 21, 2000

VALUATION BY DOT-COM STAR GURU

When there are no signposts around, you ask someone who knows the area well for directions. With present and prospective shareholders of Internet companies struggling to somehow, some way separate tomorrow's Dot-Com champions from the e-victims ready for the coming shakeout, the role of the Internet industry star analyst takes on added significance. Henry Blodget of Merrill Lynch, Abby Cohen of Goldman Sachs, and Mary Meeker of Morgan Stanley Dean Witter lead the ranks of the star Dot-Com industry analysts, based in large part on their past effectiveness in spotting today's B2C Internet stars when they were still fledgling Dot-Com wannabes. Meeker's reputation is linked in part to on-target observations about global online auction firm EBay. Blodget often comments on amazon.com, the company that effectively cemented his reputation after a longball price target was reached in record time.

Arguably, the influence of these Dot-Com gurus has expanded so much that the superstar analysts can actually help determine stock prices and thus market values themselves. Or at least, mitigate the effects on some of the companies they follow. The hard-hitting Mar. 20, 2000 *Barron's* cover story alleges that a dozen Internet companies are burning cash so rapidly as refinancing prospects dwindle that the firms could implode. Blodget's quick retort stopped markets, as he raised legitimate questions about the methodology used and its application. Questions that were welcomed by the article's author, senior editor Jack Willoughby. Some of the companies in the *Barron's* piece have secured additional financing since the time of the original analysis, Blodget notes. So when the Dot-Com Big Three of Blodget, Cohen, or Meeker talk, e-markets listen.

Estimated capital raised by venture capital firms (billions, left)
vs. number of VC funds raising $1 billion each year (right).

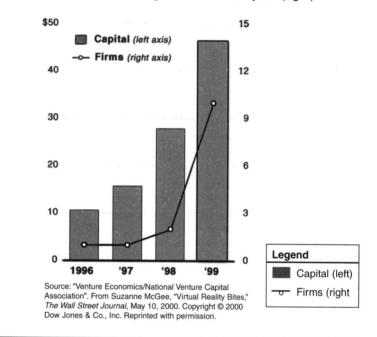

FIGURE 3.2. Follow the money. Venture capital in netPhase I: Funds and firms.

CREATING BUBBA GREATERFOOL

*March (2000) marked the peak of a six-month surge in the opening of
new brokerage accounts, many of them online. Not coincidentally, the
Nasdaq Composite Index peaked at about the same time. It has slid by
nearly a third since then and many leveraged traders have been forced
to sell . . .*

The LEX Column,
Financial Times "US Markets,"
May 22, 2000, page 32

Think of it as *My Fair Lady,* but with manic Joe Pesci in place of
Rex Harrison as the instructing professor.

And instead of smoothing the way into society, the Professor's
purpose is to continually inspire the most gullible of momentum
slaves to buy Dot-Coms at any price. *Someone* has to buy the seven-

ty percenters, those netPhase I Dot-Com companies named for their expected failure probability by January 1, 2002.

I think he's got it. Every big sting requires fools in order to work. People oblivious to the fact that they are paying good money for bad companies: cyber-shells with seven chances out of ten of collapsing and being sold for scrap.

Except that there *is* no scrap. These are knowledge businesses, which means that the true assets walk out the door at night. Or rather, they bolt as soon as they discover that management isn't going to do anything about their underwater options.[6]

Bubba has always existed for exploiters, of course. Odd lots (share purchases not in 100-share round lot multiples) reveal Bubba's identity faster than a 30% discount on Rebel Yell.™ And it has long been known that year in, year out, the odd lot short index remains one of the better predictors of stock market (and thus valuation) future direction.

You see, Bubba is a negative Einstein. A south-pointing compass. So consistently wrong in his investment sense that he is usually far more useful than a pickup truck loaded with so-called stock-picker experts!

Just do the opposite of Bubba. For years, *decades*, the real smart money (smart enough to call someone else "smart money") was content to use Bubba in no greater role. The only recurring theme about retail customers was that they were disappearing, that the whole show was institutions.

Then, groups such as David and Tom Gardner's *Motley Fool* (www.fool.com) emerged in the 1990s with what seemed to be a logical argument. If the Wise (*Fool* shorthand for neglectful brokers and financial advisers who fleece their individual accounts as easily as they breathe) underperform, then individuals can do a much better job for themselves.

Fool's causal link deteriorates somewhat under closer scrutiny. Individuals can and do often perform far worse than "smart money" institutions, as reflected by the massive empirical data of the odd lot short index. Ah, we are informed that it is trading *tactics* that make the difference, rather than *who* does the trading. But the Gardners' message that Bubba is the clever one goes down smoothly. With *Fool's* enthusiasts. It never hurts to flatter your customer.[7]

So what caused Bubba GreaterFool's role to expand? Necessity. *Someone* has to act as the buyer of last resort to fortify netPhase I market values up there in the ionosphere. Who better to play the part than someone who has never even heard of fundamental business analysis? Who better than Bubba, who likes his investment advice light and frothy even if that means fictional.

GreaterFool is the ideal buyer of shares of non-investment quality companies, Dot-Com and otherwise. Someone easily impressed by IPO share prices tripling on the first day, but who never asks *why*.

---

valueOUTPERFORMER
www.vbmresources.com

March 8, 2000

Adapted from
BEGINNING OF END FOR NET VALUE IPO GREATERFOOL?

The announcement in *The Wall Street Journal* on Mar. 8 was uneventful: "Net2000 Communications Inc. shares surged 75% Tuesday from their initial-public-offering price."

ONLY 75%? Granted, this is a sample set of one, but from time to time now as Spring awakes, one sees more (gasp) moderate first day IPO bumps such as this—instead of the more familiar doubling to quadrupling stellar results that turn otherwise reasonable individuals into a fire-breathing Purchase-Any-Dot-Com-Anytime feeding frenzy.

Given that IPO prices and share scarcity are both carefully calibrated to ensure those breathtaking 2-4x launch day price moves that ensure effusive biz-press headlines the next day, a wimpy 75% stands out like a sore thumb.

After all, Net2000 maintains a fully credentializing high burn rate, with losses reported to be deepening from a reported $13.8 million in 1998 to a far more impressive $38.8 million in 1999. Hey, if they didn't have something great to spend money on, then their burn rate wouldn't be so impressive, right. Hey, makes sense to us.

Postscript: Nasdaq Composite reached its all-time high two sessions later, on March 10.

Typically, the business of the company has a limited connection of the shareholder doing the purchasing. But when Bubba Greaterfool buys GM, the momentum reinforcement "score" is two: one for Bubb's recognition that GM makes cars, and one for the fact that Bubba drives a car. But a score of five emerges for some Dot-Com company share buyers, with a stellar six for daytraders who now see surfing for share opportunities online as their new "profession."

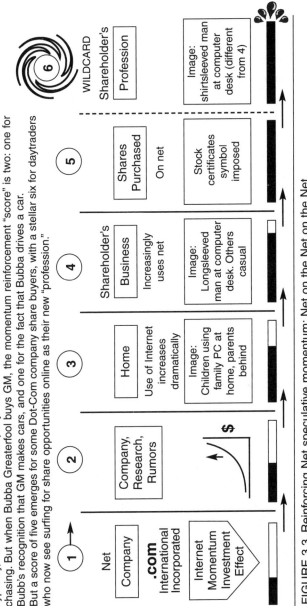

FIGURE 3.3. Reinforcing Net speculative momentum: Net on the Net on the Net.

Momentum is difficult if not impossible to sustain when senior management and other insiders are selling. With credible fundamental data about Dot-Com companies scarce to non-existent, insider sales data takes on exaggerated importance as an indirect indication of management's expectations about the future.

Planned sales of restricted share, first quarter 2000

Company	Shares Filed to Sell	Value of Shares
Microsoft	48.62 million	$4.66 billion
JDS Uniphase	21.1 million	$4.03 billion
Internet Capital Group	17.4 million	$2.05 billion
Commerce One	8.63 million	$1.76 billion
eBay	5.60 million	$1.03 billion
VeriSign	3.41 million	$685 million
Priceline	8.81 million	$604 million
Infospace	4.01 million	$592 million
Ariba	2.75 million	$512 million

Per CDA investment, from Anjali Arora, "Early Birds Fly the Coop," *Industry Standard,* www.thestandard.com, May 29, 2000, 90.

FIGURE 3.4. Momentum killer: Insider sales.

Bubba GreaterFool is easily zombified by Net buzzwords (Chapter 4) and easily persuaded by the fragile non-logic of momentum investing. It's not the price of the shares that's important. It's who else is buying.

Most important of all, our pal Bubba is someone who never, ever wakes up in a cold sweat in the middle of the night with the shocking realization that he is throwing away good money for ownership position of companies with a 70% chance of being nothing but air. How else do you refer to a company brought to the public market before there is even minimal assurance of viability?

The mark is set up. The sting can proceed.

Yazza, Yazza, One Time Only, Don't Miss Out

Self-deception by giddy investors who assume unsustainable returns,
on the premise that other investors will be even giddier.

Robert Kuttner,
"Yes Virginia, There Is a Speculative Bubble,"
Business Week, April 17, 2000

As Dot-Com share prices settle back toward Planet Earth, post-mortem explanations abound for why some people fell for some of the nuttier guess-valuations.

There's the siren-song belief in something for nothing. Everybody's doing it. There is the inevitability argument, suggested

---

FORBES
www.forbes.com/forbes

May 15, 2000

THOUGHT CONTAGION
By Scott Woolery

Sci-fi in the Nasdaq tower? A new form of computer virus? There's no such a simple explanation for when rational markets suddenly begin to act with manic-depressive extremes. The following is an excerpt from "It's a Mad, Mad, Mad, Mad Market," *Forbes* magazine.

One intriguing avenue of inquiry in market psychology: so-called thought contagion. This explains how ideas get transmitted and gain force the more they circulate. Concepts like this may explain fads like hula hoops and they may explain some of the outlandish multiples seen in Internet-related stocks.

Aaron Lynch, an independent researcher studying the phenomenon, says the Internet (as a communications vehicle) spreads delusions about the Internet (as an investing sector). People who used the Internet a lot, says Lynch, were easily excited by its potential, and acted on wild notions with their investment dollars. They'd e-mail each other or post chat-room opinions about the latest hot stock. Next thing you know, this crowd was pouring money into businesses with little or no profit, like MicroStrategy (at 150 times sales) and Ivillage (at 50 times sales).

Or, as Lynch puts it in academic-speak: "Armed with an enriched con-centration of good electronic communicators, the shareholders of Internet companies may routinely outdo the shareholders of other young companies in belief transmission."

by stock price chart trend lines that always start in the lower left and extend to the extreme upper right corner.

And then there's One Time Only. Don't be left behind—you may never be able to buy into this company at such a low price again. The implication: miss this one shot at unbelievable personal wealth, and the door is forever closed to Bubba.

In the case of Dot-Com companies still attempting to find their value base, the One Time Only statements or inference is especially preposterous. Spectacular share prices in late 1999 and early 2000 signaled that even blue chip Dot-Com companies are struggling to establish their enduring valuation. A foundation that endures for years, not just a few trading hours.

 The Nasdaq Composite peak was reached on March 10, 2000.

 Net IPOs have slumped sharply ever since, relative to the massive backlog.

Note the abrupt decrease in gains from offering to open in 2Q00

Company	1Q99	2Q99	3Q99	4Q99	1Q00	April 2000	May 2000
Internet IPOs	8	24	27	22	26	15	13
Funds Raised **A**	$602	$2,224	$1,914	$1,680	$3114	$1,161	$846
Gain from Offering to Open	170%	65%	63%	86%	106%	26%	28%
90-day Relative Gain from Offering Price **B**	141%	117%	197%	150%	20%	N/A	N/A

Source: Chart, "The Bubble Bursts" from Jonathan Rabinovitz and Mark A. Mowrey, "IPO Market Unravels," thestandard.com, May 19, 2000, Chart Data Source: Bloomberg and *The Industry Standard*.

Notes:
A. In $ millions.

B. Average gains relative to Goldman Sachs Technology Industry Internet Index, over same time frame.

FIGURE 3.5. The first dominos fall: Internet IPOs lose momentum.

Don't kid yourself into thinking that the One Time Only pitch involves only penny shares garbage of the type pushed by mythical brokers in the movie *Boiler Room*. The message to buy, buy, buy despite shocking volatility sometimes involves the Dot-Com blue chips. On the cover of its May 15, 2000 issue, venerable *Fortune* magazine asks whether this is the last chance to buy Cisco Systems at these levels.

Such a question might border on hype if the company were anything other than the Dot-Com blue chip infrastructure leader: "No matter how you cut it, you've got to own Cisco."[8]

Endgame: IPO Death Spiral

IPOs are the first domino in the Dot-Com row. The one that causes Bubba GreaterFool's blood to boil. The Net IPO plays a particularly important role in sustaining the Dot-Com momentum market hypnotic illusion. The Dot-Com IPO is key to the netPhase I financing mechanism depicted in Figure 6.1, Chapter 6.

Favored sectors can change. Interest rates may rise. Talent shortages can create crisis conditions in parts of the Dot-Com community. But as long as there is a robust IPO market with some value stability afterwards, the netPhase I value fantasy juggernaut storms ahead. Of course, if those conditions are *not* in place, the whole mechanism begins to unwind, as suggested in the "Down the Drain" exhibit in Figure 3.6.

The IPO value wind-down has been consistent and relentless. *Industry Standard's* Rabinovitz and Mowrey report that "Between April 1999 and March 2000, Net IPOs popped into the market at an average clip of 25 a month. Only 15 made it out in April. And judging from the current pipeline (in late May 2000), May will produce no more than an unlucky 13."[9]

Mo's Ends for Bubba GreaterFool:
It's Margin Call Time

Bubba GreaterFool is broke. Busted. No cash and no place to borrow any more. Endgame for netPhase I fantasy Dot-Com valuations, because the mind-boggling individual investor daily volume that sustained those prices is gone.

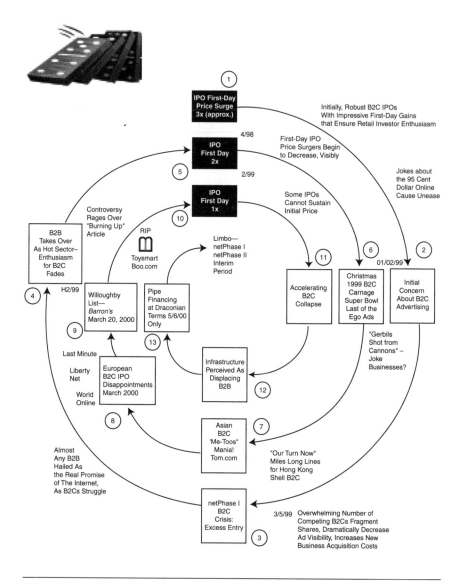

FIGURE 3.6. IPOs and momentum: B2C spirals down Q498–Q2 00.

Market soothsayers try to decipher the tea leaves of plunging daily trading volume following the crushing Spring Break of 2000. The answer lies in the fact that margin debt at the end of March 2000 was $278.5 billion, the highest level ever, according to the NYSE and brokerages. Next month, those same sources indicated a drop of $26.8 billion. That's the greatest margin debt decrease in history, in dollar terms.

"I don't think it went down because people paid off margin debt. It went down because people got wiped out," says David Carr Frank, broker with LA's Financial West Group.[10] So when it's the end of the momentum market, it's also an end to brokers' practice of scrambling to find out how their latest Dot-Com darling is faring with Bubba GreaterFool out there in the sticks.

THE FEBRUARY MASSACRE, REVISITED

Momentum markets tend to be largely oblivious to anything other than price action, by definition. Helpfully, early Dot-Com companies provide little in the way of useful data, whether public or not.

But there's one statistic that causes everyone to scramble: insider sales. A tsunami of insider sales just coincidentally occurred over the 40 days prior to the March 10 Nasdaq Composite peak. Most of the public didn't know the extent of this selling until after the five-week 34% collapse we refer to as Spring Break 2000. Just a coincidence, of course.

Of course, everyone dumping the Dot-Coms from February to mid-March 2000 just made completely independent decisions that the Net was overdue for a long-awaited implosion. No one could possibly have acted on early information. Just a coincidence, of course.

"Before Tech Stocks Tanked, Insiders Sold"

> The classic sign of any market exhaustion is that money transfers hands from the most sophisticated to the least sophisticated participants.

> InsiderScores.com President Craig Columbus
> in *The Wall Street Journal*, April 19, 2000[11]

The quote above is from an insightful Maremont/ Ewing/Egodigwe April 19, 2000, article in *The Wall Street Journal*.

According to InsiderScores.com and as cited in the *Journal* piece, insiders in the Nasdaq's largest 100 companies ranked by market capitalization sold $4.5 billion worth of shares in February 2000. That's more insider sales than for all US exchanges in February 1999. But this information didn't emerge until weeks *after* the carnage of the March 10 to April 14, 2000, Nasdaq collapse.

The explanations are always reasonable. After all, those doing the explaining are the same masters who spin the dubious theory that franchise brands can be developed on the Net in months rather than in the years that it take "terrestrial" to create Bricks 'n Mortar companies.

These are the same suits who suggest, but never promise, that e-Bankruptcy2001.com *might* become the next Yahoo! But unravel the so-called business model and you often find little more than indefensible demand projections sprinkled with Netenomics vaporprose for reasoning, words such as "scalability," "traction," and "viral marketing."[12]

The Spinners Earn Their Pay

Admittedly, this is where the spinners earn their keep. Just the idea of an owner selling any shares in a company before that company generates consistent positive cash flow is enough to make most investors' stomachs churn. If tethered analysts are talking up the stock at the same time, the revulsion deepens.

The Dot-Coms that generate losses for years and yet enjoy a king's ransom of price-to-revenue (PTR—remember, you can't calculate P/E because there are no earnings and may not be any for many years) enjoy a valuation based on the AA curve in Figure 1.3, (Chapter 1), instead of the bottom-trawler valuations AB or AC, Black Holes or Dark Models only on trust.

There's no data, just hopes and projection curves shaped like hockey sticks. The only thing that the investor-shareholder has to indicate that this is a thirty percenter (survival) rather than a seventy percenter (NIQF) company that should never have been brought to market) is the chief executive's and spinner's *words*.

---

valueOUTPERFORMER
www.vbmresources.com

April 5, 2000

BUBBA IS TAPPED OUT, E-LOCKOUT LOOMS

Momentum's hallucinatory valuation signals only work under conditions of meticulous supply-demand float management. On the upside, thin, thin share floats amplify miniscule moves, encouraging good ol' Bubba GreaterFool to jump into his pickem up truck and elope to Vegas with that there comely (but wild) Miss Momentum as retail speculators shout Yee Haa, one more Bigger Better Thing. Institutional shareholders that jumped into the Net boom in mid- to late 1999 did so only with assurance that Bubba Greater Fool was still in place, to absorb their inevitable sales. The institutions knew that share fantasy prices of 100 times losses times minus one for Year 2001's coming e-bankruptcies can only be treated as a speculative vehicle, and never as a permanent investment in a going concern. Allegedly, Peapod and Dr. Koop may no longer be viable according to their auditors. More former B2C stars will follow.

Bubba thinks about new double-wide trailers. Institutions think about exit strategy. So far, so good. At least till March 10, the "always buy Internets on spikes" advice of a full prison cell worth of instant Internet trading experts served Bubba well. But the Mar. 10-Apr. 4 ulcer-creator of a market now has even slow-witted Bubba thinking that maybe he shouldn't buy on spikes this time. Even if he wanted to, he can't. Early April margin calls mean he's wiped out. Without predictable purchasing at any price from Bubba, the float game becomes a perilous game of Russian roulette for the institutions still in.

Even the dullest pencil in that box now sees the signal and knows that a planned, orderly sale is necessary. But with only sellers left, any move by any of the co-conspirators caused the wealth of all to plunge. A new, diabolical situation for Game Theory enthusiasts to ponder. And then there's the X factor: lock-ups. To date, shares coming available because of expiration of insider trading limitations have been a benign factor. The founder of e-catfish.com has been satisfied to just count his new paper wealth each day. But the Mar. 10-Apr. 4 plunge now has Dude, the company founder, afraid that he will soon have to move out of the penthouse and back into Mom and Dad's garage. If the coming wave of lockout expirations raises fears of a wave of fear-induced insider sales, institutions will make sure they get out first. Momentum on the downside, exaggerated by the thin float.

NetPhase I was epitomized by the initial public offering that tripled or quadrupled on the first day to spark stratospheric valuations. But without the leadership provided by such IPO leadership, momentum suffers. Retail volume dries up and individual investors escape from the market.

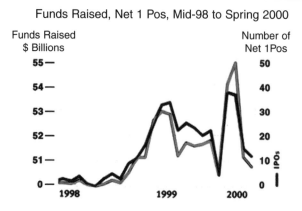

Funds Raised, Net 1 Pos, Mid-98 to Spring 2000

Source: Industry Standard and Bloomberg from Anjali Arora, "Early Birds Fly the Coop," *Industry Standard*, May 29, 2000, 90.

Funds Raised

Number IPOs
(Assumes all Net IPOs May 00)

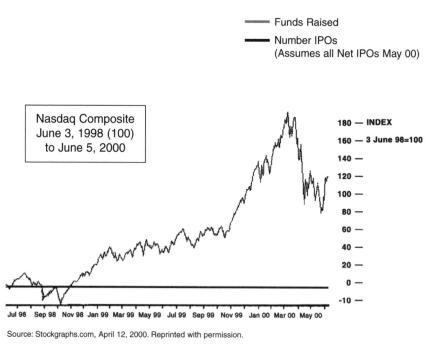

Nasdaq Composite
June 3, 1998 (100)
to June 5, 2000

Source: Stockgraphs.com, April 12, 2000. Reprinted with permission.

FIGURE 3.7. Net IPOs propel Nasdaq, mid-1998 to spring 2000.

If management and other insiders are withdrawing permanent funds from the company, there has to be a consequence some place. The Dot-Com neophyte company isn't yet generating any positive cash flow, so the cash to pay off early sellers must come from somewhere else. Is the source the marketing budget, thus jeopardizing the revenue growth rate? Is it the withdrawal from critical infrastructure investment? Or is the consequence the company cannot pursue that topnotch Corporate Key Contributor employee who could make all the difference? In the future? All of the above?

These are acute considerations if the company has not yet proven that it can survive, much less thrive. And if the company is still a private concern with no replacement funds for those that were withdrawn.

This is when a venture capitalist in times past might have gently "persuaded" the prospect's CEOs that it made sense to leave his stake in—entirely—until it was absolutely clear that any withdrawal could be offset with new cash inflows from operations.

---

www.TheStreet.com

December 8, 1999

**MAD DASH TO NASDAQ: STOCKS FLOURISH
ON INVESTING'S NEW MATH
By Justin Lahart, Associate Editor**

Take a piece of paper that is, say, 1/100 of an inch thick and fold it over. Now tale it and fold it over again—and again and again—until you have folded it 50 times. The folded-up piece of paper you ended up with would be 177,698,849 miles high—nearly twice the distance of the Earth to the sun.

Now take a stock trading at $100 a share. Add 1% to it every trading day for a year. At the end of a year, it will be trading at more than $1,200.

That's what momentum is all about: an investing style that presumes past performance actually *does* guarantee future results. It does not matter that such exponential returns are . . . as unrealizable as that folded-up paper is.

But This Is a Publicly Traded Company

There is no reduction in cash when the owners sell in the public marketplace, just a swap in share ownership. But just because the fragile company happens to be traded in a junior stock exchange somewhere in the world, is that reason to warrant doing something that would be absolutely unthinkable if that same company was still private? Prudence, if not ethics, dictate that founder capital stays until the company is solidly established as a going concern, a leader in its industry. Early bailouts may be legal but still smell funny.

Facile spinners can and do come up with scores of explanations why it's OK for early investors in a company that has not yet reached sustainable positive cash flow to sell out early.

The list of "reasonable" explanations include the one that the founders have been holding on to their restricted positions for years, and this was the first opportunity for them to receive anything approaching a fair return for their tremendous wealth-creating achievement. Another likely explanation in February 2000 was that US income taxes were due in a couple of months, and that cash was sorely needed to pay record 1999 capital gains. Then there was the argument that some "readjustments" of insiders' positions were deliberately planned to broaden the base of ownership.

Then finally, there was the fallback excuse that the lockup period for many of netPhase I's Dot-Com phenoms just happened to expire around February 2000. That argument makes it almost seem as if the sale timing was automatic, and that the insiders were merely passively following a pre-set schedule. *Hey, not our fault the market tanked.*

PIPE's Dreams

But no matter how reasonable the spin, there will always be some—including us—who contend that most Dot-Coms are fragile enough without the additional valuation burden of the potential negative signal to the financial marketplace of unexpected sales by insiders. Especially as the lack of other data multiplies the importance of insider sales as an indicator of management's true expectations about company future performance.

TRIGGER INJURES MO, FATALLY

No, this doesn't have anything to do with Roy Rogers's horse. Trigger refers to Jack Willoughby, senior editor of *Barron's*.

Willoughby is a financial journalist with a resonant Charles Osgood voice but at 78 speed. Willoughby seems to be like that professor you remember fondly from university days, the one with that exasperating but inspiring ability to slash through all that blather with his simple truths and even simpler declarative statements.

But Willoughby might go for the jugular of anyone who tries to compare him to some turncoat academic. Those are the cheerleader profs who functioned as hired gun consultant-advisers during the 1996 (birth) to Quarter 1 2000 (death) of netPhase I.

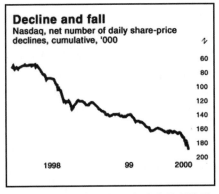

"After the Gold Rush," *The Economist*, April 22, 2000, 70. Copyright © 2000 The Economist Newspaper Group. Reprinted with permission.

Figure 3.8 Nasdaq composite: Net number of declining companies, daily share-price basis, cumulative.

The *Barron's* senior editor abhors those senior academics who sold out their Miller–Modigliani souls (along with knowledge of valuation truths that comes along with that knowledge) for a two-minute spot as a talking head "expert" on biz-TV. Those who made it sound almost reasonable that chronically unprofitable Happybang.com was selling at 200 times revenue. At least to Bubba GreaterFool. But the joke is now on Willoughby as he has become one of those media interviewees in the aftermath of his jarring "Burning Up!" piece.

Willoughby helped spark the beginning of the end of netPhase I. During that period, almost any non-investment quality e-company with a CEO who had a pulse and a story slick enough to be morphed into a (temporarily) credible business model could generate billions in IPO fantasy money.

In effect, the *Barron's* article implied that many business-to-consumer (B2C) companies were now low to no-value shells with less than a few quarter's cash before Endgame, with specific companies cited.

If that was as far as the Willoughby articles went, no problem. B2Cs were already dead and buried for several months before the March 20, 2000, article.

What infuriated many Net zealots still trapped in long positions was that Willoughby also confronted the latest Dot-Com darling category (at that time), business-to-business (B2B). One could almost hear Chairman Mark Walsh shout from the Pennsylvania headquarters of B2B leader VerticalNet as that company was included in the Willoughby List of companies that might conceivably run out of cash before they become self-sustaining Net champion businesses, according to Trigger.

Now the Willoughby List ranks up there with the CalPERS watch list as a roster with sufficient clout to instantly raise a chief executive's blood pressure by twenty percent. Or, about the same percentage plunge in the typical Dot-Com company's share price immediately following inclusion on the List.

One of the reasons that Willoughby has since been on the receiving end of *You're Killing Me!!* shrieks from melting speculators is that he violated the unspoken rule that the Dot-Com darling category of the time should be treated with reverence and never, never trashed in the business press before the crash of that Net segment occurs. Afterwards, its fair game, as the tonnage of past April 7, Zoo "Dot-Com" articles attests.

OK, OK, the Net zealot-defenders concede. If there's some Internet excess that needs blowing away, it's over there—with those out-of-control B2Cs. They're the ones who blew their backers' wads with ads showing gerbils shot from cannons.

But B2B is different. Unlike B2C, these guys actually wear ties sometimes—not just those longsleeved T-shirts with ties painted on them.

---

valueOUTPERFORMER
www.vbmresources.com

March 15, 2000

MOMENTUM-TOAST.COM

"Without the $83 billion gain in [brokerage house] margin debt since October, the bull market would be toast by now," says Charles Biderman, head of TrimTabs.com, a research firm that tracks money flow into and out of the market, as quoted in Bloomberg.com. Biderman's comments were directed to Net, computer, and telecom companies on the Nasdaq.

During that period borrowing rose 45 percent. But not to worry—market capitalization overall increased 10 percent and that's on a far larger base. But the Greater Fool theory—Internet Millennium version—may be ready for its correction. GF holds that retail (individual investor) demand remains so hot, so consistently, that stratospheric price/revenue multiples are readily confused by some as permanent value.

But Bubba now has to pay for that new Harley he bought during the boom, and he's stretched thin on credit—not just record brokerage house margin debt but also personal credit card borrowing. To make matters worse, he can no longer treat Nasdaq as a bank or his speculative portfolio of turkey.com stocks as a savings account. Schizophrenic price spikes up and down signal that the period of predictable momentum market trading is coming to an end. Trading markets—which trend sideways with no predictable direction—eventually collapse into panic if individuals set the market tone, such as now. At some point Bubba gets whipsawed one time too many and decides to dump it all.

AS MO'S HOLD OVER DOT-COM MARKETS UNRAVELS, FLIPPING INCREASES

When archeologists of the 25th century uncover those time capsules planted way back in 1999-2000, one question will be dominant: How did those market Rasputins of that ancient era cause valuations of non-viable companies to soar to nosebleed heights?

Ancient scrolls revealed that as early as January 1999, numerous sources warned that seventy percent or even more of Dot-Com companies brought to public market from 1996 forward were dead when they were created. The seventy percenters were *never* financially nor operationally viable, although that minor detail didn't prevent IPO packagers of the time from bringing e-Bankruptcy2001.com to market as fast as possible, for as long as Bubba still had cash.

Tight Discipline Needed to Maintain
NetPhase I's Managed Dot-Com Marketplace

In particular, the 25th-century archaeologists wonder about the mechanisms behind such a strange state of affairs. Their hypothesis is that these things called IPOs played an extraordinarily important role in the value wizards' grand designs.

The first goal was to create a Buy-At-Any-Cost buying panic among the masses. So the IPO shares tripled or even quadrupled on their initial day of trading, igniting dreams of personal wealth of that scale or greater.

But the second role was especially diabolical, the archaeologists conclude. The temporary high valuation illusion could only be sustained though artificially short floats (very few shares available for daily trading)—"stillbirth.com." So while GreaterFool might be permitted to buy a few stillbirth.com shares on IPO day, he couldn't sell them. Bubba had to be content to go home and just calculate his paper profits that night, but never to actually cash out to make his paper gain.

Why? Because if such action were taken by many GreaterFools, the dominos would fall (as shown in Figure 3.6).

The carefully constructed thin float managed market conditions was wrecked. Share prices would plunge, pulling down "values" from Disneyesque illusion levels back to far lower actual levels. Some GreaterFools would even wonder why they were putting money into shares of pre-bankrupt companies in the first place.

You Can Get 'Em
Only If You Don't Sell 'Em

The 25th-century archaeologists conclude that a key discipline to keep the dominos from falling was something called "flipping." This refers to the practice of selling IPO shares and pocketing the cash. Bubba GreaterFool acting to bank that first day IPO price surge, rather than just hearing about it on the evening business news and nothing more.

There could be no legal prohibition against flipping, so the wizards all said that any GreaterFool who committed this dastardly act risked being excluded from any future IPO share allocations.

For years, this bluff was enough to keep the GreaterFools in line. But in the first two months of 2000, managed-market discipline began to crack.

At first, there was just a trickle of shareholders who "flipped" their IPO allocations on the first day or soon afterwards, pocketing their gains. They probably suspected that $1,000 per share was a tad much for a company that had never proven its viability. Or, the errant GreaterFools could have figured that the illusory valuations were due for a fall to earth, so who cared if they were excluded from future IPOs?

But ten flips led to a hundred and then a thousand, as the other IPO shareholders certainly weren't going to let others cash out, potentially leaving them holding Dot-Com shares literally not worth the paper that the certificates were printed on.

Then all of the carefully managed Dot-Com IPO market, false valuations supported by the carnival shell game also collapsed. No more tripling of first-day Net IPO share prices. For a while, no more IPOs.

THE E-LASTIC THWAAAPS
IN THE OPPOSITE DIRECTION

Ah, when extreme momentum markets come undone. Jack Willoughby described the possibility that one-time Dot-Com darlings without a true business might implode all the way down to "salvage value." NYU Stern School valuation expert Aswath Damodaran's phrase is "liquidation value" in a discussion in April, shortly after the crash.

What are they talking about? The e-lastic rubber band snap-back effect as Dot-Com markets THWAAAP back in the opposite direction, a reaction to years of nosebleed valuation excess.

Momentum markets propelled into outer space by the volatile mix of hype, emotion, and artificially thin, managed floats can easily lurch back in the opposite direction as soon as upward pressure suddenly stops.

The elastic thwaaaped over in the five-week Spring Break period, as the March 10, 2000, Nasdaq Composite peak was revealed to be an exhaustion gap. The message was clear: Those seventy-plus percent failure rates are not exaggerated. Every day, another few seventy percenters collapse, as the false fluff is squeezed out of the market.

With no artificial force to keep Net managed markets in line, the e-lastic thwaaps all the way back. The only absolutely reliable basis of value when there are no better indicators is hard assets. But the virtual company's assets walked out the door weeks before, literally. Suddenly, mindless faith in anything with a Dot-Com label is turned inside out.

Instead of sure-thing profits, "Dot-Com" instead signifies 70-95% losses to those Bubbas and others caught long in the market with valueless shares in overreaching companies. The thin float that amplified share price to the upside weeks before now exaggerates downward momentum with each minor sell order.

For months after the March-April Dot-Com valuation reversal, tethered investment analysts argued that the "Nets are Oversold." But the markets proved unresponsive as demoralized individual investors blamed everyone except themselves for their Net share trading losses.

Willoughby's *Barron's* article brought a mixed reaction, and many of those reactions can be seen in the follow-up letters on *Barron's* online Web site. One of the biggest criticisms was that the analysis was flawed because it was based on past historical data, not updated information and future prospects. Another criticism was that the so-called burn rates (rates of cash depletion) were based on indicated cash flow rates only: conditions that may no longer be applicable. Criticism 3: Such "burn rate" analyses often fail to take into account new financing arrangements.

In our discussion, the *Barron's* senior editor acknowledged that some of these criticisms of "Burning Up!" were on target, but he was convinced that his approach was largely correct nonetheless. Willoughby insisted that reliance on statement data was particularly important to counteract Dot-Com communications, based on little if any hard data.

The validity of Willoughby's approach and others citing the Dot-Com burn rate crisis overall have been supported by follow-up analyses in TheStreet.com and elsewhere. The UK office of PricewaterhouseCoopers conducted a similar study a couple of months later, also warning of even more dire burn rate conditions in the B2C-dominated European Net public company exchanges.[13]

SOME INDICATIONS OF IMMINENT DOT-COM SHAKEOUT

Whatsamatter, Nasdaq burn rate victim? Did those mean Dot-Com spin-doctors fail in their efforts to deflect concerns about pre-bankrupt companies brought to market?

When you ask whether www.Happybang.com will have enough cash to make it through the next six months, are you inundated with so many new cyber-buzz phrases that your head spins?

What's a Bubba to do? In the deliberately managed, information-deficient momentum nonsense markets, one can only look for the *indirect* signals of a second severe Dot-Com collapse.

Here are some possible signals, along with our tentative prescribed actions:

1. Her Majesty, the Queen of England, becomes a daytrader.

    Two hundred separate trades of Cisco a day, huddled over a terminal, a quarter here, a half there? Not quite. Her Majesty has been described as having a stake in an online site that sells satellite pictures via downloads, among other Dot-Coms.

    Action:

    Since it's potentially off with your heads for anyone who sticks ER II with securities that plunge in value, you can bet that those advisers will only put Her Majesty in a sure thing. Sounds like sure odd lot short indicator to us. Selllllll!

2. Bubba gets a real job. Again.

    April margin calls wiped out Bubba GreaterFool; he had to sell the doublewide trailer. But even while living in a barn, Bubba kept watching those reruns of *Maverick* and subscribing to those Buy-Internet-on-Dips investment adviser services with dreams of making a comeback as a professional trader, some day. But treacherous sideways markets wiped out Bubba's beer money and enough is enough. He's going back to his old job, where gasoline pumps are always flowing, OPEC permitting.

    Action:

    The difference between a momentum market that peters out and one that soars is a solid foundation of lemming buyers who are perpetually in a buying frenzy mode. Forced exit of these buyers-of-last-resort removes the froth from overvalued Mo markets. Sellllllllll!

3. Founder of e-Bankrupcy2001.com registers to sell shares.

    Despite the Spring Break dive, company spinners are quietly talking up the prospect of a return to pre-March 10 greater

nosebleed levels. But company founder Ed Mult: lPO registers to sell a significant portion of his remaining shares.

Action:

Is it reasonable to dump shares while pliable investment
analysts controlled by the company talk up stock as a
double-your-money buy recommendation at the same time?
Thought not. Selllllllllllllll!

4. Happybang.com makes a special point of announcing cash
    and equivalents balances without being asked.

    No one asked them to. But as burn rate victim companies are
    dropping like flies, Happybang.com's spinners just thought
    you'd like to know that management has a big pile of cash on
    their desks. So none of that burn rate danger talk.

    Action:

    Does IBM go out of its way to call up CNBC to tell them about
    how much cash they have today? Exactly. Selllllllllllllll!

5. Some naive Old Economy e-procurement companies become
    frustrated with net losses, quit.

    The Old Economy companies rushed into industry e-procure-
    ment groups in 1999-2000 in hopes that they could earn their
    online spurs easily—just by making an announcement and
    nothing more. It is only later that Dinosaur Widget
    Corporation discovers that running an online business is a lot
    tougher than it looks. Stick to your knitting is a basic business
    success principle and not expanding into some whiz-bank Dot-
    Com company, the CEO of Grommet International declares.

    Action:

    This stick-to-your-knitting retreat of Dinosaur Widget lowers
    the possibility of B2B slipping to the status of a low-value Dark
    Model category (Chapters 1 and 4). The withdrawal of naive
    entrants decreases the threat of over-competition caused by too-
    easy market entry. Buyyyyyyyyyyyyyy!

Notes

1. Faisal Islam, "Wall Street's Party Pooper," *The Observer* (London), May 28, 2000, B5. Shiller is the Stanley B. Resor Professor of Economics at Yale University (Princeton, New Jersey: University Press). Shiller's perspectives on the shake-out implications of the 1996-2000 part of the Dot-Com boom are examined in Chapter 6 of this book, "Which Shakeout?"

2. Originally published in 1841 as *Memoirs of Extraordinary Popular Delusions* (London: Richard Bentey).

3. Ibid.

4. Interview by VBM Consulting, April 13, 2000.

5. "The Wall Street Journal Report," CNBC, May 21, 2000.

6. Penny wise, pound foolish: with less favorable US accounting treatment at this writing for repriced options compared to those originally granted, some management attempts to make lemonade out of lemonade by trying out the theory that the employees who stayed behind are the loyal, really productive talent. If that apology sounds familiar, it is because it was last used by the bricks 'n mortar company that lost its key people to soaring Dot-Coms just three years ago. Now as then, the Rule of Adverse Selection tends to apply to those who are left behind.

7. This is grossly and probably unfairly simplified, so you should go to the site yourself to understand the popular Web sites' guiding principles. Also see Gardner and Gardner, *The Motley Fool's Rule Breakers, Rule Makers: The Foolish Guide to Picking Stocks* (New York: Simon & Schuster, 1999); David Berger, with David and Tom Gardner, *The Motley Fool UK Investment Guide* (London: Boxtree, 1998).

8. Andy Serwer, "There's Something about Cisco," 38.

9. Jonathan Rabinovitz and Mark A. Mowrey, "IPO Market Unravels," *The Industry Standard* (www.thestandard.com), May 29, 2000, 58.

10. Sharon Walsh, "Some Hear a Margin Call of Doom," *Washington Post*, June 1, 2000, E1.

11. Mark Maremont, Terzah Ewing, and Laura Saunders Egodigwe, "Before Tech Stocks Tanked, Insiders Sold," 1, 9.

12. Vapor model(z) are described more extensively in Chapter 4, "Netenomics and Vapor Modelz."

13. See Carlos Grande, "UK Dotcom Cash Running Out," *Financial Times*, May 17, 2000.

Chapter 4

NETENOMICS AND VAPOR MODELZ

"Let's be honest and admit that the 'New Economy paradigm' affected the rational judgment of a lot of small and institutional investors alike."

Investor in controversial
Internet Services Provider World Online,
which closed on June 16, 2000,
at Euro 14.85, 65% down from the
IPO price at launch on March 17.[1]

Every major movement with broad economic and social implications brings its own set of jargon. During netPhase I, those seeking to ensure that the VC-IPO deal assembly line lasted as long as possible counted upon dubious pseudo-economic phrases and Net "business models" to sustain the mass hallucination.

WELCOME TO NETENOMICS 101

Welcome to your class in Netenomics 101, where you can create instant valuation principles out of thin air. Some of the more alarming baffleprose of this type is shown in Figure 4.1. One of these, "scalability," and several others, are explored in the pages that follow.

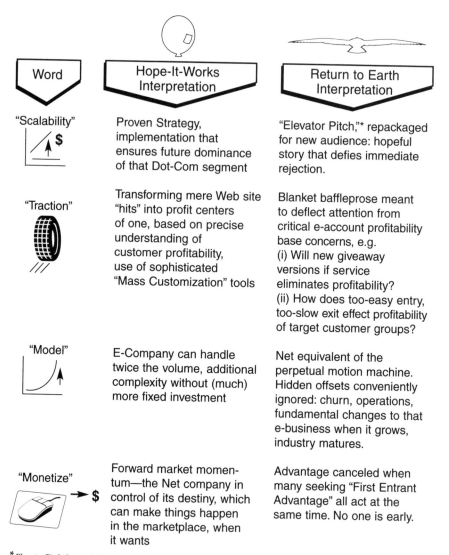

Word	Hope-It-Works Interpretation	Return to Earth Interpretation
"Scalability"	Proven Strategy, implementation that ensures future dominance of that Dot-Com segment	"Elevator Pitch,"* repackaged for new audience: hopeful story that defies immediate rejection.
"Traction"	Transforming mere Web site "hits" into profit centers of one, based on precise understanding of customer profitability, use of sophisticated "Mass Customization" tools	Blanket baffleprose meant to deflect attention from critical e-account profitability base concerns, e.g. (i) Will new giveaway versions if service eliminates profitability? (ii) How does too-easy entry, too-slow exit effect profitability of target customer groups?
"Model"	E-Company can handle twice the volume, additional complexity without (much) more fixed investment	Net equivalent of the perpetual motion machine. Hidden offsets conveniently ignored: churn, operations, fundamental changes to that e-business when it grows, industry matures.
"Monetize"	Forward market momentum—the Net company in control of its destiny, which can make things happen in the marketplace, when it wants	Advantage canceled when many seeking "First Entrant Advantage" all act at the same time. No one is early.

* Elevator Pitch: Instant high-pressure share sales pitch so-named because of where the target buyer is sometimes cornered.

FIGURE 4.1. The tyranny of Net bafflewords hoped-for interpretations, back-to-earth reality.

Metcalfe's Law

The granddaddy Net principle—sometimes called "network effect"—is named after Bob Metcalfe, co-founder and former chief executive of 3Com. The 'Law,' as generally interpreted, goes as follows: the value of the network enterprise increases with the square of the number of participants.

Sounds good, and is universally cited by every self-respecting Nethead. Metcalfe's Law even rates periodic interpretation and comment from *Wired*'s and MIT's Professor Nicholas Negroponte.

Whoops. As also explained in Chapters 6 and 7 in addressing the changing nature of competition in e-procurement, Metcalfe's Law only works in the case of monopolies and oligopolies. In most markets, the Net spawns the exact opposite conditions: ruthlessly competitive markets subject to multiple waves of fragmentation, thanks to too-easy entry and too-slow exit by entrenched competitors.

In theory, it's great to think about setting up your own worldwide online flower ordering and delivery network. You don't have to be a contestant on Regis to know that if you completely control a market, additional customers can be added at decreasing marginal cost.

Unfortunately, the problem is that a dozen others already thought of your online flower business first and are busily deploying their *own* Web-based business models, fragmenting demand. NetPhase I nosebleed valuations make the excess entry crisis far worse. One day, your own mom tells you she has this great idea for an online business, and she's just spent your college money on a server, and, well dear. . . .

Sure, that report from Rings O' Saturn Research showed that the eventual demand for your business is two trillion dollars by 2006. And Rings can always be counted on to be accurate to the nearest trillion or so. But that full long-term market potential takes years to develop. In the near term, demand is so fragmented that no one reaches critical mass and all participants risk going broke.

Excessive competition is behind the now characteristic pattern of a severe split between Net victors and victims. In a B2C segment of, say, six competitors, today's emerging pattern is one stellar success, one challenger barely at the cash flow break-even line, and four cripples awaiting elimination.

Last-generation search engines not associated with major portals. Commodity dial-up ISPs. And—oh yes—flowers. In B2C sector after sector, Metcalfe's Law turns out to be just more Net hype that appears great but doesn't work.

Ah, but Metcalfe hailed from the one part of the Net that lends itself to monopoly-oligopoly type-structure: e-infrastructure. As explained in Chapter 6, Cisco Systems was broadly perceived as the sole provider of huge core routers before Scott Kriens and Juniper Networks came along. Juniper's recent market share is generally estimated at 20%.[2] Today, the result is a duopoly, a market in which Metcalfe's Law actually applies.

Class Grade (for your repeated use of "Metcalfe's Law"):

A: if you restrict usage only to large-scale segments of the e-infrastructure segment, such as the Cisco-Juniper core renter segment

B: for B2B

F: for B2C markets plagued by excessive new entry yet slow by withdrawal, unless forced by withdrawal of financing

Viral Marketing

Brad Wieners of *Wired* refers to RocketTalk as the showcase example of this alarmingly named Netenomics principle.

RocketTalk's business plan called for offering free software at www.rockettalk.com. In the past, the software was designed to allow you to download music to share with your friends. But with Napster entangled in litigation, it is of course just a coincidence that RocketTalk Beta Release 1.6 (mid 2000) features other applications, such as streaming video downloading.

RocketTalk founder Jeff Weiner (a different last name) says, "we are a hardcore believer in viral marketing," which to the best of our understanding means making personal recommendations only, and at nanospeed, on the Net.

Wired's editor points to Colorado's Blue Mountain Cards as the quintessential viral marketing example. Founded with late

1960s idealism, the business is often cited as the ideal example of Net high-speed growth by word of mouth.[3] Oh so egalitarian, at least until it came time to cash out.

Two problems limit the plausibility of this particular bit of Net baffleprose. First is competitive noise: The same din from rivals that caused Dot-Com advertising costs to soar and ad effectiveness to plunge is also a problem here, as too many word-of-mouth companies enter. There are few barriers to entry, and the results show: massive overkill as opinion-setters who might sustain growth by word-of-mouth are besieged with requests.

Second, viral marketing can and sometimes does operate in reverse. Put out a release that causes the Palm Vs to crash when

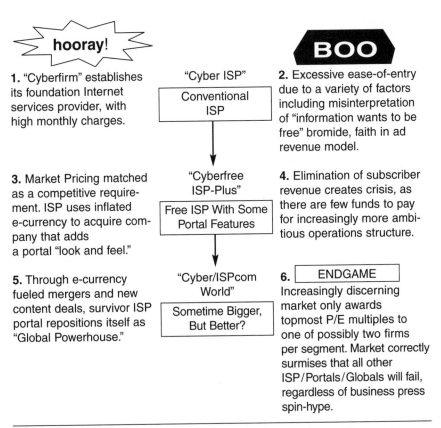

hooray!

1. "Cyberfirm" establishes its foundation Internet services provider, with high monthly charges.

"Cyber ISP"

Conventional ISP

2. Excessive ease-of-entry due to a variety of factors including misinterpretation of "information wants to be free" bromide, faith in ad revenue model.

3. Market Pricing matched as a competitive requirement. ISP uses inflated e-currency to acquire company that adds a portal "look and feel."

"Cyberfree ISP-Plus"

Free ISP With Some Portal Features

4. Elimination of subscriber revenue creates crisis, as there are few funds to pay for increasingly more ambitious operations structure.

5. Through e-currency fueled mergers and new content deals, survivor ISP portal repositions itself as "Global Powerhouse."

"Cyber/ISPcom World"

Sometime Bigger, But Better?

6. | ENDGAME |
Increasingly discerning market only awards topmost P/E multiples to one of possibly two firms per segment. Market correctly surmises that all other ISP/Portals/Globals will fail, regardless of business press spin-hype.

BOO

FIGURE 4.2. Finding the elusive profitable Net model: Hooray and Boo.

connected and every customer knows about it days before you. Damage control is tough if not impossible on the Net. It might be said that first-generation PointCast "push marketing" (an early Netenomics term since killed off) software was the victim of viral marketing as rumors spread almost instantly that the software might cause hard disk crashes.

---

valueOUTPERFORMER
www.vbmresources.com

May 5, 2000

Adapted from
TALK UP THIS DOG WHEN YOU GET ON TV, WILL YA?

Arthur Levitt, chairman of the US Securities and Exchange Commssion, announced on May 3, 2000, that the SEC would soon issue tougher guidelines regarding full disclosure of firms' positions and interests in companies talked up on financial news television by company star investment analysts. Fairly complete disclosure rules are already in effect for print statements, regarding both the writer's financial interests as well as interests of the firm. But admittedly somewhat less exacting requirements are in place at present for television—not a particularly good medium for small footnotes about holdings and past underwritings, no matter how fast CNBC's Ted David can talk..

Joe Isuzu-style on-screen print disclosures, instead?

It is evident that Levitt and staff believe it is important that investors know that the same firm that employs the bubbly analyst now on camera talking up the attributes of e-Bankruptcy2001.com also brought that dog public last month. Leave it to the investor to connect the dots there, to guess for himself whether or not Distinguished Investment Banking House Inc. is exerting any pressure to ensure that the swan dive in e-Bankruptcy's shares end soon, or else. There seems to be no single event that prompted the SEC's indication. Perhaps Levitt is trying to see whether "change before you have to" is just a Jack Welchism or whether financial TV concerns will take heed—including CNBC, jointly owned by General Electric and Dow Jones. Some "star" investment analysts were especially visible in April to support "long-term buy stories" for a couple of disastrously disappointing March European Dot-Com IPOs.

Postscript: After the May 3 Levitt announcement, there did appear to be some greater deliberate effort to ensure that CNBC guests were asked to disclose their positions. We would prefer on-screen Joe Isuzu-style graphs flashed while the talking head is still carrying on. E-BANKRUPTCY2001.COM'S SHARE PRICE IS OFF 94% FROM ITS 52-WEEK PEAK AND THIS GUY IS TOAST UNLESS HE CAN CONVINCE YOU

Class Grades:

B: but as support approach, only.

Hint! Don't blow much of the company's marketing budget on viral marketing—it is too easy for competitors to imitate.

Scalability

Jim Seymour (jim.seymour@zd.com) of the Seymour Group, consultants, makes an important distinction between *engineering* scalability and *business-model* scalability in his discussions with us and in his column at TheStreet.com.

Cutting hairs? The Texan insists not. Engineering scalability here refers to the capacity and resiliency of a network to handle increasing volume until, at some point, the operator must dig deep and increase the scale and cost of critical investment up to a higher plateau. The operator must break down and buy that new core router.

Regarding business-model scalability, Seymour cautions that:

> [This] has a completely different, though clearly related meaning. In the business world, and especially in Web businesses, managers speak of the scalability of their revenue models, by which they mean that after reaching a certain, predictable mass in terms of capital investment and numbers of users signed up, *they can then serve many more customers with almost no additional costs* [emphasis added] . . . Essentially, if not quite, zero.[4]

Net alchemy. Even better than the notion of turning lead into gold is the hallucination that once someone makes a single major front-end investment, then no further investment is necessary. Under such assumptions, the marginal cost of acquiring new customers plunges. Acquisition costs per customer plunge toward nearly zero.

To most, such theories long ago went the way of the perpetual motion machine. The Net holds tremendous potential to change the internal economics of businesses implementing the right Internet programs (Figure 7.1, Chapter 7), but (near) zero marginal cost? We've got a virtual Brooklyn Bridge we'd like to talk about if you swallow that.

It is that if the company/business plan is "scalable," then additional fixed investment decisions can usually be deferred for a while, as the market grows into the Dot-Com's capacity that is already in place. But additional fixed investment must eventually be made, at some point, or growth stalls. The growing segment is abandoned to the competition.

Class Grade:

B: But only if your use of "scalability" corresponds to the limitations of the engineering interpretation.

First Mover Advantage (FMA)

You are expelled from school simply for asking about this turk-e.

"FMA" is one of the welcome casualties of Spring Break 2000 and a particularly lethal form of Dot-Com baffleprose. Ever since the market's netPhase I hypnotic trance was snapped in the weeks after March 10, 2000, any Dot-Com spinner spewing "First Mover Advantage" is likely to hear a brusque retort from private financiers "Yes—first to bankruptcy."

But that's today. In Net pre-history of 1999 and before, Netscape, Spyglass, Digital Equipment (in the form of its early AltaVista portal), Boo.com, CDNow, and Peapod all were proclaimed by Net zealots as achieving FMA in one form or another. How did those early Dot-Com darlings prosper? Most didn't, or haven't. Because FMA is incidental, rather than causal, to Dot-Com success.

Is Amazon.com an example of FMA? Try again. Barnes & Nobles dropped the ball along with an early chance to blow away Bezos & Co. The failure of a natural rival to mount a true challenge is not at all the same thing as FMA.

Net First Mover Advantage means nothing because of entry speed. It doesn't make any difference that you're first to market. The companies that arrive second, third, and fourth will each sep-

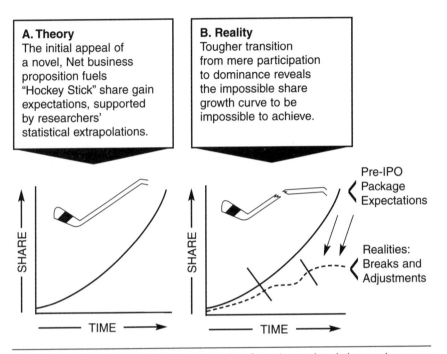

FIGURE 4.3. The "Hockey Stick" is broken: Dot-Com demand and share gain curves face tougher scrutiny.

arately blow you away into last week if you make the mistake of actually listening to any of your own FMA market propaganda.

In those hazy, crazy days of netPhase I easy financing (e.g., 1999), when Net high jargon still reigned supreme, we asked those who founded an excellent me-too clone of a US auction site to describe their firm's key advantage. You know the response already: FMA.

Business Arithmetic, Reinvented

Growing understanding that discounted free cash flow propels corporate value—and NOT earnings per share (Chapter 1, Figure 1.5)—means increasing emphasis on cash flow-oriented financial data.

The good news is that more and more valuators come to rely on methodology proven for decades, rather than on homespun counterfeits tolerated temporarily because of the Net's novelty.

ZD INTERACTIVE
www.zdnet.com

April 28, 2000

BE WARY OF NEW DOT-COM PROFIT PARADIGM SHIFTS

by Larry Dignan

Now that profitability—or at least an alleged path to profits—is an investor obsession, some Internet companies are trying to push a profit paradigm shift. These companies mention the "p" word, cook up newfangled calculations, and hope investors overlook the real bottom line.

First it was EBITDA (earnings before all the bad stuff), and then it was cash EPS (earnings without some of the bad stuff). Now companies are trying to pass off gross profits (selling goods for more than we paid for them), profit vapor, and just thinking about profits as the real thing.

The real bottom line is getting farther and farther away. Here's a guide to the latest Dot-Com profit stunts:

The Gross Profit Chatter

We can't recall ever seeing gross profits played up until this week. Hmmm. Maybe Dot-Coms reckon that any profit will do. Don't get too enthusiastic about gross profits. Drugstore.com (Nasdaq: DSCM) and Buy.com (Nasdaq: BUYX) went the gross profit route with their earnings reports. Drugstore.com tried the gross profit trick 38 words into its earnings release.

"Drugstore.com also achieved a positive gross profit (defined as net sales minus cost of sales) of $1.1 million, or 5 percent of total sales," the company said. The company basically said that it sold goods for more than it paid for them. Many money-losing companies can make that claim.

Buy.com used the same stunt and even gave a mock per-share figure. "Gross profit was $8.9 million, or $0.08 per share," the company said. The official bottom line was a loss of 28 cents a share.

Both companies topped estimates and had good progress, so why try to fool us?

We Could Report a Profit if We Wanted to!

Sure you could. Juno Online (Nasdaq: JWEB) went with the "we're not profitable because we choose not to be" route with its first-quarter earnings.

"Juno's net loss in the first quarter was only $2.9 million before subscriber acquisition expenses (which expenses are largely discretionary, and can be adjusted in response to such factors as seasonal variations in the cost-effectiveness of direct mail advertising, the availability of funding, and overall market conditions)," the company said. Juno went on to say it's front-loading marketing expenses.

Later in the earnings release (much later), Juno forks over the real net loss—$1.28 a share. Most of that was marketing spending, which at last check still counts as an expense.

This "we could be profitable" theme is prevalent in the Dot-Com world. In fact, it's not hard to find a few analysts that will say Amazon.com (Nasdaq: AMZN) could flip a switch and be profitable — if it wanted to.

Profits Are Coming . . . Really They Are

This strategy is the equivalent of profit vaporware. Profits are mentioned, but there's no map of how a company will get from point A to point B. Examples of this approach are numerous. Amazon is on a path to profits but hasn't set any dates.

In CyberCash's (Nasdaq: CYCH) earnings release on Thursday, the company dropped this statement: "Our goal is to achieve operating profitability for CyberCash, and we are on target."

On target? What target? According to earnings tracking firm First Call Corp., the company is expected to report losses for at least fiscal 2001. No analyst even ventured a guess for 2002. On target in CyberCash's case could mean 2010, for all we know.

Set a Date

If you really want to impress us, set a profit date. Not setting a profit deadline is like getting engaged and never setting the wedding date.

Many Dot-Coms are getting the hint—even if Wall Street doesn't immediately respond.

Business-to-business player VerticalNet (Nasdaq: VERT) expects to be profitable in the third quarter of 2001. About.com (Nasdaq: BOUT) on Thursday said it'll be profitable in the second quarter of 2001, two quarters ahead of schedule.

EToys (Nasdaq: ETYS) reported a hefty loss in its fourth quarter but did back up its profitability talk with a few dates. On a conference call with analysts, CEO Toby Lenk said the company "will be in striking distance of break-even by the holiday quarter of 2001 (third quarter)."

Lenk said EToys will be profitable in 2002. "We see a clear path to profitability," said Lenk. "The largest of the quarterly loss is behind us. We're putting the stake firmly in the ground."

Lenk projected that eToys would be profitable on $750 million to $900 million in sales. Whether you believe the profit projections of eToys, About.com, or VerticalNet is up to you, but at least there's some accountability.

The bad news is that the shift to cash flow-based valuation is interpreted by some opportunists as an open invitation to try to disguise true performance with a whole new set of disguises: partial reporting, confusion of revenues with profits, laughable risk and term assumptions in the discounted cash flow (DCF) valuation method.

The *combination* of a creditable DCF methodology plus equally creditable input is powerful. As *analysts' interpretations* of company future discounted cash flows shape corporate valuation, Dot-Com management enhances shareholder value by supplementing reported GAAP earnings per share data with credible DCF forecasts to the extent permitted.[5]

Problem is, situations such as the 1999-2000 Staples' reporting controversy with First Call arise from time to time, and such episodes are sometimes confused with the DCF forecast data issue.

In Staples' case, the debate with online reporting service First Call, as we understand it, centered on *which* data was presented, and *how*, rather than on incompleteness of any required information. The base argument seems to be that management has the right to put its own financial information in the most favorable light possible, as long as there is also timely and complete disclosure of all required data.[6]

The distinction between merely presenting data for optimal effect and borderline distortion of data arises in the case of the more aggressive attempts to devise "adjusted" earnings. Larry Dignan's feature article from the April 28, 2000, *ZD Interactive* is presented in a tongue-in-cheek style. But the subject is serious.[7]

Sometimes, the motivation for "creative" treatment of Dot-Com performance centers around the challenge of growing a combined clicks 'n mortar enterprise.

The Dot-Com side of the business provides a frothy valuation boost for a while, but operating losses of the Dot-Com business may eventually threaten to cancel out some or most of the profits from the "Old Economy" part of the two-headed business.

Champions of GAAP earnings per share become concerned that their string of 20 consecutive quarterly EPS increases may be jeopardized. Despite the facts, some will always be convinced that EPS trends, not DCF projections, drive value.

Business Arithmetic, Ignored
(Or, Profits Are SO Twentieth Century)

A related but somewhat different "numbers" dilemma arises when the Dot-Com spin doctor throws out the improbable notion that positive cash flow doesn't really matter that much. The spinner looks up to see if anyone is nodding their head in agreement. After all, Mark Twain said that you can fool *some* of the people *some* of the time.

But there aren't many head-nodders following the 34% percent plunge in the Nasdaq Composite we refer to as Spring Break 2000. Once upon a time, proclamations that *Profits Don't Matter* might have identified the bold 'n brash Dot-Com value star who disregards short-term results in favor of those things essential to the business.

That hypnotic spell is now broken. Fling out the *Profits Don't Matter* in a meeting with financiers trying to shore up the company's cash position because IPOs are no longer available, and the proclaimer might find that he is the one flung—out of the room.

To many, *Profits Aren't Important* and similar clever netPhase I themes are symbolic of all that was wrong with the system in that they sped future bankrupt companies to the IPO marketplace.

As with most of the other Netenomics phrases, there's a grain of sanity here. Fast-growing, high potential capital-intensive businesses are expected to show investing-in-the-future losses in early years. Unless that company's profit pattern mimics the early years' dip in "soup ladle" curve (Figure 1.1), observers who knew the pattern of profitable companies fear that the later, high profit stages of that curve will be missed, also.

Then there's the misguided corporate beancounter who turns down all investment projects that do not appear likely to reach profitability in the first 12 to 18 months. Initially, he fools himself and others into thinking that he's creating value, as there are fewer loss-generating projects. But the opposite is true, instead.

This myopic manager destroys value in three ways. First, through adverse selection, the projects that show unexpected profits too early also tend to be short-lived. Second, the too-narrow selection criteria causes the corporation to miss some major value opportunities. Finally, the value opportunities that are missed go to the competition instead.

FADS: FREE, ONLINE ADVERTISING, DARK MODEL

Three Netenomics terms transcend separate Internet business models. The three are "free," online advertising, and the Dark Model.

Free, and Last

The notion that giving away something for nothing is a great way to build a Web-based business is nothing new, except for the Web part. For years, eager marketeers have assailed their bosses with great plans to open up all new territories with massive giveaways. *They will buy something from us in the future at a profit* is always the justification.

In Chapter 1, we suggested that self-interest is the key to interpreting individual valuation schemes especially in the case of the Dot-Com company temporarily "valued" at, say, 100 times revenue multiples when that company will probably go bust within two years.

Self-interest also dominates in the *free* description. Except that instead of a salesman, there's a Dot-Com CEO who knows that the scarcity of solid data means that he can fool at least some of the financiers. Giveaways create value? Sure, dude.

At least during netPhase I, this spin was possible. The period following Spring Break 2000 is another matter—as described in Chapter 6. There's also the Net-cultural aspect of *free*, which seems to have endured from the early days when the Net depended on selflessness to survive.

Separate rhetoric from reality, and companies giving away a "free" ISP (Internet services provider), information service, or the like must generate some profits to survive. Online advertising (see below) is one possible revenue source. The backup argument is the dubious concept that having been given something once, twice, or three times for free, B2C or B2B customers will now buy that product/service (or something close to it) for cold, hard cash.

No chance. Reinforced by the *free* Net culture, businesses instead risk becoming profitless shells as they discover sometime later that they have instead conditioned their customers to expect that nearly every future service they demand will also be provided to them as valued customers, without charge.

Another rationale for *free* is sometimes cross-marketing. This is the marketeer's dream, that appeal of one unrelated product creates demand in another product or service. Cross-marketing is only marginally achievable at best in terrestrial markets. Online, the concept is a non-starter.

Sounds good, doesn't work.

Once a segment "goes free," there is no return. Just *try* to resurrect browsers as a charge-for market after Microsoft made it a giveaway. Although we admire services such as TheStreet.com who try to charge fees when lesser competitors give their services away for free, we fear that the Net is now a land of lowest common denominator pricing. Count on less knowledgeable customers plus saturation advertising to sometimes blur the distinction between legitimate services and pretenders.

Advertising:
Demise of 95-centDollar.com Dozen

If you think you have an original Net idea, it's only because you don't know about the two who are already implementing it. We actually thought once that we originated the story of the pretend Web site that makes a business by giving away dollars for 95 cents each and then receiving seven cents in ad revenue, all with zero development cost (this is where the magic of viral marketing can work, fast).

By last count, we were about the thousandth to take credit for the concept.

But concepts like the 95-centDollar.com "site" endure, sustaining the tenuous logic of nurturing a business from advertising alone. This is a form of support that even its fiercest champions still described as tremendously underdeveloped, as of mid-2000.

But that's only half of it. We see recurring instances where corporations trying to justify a new B2C operation or project set a maximum for the amount of advertising revenue that they will accept in the justification model to well less than 50 percent or less. At one client firm, it is 25%. Seventy-five percent was the maximum prior to Spring Break 2000.

Whatever the reason—excess competition, advertisements that don't work, reduced ad budgets in that more stringent post-Spring Break era—few will argue that a major change in reliance on advertising as a revenue source has occurred. Even before the March 10 Nasdaq Composite peak, when year 2000 Super Bowl marked the last hurrah for ego-trip, ineffective ads from Dot-Coms with more cents than marketing sense. Advertisements for Dot-Com companies on previous generation media remain nonetheless: television, radio, billboards.

Dark Model:
Value Endgame, Even before You Get Underway

Our contention is that there are many more hidden profitless industry segments around than many would admit, and more are coming daily. See Figure 4.4, Slippery slope: Value destruction in "Dark Model" companies, units. Even though Web hosting is still far away from achieving its full potential, the tough truth is that excess entry opportunities position this as the new low-profit Dot-Com sector, following in the footsteps of dial-up ISPs and wholesale Net access as the next profitless shell industry.

The notion of Dark Models is fiercely contested by everyone trapped in one. Commitment to maximizing shareholder value ends when it threatens that person's job.

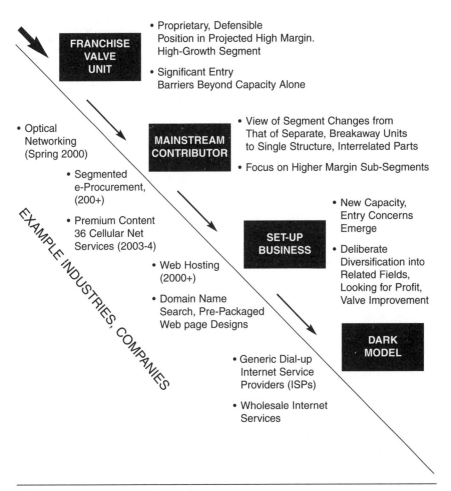

FIGURE 4.4. Slippery slope: Value destruction in "Dark Model" companies, units.

IDENTITY, PURPOSES OF
DOT-COM VAPOR MODELZ

Business Model. The words roll easily off the tongue of the Dot-Com company management and even more smoothly off the silvered tongues of its spinners and financial intermediaries. *Don't blow it on CNBC tomorrow when you answer the "business model" challenge question: This IPO must soar.*

Business Model. Somehow, what was one of the most ordinary business terms prior to 1994 now assumes magical dimensions. The model is key to billions, assuming that it is perceived to be the equivalent of a guaranteed successful marketplace strategy for the future. The stage is set for a lucrative Initial Public Offering.

In Dot-Com pre-history—that is, before the mid-1990s—"business model" meant nothing more than one hypothesis about how that business might operate into the future. A broad description of the business and little more, with no clue about whether that model was complete or correct, or even adequate in terms of covering the key questions central to that firm's future survival.

Business model. We have absolutely no idea how this mundane phrase came to be elevated to mean so much more, but it did. During the heyday of netPhase I, the perception was that the model was close to a magical prescription, a unique selling proposition plus segment dominance combined. A solid blueprint assuring maximum shareholder value with a minimum of difficulties.

Since those halcyon days, *business model* has slipped to depths of the corporate vision statement, and you don't see much of the latter today as just the word "vision" is a laughing stock in most management circles. Today both *business models* and *vision statements* identify the obtuse manager who puts form far before function. And worse, who cannot tell the difference.

Dot-com business modelz (we add a "z" to avoid confusion with legitimate, exacting simulations and analyses) are next, as cartoonists parody kids who make a business out of selling assets of bankrupt Dot-Coms. The joke would be funnier except that such vulture companies represent one of the faster growing Dot-Com segments after the Spring Break 2000 crash. The Dot-Com makeover—reconstructing the core Web-based business to improve prospects for future financing—emerges as a growth category from mid-2000 forward.

Some reconstruction is legitimate. But other efforts are valueless surface adjustments. For example, re-packaging the company's business model so that an investor will add more funds to keep old e-Bankruptcy2001.com alive a few months longer. Perpetrators of this shell game are some of the same oily consultants and other parasites who designated themselves as experts in developing new Dot-Com business concepts just a few years earlier.

But that still doesn't answer the question of how it is that such baffleprose was ever believed in the first place. Answer: *Investors want to believe it's true.*

Remember, the business model is just a slightly formalized version of the five-minute elevator pitch that each Dot-Com exec can deliver unconsciously. The model isn't designed to be plausible. Most aren't. It is merely intended to suspend disbelief, temporarily. Nothing more is necessary.

It doesn't make any difference that the first wave of medical information Web sites, such as DrKoop.com (Figure 1.7), had an Achilles' heel from the beginning because major medical organizations could always outflank the first-generation sites. Few raised this concern in 1996-99. It took the millennium plunge in the stock price to raise concerns about the business model.

In March 2000, Kate Bulkley asked management of online travel and reservations service Lastminute.com about its business model a few days after that company's controversial IPO. She questioned the logic underlying that Dot-Com's business model, as similar services were already available from many other online companies and channels at comparable prices. As the CNBC reporter suggested, Lastminute.com is a self-described online "aggregation," which goes against a basic business appeal of the Net to get rid of the middleman.[8]

Some Dot-Com management relegate preparation of business models to third parties, treating the documents as a bureaucratic nuisance. The result is business *modelz*: long on Dot-Com hyperbole, short on intelligence—ensuring that the business is not a seventy-percenter.

This is a massive mistake. The business model is the closest thing to hard performance data that many Dot-Coms encounter in their early years, whether the company is an online only standalone or a clicks 'n bricks hybrid.

The fully-adequate business model is not some passive document for some junior staff number-cruncher to unconsciously process. The fully effective business model is the equivalent of a medical chart monitoring the status of a critically ill patient in a hospital, along with key tactics for what could be done, what *should* be done to ensure that the patient not only *survives*, but *thrives*. Absence of an effective new business model relevant for the new circumstances means that future viability is unproven. This deficiency may not hinder the Dot-Com in securing financing during money-mad periods such as netPhase I, but as financing becomes scarce the zero company model receives nothing.

IPO DAY AT CNBC

Dot-Com all-smiles management accepts the gracious congratulations of the TV presenters, along with the perfunctory New IPO interview.

The Dot-Com CEO has every syllable of his business model explanation down pat when CNBC's Bill Griffeth asks the fateful question on camera, *"Tell us something about your business model . . ."*

The verbal download that follows takes about 30 seconds. The pitch has been timed before, as the CEO knows that he only has three minutes or so on screen. This could be E-Bankruptcy2001.com's only chance for national exposure. There are always other Dot-Coms crowding the airwaves, seeking to capture the public's imagination and, eventually, their funds.

The other reason for fast-paced delivery is more pragmatic. Rapid-fire delivery makes it harder for challenges to be mounted. So, in one breath and best carnival-barker rapidspeak:

> BILL, Rings O' Saturn Research says that by 2004, every person in the universe will possess at least two of these indispensable items at 90% net margin, not to be confused with our cost of sales and churn rates, which are also 90%. We have first mover advantage and scalability and fully monetize our network effects. No one else can get in to the critical demand for Digital Online Only Migrane detectors—the DOOM market. Bill, there are technical problems with our raw killer ap.

But we're confident that our technicians can fix the problems if we re-price their share options. We expect to become profitable by first quarter of 2005 because we can't get away with any date later than that. BILL (exhale).

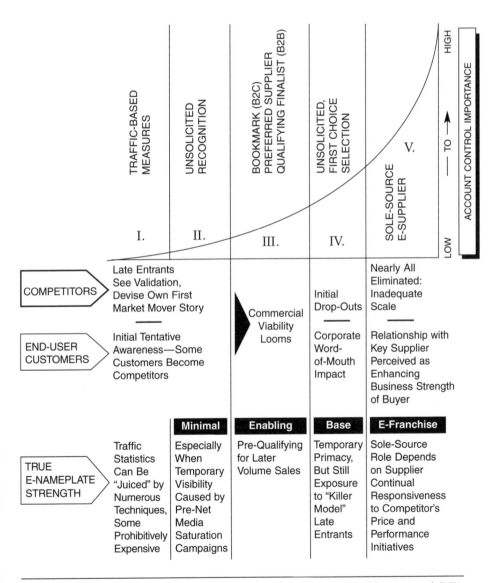

FIGURE 4.5. Building the champion Dot-Com company model: Why mere visibility does not neccessarily mean a viable business.

How can they get away with this? Comparisons to more unbelievable business models are unavoidable, so there is some gentle follow-up questioning. For example, Mark Haynes or someone else will ask: *So what makes your model so special—when this is the seventeenth search engine in a segment that can support six at most?* Of course, in media-friendlier form.

DEBUNKING THE INTERNET VAPOR MODELZ

Following is adapted from a July 1999 VBM Consulting article (www.vbmresources.com), which helps explain why those who develop worthless models that have no relevance to the real world sometimes believe that even this deficiency cannot jeopardize their chance at IPO riches.

In the software community, "vapor" refers to a new update version that exists only in the mind of the developer. A trick, intended to divert and distort buyer behavior. The tactic may work temporarily but crashes (literally and figuratively) soon after.

A comparable series of developments emerge in the case of the whiz-bang Internet businesses, which are unprofitable today and possibly forever. "Model" replaces the word "vapor" in the case of these commercial releases.

Not to worry, all you new Internet company investors and founders. Even if the truth is already suspected by most, the secret will not get in the way of floating some ten-month-old company that in the past would not even qualify as a serious prospect.

After all, why shouldn't a pre-bankrupt company have the same chance at IPO riches as a company that actually might survive?

You see, there are lookouts on the corner ensuring that this particular heist succeeds. London City investment bankers drool at their Manhattan cousins' ability to secure lucrative accounts by providing access to the soaring first-day IPO profits. Never mind that the average individual Bubba investor has no chance at all to participate, or that the IPOs first-day headlines merely draw in the next wave of suckers.

Key to the Net is its model, a spreadsheet version of how the corporation is supposed to prosper into the future. Plausible enough long enough for the initial investors to get out of e-Bankruptcy2001.com and still be smiling.

One small problem: *The models usually don't work.* Which means that the average Dot-Com company has to switch from one model to another to keep the wealth illusion alive.

See if you can spot *your* Dot-Com's business model in the list that follows:

---

valueOUTPERFORMER
www.vbmconsulting.com

May 11, 2000

Adapted from
INFORMATION WANTS TO BE FREE? WELL, SORT OF

"Information wants to be free?" Never mind that data is inanimate and can't "desire" anything. Or that if the content has any worth, no one in their right mind gives it away for nothing.

But do these considerations mean that this slogan—the millennium's version of a '60s flower child slogan—is now officially cancelled? Psion's David Levin doesn't prescribe to giveaway data. The chief executive identifies *location, time,* and *personal relevance* as the three contexts that give information value. In the process, Levin provide a beacon for growth of the Wireless Net in the future, one of the Internet's horizon opportunities.

Levin suggests that data is portable (location), available BEFORE the time needed (time), and honed to the individual's imperative (personal); then that data becomes throwaway bits. Leaving aside the "portable" aspect—Psion is a leading producer of small personal digital assistant devices (PDAs)—the other two parts of the Levin formula give clues about why some content providers create their own crises by failing to focus extremely important information to people eager to get that data on a high fee, spot basis. So while some companies make giveaways out of Net-enabled cellular phones and rush at breakneck speed to make the "e-Internet on the mobile" a profit-less market, Psion pursues the value bulls-eye, instead. And the PDA manufacturer was not even one of the firms that shelled out billions for a 3G (next generation) license.

Model 1: Chapparal

This first-to-Net pioneer has precious little else going for it. Management's IPO strategy is to capitalize on fawning trade press and explosive statistics about the first-wave of users to sign up, hopefully before anyone realizes that such near-data means absolutely nothing as far as future prospects of the company are concerned.

As of mid-1999, the UK's minimal charge Internet Services Provider, Freeserve plc., was less than a year old and already had drawn more than 100 competitors, like iron filings to a magnet.

Each rival is poised to displace Freeserve with an even cheaper, faster, better deal. In another year, that number could easily double when one takes into account commercial no-access fee services: conventional companies that use "free" for marketing pull, while the actual Internet service is provided by a separate third-party carrier on contract.

Here's a question never to ask the nervous CEO of a Chapparal Net model company:

"Can you ever make a profit when growth of the number of users flattens and the number of competitors doubles? Be prepared to hear a swift: Next! From the frazzled chairman.

Model 2: Yankee Doodle Dandy (Doo)
(So Long As They Stay Over There)

The model of an aspiring European online auction service is simple: Copy the Yanks. E-Bay, Yahoo!, and Amazon auctions have all enjoyed some success. Why not start a comparable service but without the American accent?

The coming crisis occurs when this is all the service offers, which is different from the coming American invaders.

"Buy American" never works particularly well in the US.

Why should "Buy You (Vous) EU?" be any more effective throughout Europe? Answer is, it isn't.

Net customers cut across national lines, which is part of the massive appeal of Internet commerce. The "we made it work, right" argument of the Yanks can be persuasive when extended to other parts of the world. The American invaders in auctions, online securities brokerage, insurance and travel services are parked just offshore, ready to grab the market with familiar American over-enthusiasm as soon as there is any sign of European demand.

Never ask the sensitive manager of the non-US based YDD model company:

"What happens to your business when leading US competitors enter your market with a customer proposition that is as good or better than yours?"

Model 3: Pinky and the Brain

A popular Warner Bros. cartoon features a balding rodent with an enlarged cranium who continually proclaims that he's "Going to Take Over the World." No, no, not anyone associated with a pioneer e-business based in Seattle. Brain is nothing more than a laboratory mutant with an overactive imagination and a penchant to control everything. Then again, Z-shops, www.drugstore.com? Hmmm.

This PATB model calls for entering (and later dominating) *every* Net market possible.

Sometimes because the Chaparral model is already unwinding and profits are plunging, one must leap to another model to ensure that the storyline is still intriguing to Bubba GreaterFool and—more importantly—to possible second-stage financiers.

Amazon.com expands from books to CDs to auctions, toys, drugs, and electronics, leaving its books' backside open to focused competitors (Fatbrain) and wave upon wave of online deep discounters.

The problem with becoming all things to all customers is that you ultimately become nothing to any of them. Site navigation becomes sluggish, as the number of Web site tabs and guideposts and ads resembles family photo albums after decades of neglect.

Then there's the ultimate threat of the one organization that deliberately points itself toward offering everything cheaper or less, which rarely enters a battle it cannot win. Yes, In Sam Walton We Trust.

Never ask the sensitive manager of the PATB Net model company this question:

"What happens to your business when Wal-Mart finally sets its online formula right, establishing the unassailable cost and performance advantage online that it does now in 'terrestrial' stores?"

Model 4: Everybody's Doing It, Doing It

Participants eager to join the growing Net category introduce slight, irrelevant, minor alterations that make their service cosmetically different from rivals. The distinctions mean nothing to customers. With no differences of importance between major competitors, marketplace dissolves quickly into fragmented commodity pieces. Each share is too small to sustain a business.

Even though there are far too many specialty search engines, that doesn't prevent new ones from bubbling up all the time, leading the reasonable observer to think that the motivation is less what the market *needs* than that this is something the Dot-Com entrepreneur can *do*. A treacherous trap whether starting or trying to remain in a business.

Look out for the tsunami wave of meaningless Dot-Com product/service differentiation. Search engines allow customers to sort by most popular response, most payment received from sponsors, preferred response of this or that "expert" group. Occasionally, even (gasp) a search engine that provides the best answer.

Over the near term, the danger to the investors still riding the crest of these high fliers is that another competitor will enter easily and draw away too much business. But that ease of entry suggests another, far more damaging threat: that the next generation of operating software may permit end-users to act as their own search engine managers, eliminating the need for these "infomediaries."

Never ask the sensitive manager of the Everybody's Doing It model company these questions:

"What is the minimum market share to survive, and what share do you expect to have in a year? Does the entry of new companies to the industry now fragment demand so that no one can survive?"

MOVING FORWARD

I think it's a very positive thing to have to physically drill down into business models to see if there will be profits three, five, ten years out.

Mark Walsh, chairman, VerticalNet[9]

Attitudes toward Internet businesses have changed dramatically since Spring Break 2000. The Dot-Com financing landscape has been hit by a severe earthquake, obliterating the VC-IPO model of netPhase I (Figure 6.1, Chapter 6).

Post- Spring Break 2000, the Dot-Com category is adrift, without clear future financing direction. The crisis dictates one-off holdover temporary financing just to buy some time.

Twenty borderline-viable Dot-Coms in a portfolio run by three to four major financing sources evolve into five compact competitors. These are all-new Dot-Com stand-alones and hybrids (bricks 'n clicks) formed from post-IPO Dot-Coms surviving the collapse of netPhase I, plus the rare post-crash new IPO.

But survival financing will be available ONLY to a limited number of clearly No. 1 or No. 2 segment leaders. Companies with short, verifiable paths to positive cash flow and segment dominance.

Faced with this stark new era, Dot-Com management can be excused for believing that the first priority is to scramble around in search of all-new financing sources. Nope. The same thin, thin floats used to help "guide" netPhase I market values now mean that the Dot-Com company often has less than a year's cash left.

It isn't always the burn rate that creates the liquidity crisis. Sometimes Dot-Com management gambles that buckets of cash will always be available for a company with the ".com" suffix, at any point in that firm's life cycle. Whoops, lost that bet.

First Things First

Renewed emphasis on finding new sources of financing is certainly rational and reasonable. But not always optimal.

With trickle, trickle announcements about Dot-Com bankruptcies taking over the first page of the business press every day, finding and eliminating NIQ Dot-Coms as quickly as possible becomes Priority One for survival of the Dot-Com marketplace overall. Fail to remove the weeds quickly, and growth of viable companies stalls.

Throughout netPhase I, viability of the Dot-Com ranked among the lowest priority, regardless of rhetoric to the contrary. In Net We Trust prevailed. Even if the business model seemed childish, the mistaken belief flourished that this group of companies could continue to defy long-established survival percentages for start-ups at similar points in their development.

That delusion is now blown to smithereens. The opposite extreme assumption takes its place. Unless the financing or investor group management is convinced otherwise, its assumption is that the Dot-Com is a seventy-percenter with bankruptcy just around the corner.

Any proof to the contrary must come straight from the company's leadership, and must be clearly supported by verifiable intelligence from independent sources. No more perceptions-management exercises that duck basic questions about today's profits and tomorrow's prospects. Management in a B2B sector that thinks that mere access to business data alone is enough to displace Mark Walsh's VerticalNet in that relationship-driven segment are better off learning the tough truth now, rather than later.[10]

Requisite Mindset:
Your Model Is Already Broken—
Fix It Right Or Disappear

Extended debates about whether or not the incumbent Dot-Com model "still works" merely increase chances of failure to nearly

100%. If not because of previously unseen challenges from competition, then because of cash starvation.

Radical, independent reform of the business model is not some bureaucratic distraction but rather, a pre-condition for present survival and future possible success. With questions of viability soft-pedaled in the past, direct financiers and others are not about to allow themselves to be fooled a second time.

The Dot-Com company that fails to radically challenge *all* parts of its business model after Spring Break 2000 and *before* pursuing new financing effectively is throwing in the towel. Giving up. Every day, management stresses the importance of operating at "Internet speed." Of understanding that industries, companies, and individuals face 180-degree changes every quarter or so. Failure to apply that same perspective to the corporation's blueprint for future survival and success is tantamount to saying that this company cannot succeed.

The "right" plan? There is no template model for re-making. Any standard formats and canned combinations of just the right magic words, content, and concepts died along with netPhase I. However, Figure 4.6 ("Click Ass: Identifying the Dot-Com models that work") shows six characteristics that we find to be most important.

Questions Designed to Separate the Value-Creating Dot-Com From Its Value-Destroying Cousin

There are some common sense questions that can help separate the non-viable Dot-Com doomed to fade into history from its "In the Black" relative. Two such issues are examined below:

1. Is there any solid connection between expenditures made and capturing additional share?

    Numerous B2C late-to-market IPOs splashed out millions in TV and billboard advertisements during the critical Christmas 1999 season in a high-risk attempt to grab market share. New York Web traffic analysis company Media Metrix suggests that most of these desperation gambles by

Several key characteristics emerge as critical for developing the new or reworked business model that is far more than just a financial PR exercise. Following are a few of those elements:

1 MINIMAL USE OF NET-PHASE I JARGON, JUSTIFICATION

Reliance on buzz words hides incomplete thinking. What else have they missed that is critical to future success?

2 FOCUS ON FUTURE SEGMENT DOMINANCE, NOT MERE PARTICIPATION

With only No. 1 and No. 2 receiving highest valuation (and sometimes, the only Dot-Coms surviving), there's no third place.

3 ANTICIPATE HALVING OF REVENUES WITH COSTS DECREASING LESS

Failure to reflect excess entry is arguably the greatest deficiency of "Modelz" today. But if the original budget had any integrity, most costs are already lean and cannot be cut much further without weakening the business.

4 FINANCIALS BUILT ON **BOTH** A TOP-DOWN (RESEARCH HOUSE) AND BOTTOM-UP (CONFIRMED ACCOUNTS) BASIS, OVERCOMING LIMITATIONS OF EITHER APPROACH

Reliance on attaining a miniscule percentage of a massive market looks impressive but may be irrelevant if the base is very small.

5 FOR B2C: ADVERTISING REVENUE COUNTED ON CASH-RECEIVED BASIS ONLY MAXIMUM OF 25% OF REVENUE 10% OF MODEL CASH FLOW.

Major corporations are dramatically revising their B2C models to reduce dependence on ad revenues because eyeballs aren't profits. The model that overrelies on ad revenue is pre-bankrupt.

6 ANTICIPATE FULLY THE ENTRY OF BRICKS 'N CLICKS HYBRIDS TO THIS FIELD.

Hybrids' success to date mandate assumption that this will be dominant path to market.

FIGURE 4.6. Click ass: Identifying the Dot-Com business models that *work*.

little-known Dot-Coms failed as eyeballs gravitated to familiar "Old Net" (e.g., better established) household names, such as amazon.com and eBay.

The sense of bets made and lost was confirmed on a spot basis as the gambling B2Cs' post-Christmas excuses turned into dust. One brassy Dot-Com manager explained that the millions spent during the season accomplished exactly the intended result, even though his firm was nowhere on the Media Metrix list. Sure, that could happen.

2.   What are the barriers to entry, if any, and who within the segment are the most successful at erecting those barriers?

Market share gains are for nothing unless shares can be defended. With rare exceptions, first-to-market status alone fails to deflect competitors. To the contrary, the fact that the market has now been "legitimized" may actually increase competitive intensity. Unless the Dot-Com is one of the few corporations that have erected insurmountable barriers against churn, outlays splashed out for market share can easily disappear down the drain.

Direct, objective verification is essential to distinguishing the value-destroying Dot-Com from its value-*creating* cousin.

Everyone claims to possess infallible "glue" to retain today's customers. But be wary of churn, as new customers displace old ones with little market benefit. The "free" ISPs growth rate of new subscribers is only one statistic for assessing enduring strength. With dial-up ISPs a commodity Dark Model, key is how many are retained, as well. The question is not just who *attracts* the new customers, but also who *retains* them.

An even worse situation arises if nobody has discovered the key to preserving share gains once achieved. That situation in many B2C markets and some B2B segments points to a cyber commodity market, in which all participants are rendered unprofitable. If not today, then tomorrow.

Notes

1. Neal E. Boudette, "World Online's New World" *The Wall Street Journal Europe*, June 19, 2000, 25.

2. David Parsley, "The Man Who Would Take On Cisco," *The Sunday Times* (London), June 4, 2000, 3.13.

3. December 7, 1999, VBM Consulting interview with Brad Wieners. Also see his "Pass It On," *Wired*, July 1999, 60.

   First we thought that viral marketing originated with Blue Mountain, as Wieners suggested to us. But then we saw the biography of Timothy Draper, at the IBF Private Equity Internet Investment Seminar, April, 2000. "His original suggestion to use 'viral marketing' in Web-based e-mail to geometrically spread an Internet product . . . was instrumental to the success of Hotmail . . ."

4. "Sussing Out Scalability, Real and Claimed: Part 1," May 3, 2000, www.TheStreet.com.

5. **Combination**

   The importance of *combination* of methodology and input are referenced here because of distortion problems associated with "Contaminated DCF" as described in Chapter 1. A powerful base valuation methodology such as Adjusted Present Value (T. Luehrman., "Using APV, A Better Tool for Valuing Operations," *Harvard Business Review*, May- June 1997, 145–154), or some of the other generally available standard valuation models, is only as good as the input used in that model.

   Assume a 10-15–year lifespan (t) for valuation purposes when businesses in that industry disappear every three years, and gross valuation inaccuracies are assured. Similarly, faux-data inputs for risk, growth rate, profitability, and assumed returns on fixed investment, R&D, and advertising components of the valuation model can and do destroy valuation credibility.

Analysts' Interpretations are What Count

In *Cash Flow and Performance Measurement*, (Morristown, New Jersey: Financial Executives Research Foundation [FERC], 1996, 11), author Henry A. Davis refers to his multi-company research: ". . . value is best understood by institutional investors with a long-term perspective who base their analysis primarily on their estimates of future cash flows discounted at the company's WACC (weighed average cost of capital)."

The Dot-Com company that fails to provide full and complete cash flow guidance to analysts limits its access to future financing in today's more stringent funding environment.

6. No statement or inference made here suggests in any way that Staples' data or disclosure was incomplete or misleading in any form, degree, or manner.

7. For additional insight into some of these alternative measures and their uses, see Steve Harmon, "The Metrics for Evaluating Internet Companies," originally developed February 23, 1999, from *The Internet Stock Report*, May 16, 2000.

8. Media darling LastMinute.com went public at the beginning of the five-week Nasdaq plunge referred to in this book as Spring Break 2000.

    Within days of the disappointing IPO, the online travel service became a magnet for general criticism directed at late netPhase I B2C IPOs that just made it to market before the crash.

9. Larry Dignan, "B2B Stocks: From Boom to Bust to Boom Again," *ZDNet Interactive Investor* (www.zdnet.com), April 21, 2000.

10. Arlene Weintraub, "The Be-All and End-All of B2B Sites?," *Business Week*, June 5, 2000.

Chapter 5

WHICH SHAKEOUT?

We're on the verge of the biggest deployment of technology in 40 years and the biggest structural change in the economy in 50 to 70 years. Today e-commerce is only 2% of the [US] economy. In five years, I think we'll see 20%. Last year was the first year of recognition of the whole (business-to-business) space, so now you're talking about only the second year of a bull market.

Alberto Vilar,
technology fund manager,
Amerindo Investment Advisors.[1]

We all knew there'd be a shakeout this quarter. We just didn't think it would include us.

David Lloyd,
Toysmart.com CEO. Dot-Com—Born 1996,
Died May 19, 2000.[2]

Whether or not there will be a further shakeout of the shakier parts of the Dot-Com boom is now an irrelevant question in the aftermath of the five-week Spring Break. The combination of a swift 34% collapse plus the exit of retail investors relegates netPhase I valuations to nostalgia.

Now debate rages over whether the market is primed to make a further revaluation downward back to earth or whether the interim trading rage continues.

As noted in Chapter 1, self-interest continues to reign supreme during the post-Spring Break period, when it comes to Dot-Com valuation. Packagers of IPOs and other intermediaries who insisted that Dot-Coms were not overvalued in early March 2000, now insist after several downward corrections that the Nets are not *really* overvalued.

But actions speak louder than words, and the Dot-Coms have not rebounded since the peaks of early March. The back of Net excess is broken. Question now is, what's next?

THE END OF E-CAMELOT

NetPhase I was a magical time. A wonderful era when Stanford dropouts, online mountain dwellers in Colorado, and Generation X-Y's pre-millennium version of the 1960s flower children-programmers all converged to pursue *the dream.*

Valuation Alchemy:
The Future Revenue Number —
Whatever You Wish It To Be

Instant meetings via PC. Simultaneous, almost intuitive user access to research, knowledge-based products, even channels of commerce. The Internet era is as different from the period preceding it as the eras that market invention of the wheel, electricity, and the automobile.

Part of the Net magic was that instead of being tethered by the past's proven rules of valuation, those rules were blown to smithereens with little protest, so long as throwaway jargon such as "new paradigm" was liberally tossed about. In e-Camelot, your e-enterprise was worth whatever you wanted it to be worth.

People laughed at the *Alex* cartoon showing a whimsical Dot-Com company IPO price being set by thousands of lackeys all "hitting" the site all night to generate enough fake activity for the desired IPO price (shown in Chapter 1). But that laughter hid winces. Some techniques for manipulating IPO prices were almost as outrageous as the cartoon parodies.

New Emphasis:
Ensuring Great Dot-Com Companies,
Not Just Successful IPOs

One "wonderful" aspect about e-Camelot was that tomorrow's pre-destined bankruptcies were just as likely to receive massive financing as future successes. Just swell for those wizards knowlegeable in the black science of market hype to create a great IPO—wizards who know nothing about creating enduring business wealth in the years following that public offering.

There are two reasons for this last, wonderful alchemy condition. The first is that few in the kingdom could distinguish tomorrow's e-bankruptcies from the e-champions. No one could tell for sure whether egruel.com was one of the 30% of online companies that might survive versus the 70% doomed to crash and burn.

Survival is all a matter of managed perceptions, right sire? Don't go to all that bother of trying to build a sound Internet business. Just hire a skilled manager who is especially adept at analyst-bluff. Then grab some valuation formula manipulators who are adept at fitting discounted cash flow models containing fantasy numbers to generate the desired valuation.

The second wonderful aspect of this alchemy is that the world is so awash in cash that it doesn't matter if the company crashes and burns five quarters after its IPO. Just ensure that there's enough time after the lockout period expires for the "founding investors," deal-arrangers, and others to dump their positions at a profit, before the bad news from auditors declare that "we have doubts that egruel.com is a going concern."

The End of the netPhase I Easy Money
The End of Seventy Percenters' Access to Public Markets

Then the unthinkable happened. A triple whammy marked the beginning of the end for e-Camelot.

First, the mop-haired overlord of e-Camelot empire lost a tough ruling to Klein, the Dark Duke of DC. And while the Lord Gates had showed incredible resilience in ages past, one couldn't help but sense that this time things were different.

Phrases in the judge's decision sounded as if they had been ghostwritten by Sun Microsystems' spin doctors. The preliminary judgment that Microsoft violated the Sherman Antitrust Act exposed Gates & Co. to massive distraction caused by private shareholder suits. Lord Gates now shared another distinction with John D. Rockefeller.

The second crisis for e-Camelot to stumble was the undermining of the Net Vapor IPO, the realm's ultimate source of wealth. The secret was known by everyone, discussed by no one. E-Camelot's stable of worthless companies valued at fortune levels depended on the foolability of GreaterFool serfs, roped in by alluring IPOs.

The GreaterFool attains his title because he will always buy what you are selling, no matter how high the price—as long

---

valueOUTPERFORMER
www.vbmresources.com

May 22, 2000

JUST A COINCIDENCE, OF COURSE

March 6, 2000, was four days before what turned out to be the Nasdaq exhaustion gap peak on March 10. And March 10 was the beginning of the treacherous five-week 34% collapse that proved once and for all that the Dot-Coms were fallible. March 10 was also the end of that crazy, wild, wonderful naive period when Dot.com meant Get Rich.

March 10, 2000, was the END of netPhase I. And the beginning of a transition to something else, something more sustainable. A key event four days earlier on March 6 was that CMGI's AltaVista announced its own new form of "free" ISP service in the United Kingdom.

Something over there, but not without notice worldwide. The trickle of concern that the "free" model simply meant unprofitable future operation extended beyond just United Kingdom's Freeserve, to broader concern about whether everyone had been wrong about the "free" model, everywhere. But the timing? Merely a coincidence, of course.

as he thinks that price might go higher. Invaluable for Ferret International and other institutional investors in the kingdom, secretly selling their shares in the realm's Dot-Coms just as the GreaterFools are buying.

The GF dreamed of replacing his sad mud hut with a doublewide Winnebago. The sellers at Ferret International were just grateful that there was a buyer of last resort available to cancel their mistakes.

International Ramifications

But then the Net IPO market became a bad joke in Hong Kong in January-February 2000. And crashed in Europe in March 2000, when greed caused IPO overpricing, and eventually a series of launch day disappointments that severely eroded confidence in the Dot-Coms. The GreaterFool looked to headlines proclaiming that the share price of egruel.com has quadrupled on its first day as a public company before he also buys. More doubling of the IPO price on launch day caused the GreaterFools to bail out, ASAP. The price in a manipulated Dot-Com IPO is supposed to *soar* on the first day of trading.

IPO weakness in Europe and Hong Kong began to wash over into that Land of Mammon within e-Camelot, the US. As one US-fund manager noted, in 1999 there were just a few Internet IPOs. Breakaway demand to buy *anything* Dot-Com ensured that nearly all soared.

But high prices caused a flood of new Dot-Com IPOs— enough that even a few of the pliable GreaterFools began to be more discerning in 2000.

The third crisis occurred when some of the kingdom's loyal scribes who once did nothing except trumpet the wonder of e-Camelot suddenly became tougher. Douglas Crook of Prudential Securities had the temerity on March 31, 2000, to suggest that not all was well in the B2B e-procurement world. Crook noted that instead of commanding all future profits for online procurement, stand-alone companies such as Commerce One faced tough price and function competition in e-procurement from end-user companies and competitors such as Microsoft.

Lord Gates once demonstrated great skill at determining the precise price that assured him dominant market share in any market: *zero*. So much for profit margins, sector-wide. Crook even suggested that some customers themselves would become tough competitors.

More and more disloyal messengers followed the Prudential precedent, threatening to undermine e-Camelot completely. The Internet may be here to stay, but that doesn't mean that all of the Phase I participants will. And certainly not tomorrow's teetering Dot-Com bankruptcy, temporarily propped up during the e-Camelot period of funny number "valuations."

Shed a tear for the end of e-Camelot. But this is not the end of this wonderful story. For those willing to build great Internet

---

valueOUTPERFORMER
www.vbmresources.com

April 24, 2000

HUMBLE PIE (APOLOGIES TO DON MCLEAN)

Still wondering about that fundamental Dot-Com revaluation that started with the Spring Break Nasdaq slump in mid-March 2000? Go ahead and sing the following, to the tune of Don McLean's, '70s classic, *American Pie*. The remake is from Janice M Hitchens at London's Flemings. Her title: *Humble Pie*. From Damien McCrystal, "A Piece of Pie," *Sunday Business* (London), Apr. 23, 2000

A LONG LONG TIME AGO / I can still remember how the market used to makes me smile / What I'd do/ when I had a chance / is get a cash advance / Add another tech stock to the pile.

But Alan Greenspan made me shiver / With every speech that he delivered / Bad news on the rate front / Still I'd take one more punt. I can't remember if I cried / When I heard about the CPI / I lost my fortune and my pride / The day the Nasdaq died.

So bye-bye to my piece of the pie / Now I'm gettin' calls for margin / Cause my cash account's dry / It's just two weeks from a new all time high / And now we're right back where we were in July.

companies and not just devise frothy Internet IPOs, the future remains bright.

POP! GOES THE INTERNET VALUATION

Now I'm not too smart, but I'm smart enough to figure out that it's tulip time.

H. Ross Perot to Bonnie Azab Powell
about Dot-Com valuations in January 2000
Red Herring, 41.

The Nasdaq Composite's peak on March 10, 2000, marked the end of netPhase I illusory valuations. Within five weeks, Nasdaq slumped 34+ percent. Far too much, far too fast to be excused away as a fluke: netPhase I's back was broken and everyone knew it.

No longer would Bubba GreaterFool be in a buying panic to purchase Dot-Coms with 70-plus percent failure probability at any price, any time. Margin calls in early April 2000 wiped Bubba out. Guess it's back to a real job, maw.

AOL/TWX:
Early Cracks in the netPhase I Foundation

But Nasdaq's exhaustion peak was telegraphed two months earlier by AOL's announcement of its intent to acquire Time Warner.

The acquirer was hit with an immediate 30% discount in value, based on AOL's pre-bid price in the few trading days immediately before the January 10, 2000, announcement.

Conversion of cyber-currency to the "harder" equity of terrestrial companies represents one way to value the Dot-Coms (Figure 1.9) when other valuation methods are unavailable, inadequate, and/or subject to manipulation (see Contaminated DCF discussion in Chapter 1 and John Kay article, also in that chapter).

Privately, the question of valuation methods spread like wildfire following the early January announcement. Now, if a Dot-Com star such as AOL faces a mandatory 30% value discount when

THE INDUSTRY STANDARD
www.thestandard.com

April 5, 2000

THE VULTURES ARE CIRCLING (excerpts)
By Bernhard Warner (©)

VBM Note: Think that the Dot-Com netPhase I shakeout means an end to new Internet industries? Think again. This piece from **The Standard** *caught our eyes as it describes the new Dot-Com businesses that are prospering from the Year 2000 transition period.*

The newest growth market is providing services to bankrupt Internet companies. Auctions of liquidated and distressed assets are gaining ground on the Net.

Predictions of Dot-Com failures may chagrin investors, but Chris Celentino doesn't mind them one bit. That's because corporate liquidation is his business. A partner at Luce, Forward, Hamilton & Scripps in San Diego, Celentino says his law firm is staffing up to handle bankruptcy proceedings for Internet companies.

Demand for his firm's expertise is increasing. "Dot-Coms are seeking our services because they're having a tough time paying lenders," adds Celentino. The firm is also getting calls from vendors who haven't been paid and from venture capitalists who need help recouping funds from their failing investments.

Having splurged on everything from cheeky ads to Herman Miller chairs, some online plays, particularly e-commerce outfits, are having trouble paying their bills. To keep from going out of business, some are exploring bankruptcy protection—a practice that's all but unheard of for Net firms, until now.

New York-based Beautyscene.com, which launched in August [1999], went that route last month. Having piled up big debts following a go-for-broke Christmas ad push, the company's only choice was to reorganize. Seeking protection from creditors in the California courts, the site was recently sold to an undisclosed buyer.

In February [2000], Net backbone provider Apex Global Information declared Chapter 11 bankruptcy in a Michigan court to protect itself against creditors it owes $45 million.

So far, the number of Net bankruptcy filings are few, lawyers say. But they expect that to change. "If the market softens and equity financing starts to dry up, I definitely expect to see the Dot-Coms use Chapter 11," says Warren Agin, a partner at Boston-based Swieggert & Agin.

When that happens, those companies can turn to the Web, specifically to auction sites geared to businesses in bankruptcy. One such venue, Bid4assets.com, launched in November [1999].

attempting to convert its cyber-currency in the real money, what is the deeper discount required for lesser Net companies? 40%, 50%?

And how long will it be before the lightning strikes?

Two months.

January, 2000:
The Announcement

The $327 billion dollar acquisition of Time Warner (TWX) by America Online (AOL) was heralded as the watershed event of the Internet age. January 10, 2000, was the day when content and conduit finally converged, with particularly devastating market effect. Especially for competitors now scrambling to find their own dance partners.

The rivals' dilemma was acute: no other combination of two companies appeared to come close to matching the AOL-TWX combination in terms of sheer Net clout. If content is king, as both

---

Case in point: The domain Planetrock.com (one of the assets that bankrupt Net firm Websecure was forced to sell) sold in January for $28,000 to a Net radio show through Bid4assets.com.

Another firm, Epiq Systems, develops software for bankruptcy trustees to manage the sale of liquidated assets. It also posts clients' assets at Bankruptcylink.com, where shoppers can troll for bargains ranging from boats to foreclosed property. A public company, Epiq's stock peaked at $15.38 in early January, just as prominent e-tailers Amazon.com and eToys began their swoon. Shares remained steady last week, hovering above $11. "We're countercyclical," says Chris Olofson, president and COO. We love it . . . when we see assets being liquidated."

These firms represent a new online cottage industry—one that, like eBay, collects fees for transactions that take place on the companies' sites. In this case, thought the goods for sale once belonged to individuals or companies that can no longer afford to keep them. Last year, the total value of Chapter 11 assets was approximately $59 billion, according to Bid4assets.

Expect the online market for distressed assets to grow as more Dot-Coms go under. Says Harold Bordwin, present of Keen Strategy Advisors, which consulted on the sale of Beautyscene.com: "Out of the contacts we made the past several weeks, we have two potential new clients. That's encouraging."

Oracle's Larry Ellison and Disney's Michael Eisner proclaim, there are few knowledge assets as potent as Time Warner's stable of commercial brand star names, ranging from Bugs Bunny to CNN, with *Time* magazine and *Fortune* magazine in between.

Marry that visibility with AOL, the world's favorite way to access the World Wide Web, and one result is the equivalent of a full employment act for financial pundits. The first two weeks following the merger announcment were dominated by Marriage in Heaven fawning articles by reporters mesmerized by the sheer immensity of the deal, even by Silicon Valley standards.

That phase was followed by weeks of inevitable speculation about who would come next, followed by articles exploring whether the disparate cultures of the immensely different companies could be reconciled to make the deal work.

Convergence Theme

Never mind that "convergence"—the theme most frequently cited when the AOL/TWX deal broke—is a dubious concept, having soared and crashed before in both telecommunications and electronics industries. While executives of expensive deals cite technology convergence as a central part of the rationale for their transactions, end-user customers generally could not care less.

While world telecom giants touted combination services, such as voice-data-image ISDN, customers pushed instead for high-speed data links, burdening Integrated Services Digital Network with the tongue-in-cheek description in the marketplace that persists to this day: Inferior Services customers still Don't Need.

Dot-Com AOL paid a 70% acquisition premium for media giant TWX, despite the fact that few acquisition lessons are clearer than the point that deals between unrelated companies usually fail, miserably. Also, the greater the acquisition premium in percentage terms (amount paid compared to pre-bid market value), the more precarious the deal. In retrospect, it is apparent that few deals with acquisition premiums above the 35% level succeed. AOL paid *double* that amount, in percentage terms.

In January 2000, valueOUTPERFORMER (www.vbmresources. com) speculated about the real implications of the AOL-TWX deal. The assessment: AOL-TWX was the long-awaited pinprick that started to deflate the Internet valuation bubble. And dramatically, as pinpricks tend to do.

Revaluation by Acquisition of Harder Assets: The 30% Haircut

AOL's acquisition terms translated into an immediate 30% reduction in that company's value, a reality confirmed in part by daily stock market "adjustments" in sessions that started January 11, 2000. Valuing the transaction? The marketplace was already doing that job.

At approximately twice TWX's market capitalization as of January 7, 2000 ($163.2 billion compared to $83.5 billion), AOL was expected by many to command around two-thirds of the equity of the combined company. Especially when the Net's "hot" status and Time Warner's sorry track record of Net innovation, with its defunct Pathfinder site, were taken into account.

But instead, AOL settled for only 55% of the new cyber conglomerate. Which means that AOL's cyber-currency is apparently worth only seventy cents when Steve Case and Bob Pittman attempt to purchase terrestrial assets with their funds.

Statements from analysts confirmed the concerns about the value implications of the proposed AOL-TWX linkage. Fund manager Schroders immediately downgraded America Online, commenting that the terms of the deal made it impossible to ignore some of the aggressive prior valuation levels of this Dot-Com, and by implication, other Internet high fliers as well. James Bollinger of California's EquityPartners.com expressed similar sentiments.

For Net zealots eager to quash anything that might suggest that the bubble could burst before they could get out, the timing of AOL's ad hoc value reduction couldn't have come at a worse time.

In January 2000, business-to-consumer (B2C) companies were already reeling because of their big bet they made and lost.

Desperate to gain market share by trading venture capital and IPO equity for advertising, scores of invisible Dot-Com companies all launched US media blitzes for the Christmas 1999 holiday season.

Problem is, they all did it at the same time, canceling each other out. All that most consumers remember is noise. Advertising agencies thanked their lucky stars for their windfall riches as Dot-Coms flush with cash failed to check out the competitive environment for Christmas advertising.

---

valueOUTPERFORMER
www.vbmresources.com

May 29, 2000

WATCH OUT FOR THE CHICKEN LITTLE VIRUS!

It has just come to our attention that a brand new computer virus believed to be originating from Asia is now spreading wildly throughout the world's Internet-linked systems and even the terrestrial and TV business press.

Formal name: The-Dot-Coms-Are-Toast-How-Many-Times-Does-The-Rubble-Have-to-Bounce-Before-You-Realize-That-Turkey? virus. Or Chicken Little virus for short. This pestilence infiltrates your PC in the form of a seemingly innocent report, column, or biz-news sidebar, usually from someone with a job title that connotes some (prior) credibility: a biz-news editor, a behavioral scientist dabbling in market manias, bears who missed the entire 96-99 major market move and now want revenge.

Having observed that the Nasdaq Composite took out BOTH of the "Spring Break 2000" (Mar. 10-Apr. 14) intra-day and closing lows during the week of May 22-26, 2000, those releasing the Chicken Little virus now proclaim that Dot-Com valuations will soon become dust. The Sky is Falling! These Chicken Littlemen claim that a 2000 (the year, not the Nasdaq Composite, at least we hope) soft-landing on a sustainable, albeit lower, Internet company valuation tier, is impossible.

But the antidote for the Chicken Little virus is simple. Tell yourself that a fundamental clean-out and revaluation of the Dot-Coms is NOT an Internet Armageddon. But rather, a tough, deep pruning necessary to let the roses bloom while getting rid of the thorns and choking clutter. The Net is is here to stay. Which is more than can be said for the creators of Chicken Little virus.

Burn Rate Liquidity Crisis Anticipated

The consequence is that scores of these companies now have only a couple of months' cash left and no realistic prospects of a savior secondary financing. Market enthusiasm and vencap funding shifted to business to business way back in September-October 1999. That's decades ago in Internet time.

Prospective spring 2000 headlines facing some of the staggering B2Cs that came to IPO market after mid-1998 represented a spin doctor's worst nightmare. How 'bout "Most 1998-1999 Business to Consumer Net Businesses Now Facing Financial Ruin."

But if the Christmas 1999 ad debacle caused sleeplessness among Dot-Com faux-valuation wizards, the AOL pinprick caused ulcers. As of spring 2000, AOL, Cisco, Dell, and a handful of other top tier Net and Net-related companies have enjoyed special insulation against volatility. These are the Golden Nets, the household name businesses that preserve the Dot-Com promise, even as mediocre businesses with nothing to them except that they are online proliferate.

The Christmas debacle raises serious questions—both about survival of the firms that went on a spending orgy and lost, and about the viability of the revenue/advertising "model" that has been a foundation of B2C since the beginning of the Internet boom. If new customers cannot be attracted using the most expensive (and presumably the most effective) advertising means, then page visits, outside revenue, and any chances for future profitability instantly disappear.

THE DOMINOS BEGIN TO FALL

Once the Dot-Com IPO foundation was undermined, the entire netPhase I financing structure begins to unravel. Jonathan Cohen of Wit Soundview described the situation: "The public and private markets are related incredibly closely. As soon as some of the real (Nasdaq) market damage began to happen back in April [2000], venture capitalists began to withdraw."[3]

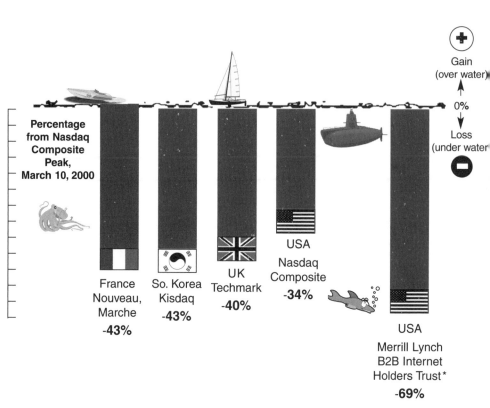

Gain
(over water)

0%

Loss
(under water)

**Percentage
from Nasdaq
Composite
Peak,
March 10, 2000**

France
Nouveau,
Marche
-43%

So. Korea
Kisdaq
-43%

UK
Techmark
-40%

USA
Nasdaq
Composite
-34%

USA
Merrill Lynch
B2B Internet
Holders Trust*
-69%

*A 68.6% decline from March 10, 2000 to April 14, 2000. Trust tracks 20 companies.

FIGURE 5.1. No fun on Spring Break 2000: Percentage decrease from year 2000 peak, to April 21, 2000.

Cohen was in the eye of the Dot-Com devaluation storm as a key speaker at an Internet conference in Manhattan held during the second week of April 2000. The beginning of that week (April 10) was characterized by the usual venture capital bluff and bluster. By Dot-Com Black Friday, managers of Dot-Com start-ups seeking funding were already finding that their calls were no longer being returned from the same VCs who pursued them so urgently just a few weeks earlier.

Endgame. The venture capitalists who define "valuation" within the bounds of their own self interest look to a projected IPO price as the keystone element in their analysis and pricing to Dot-Com entrepreneurs, as described in Chapter 1. So when the IPO market is damaged to the extent that projected IPO pricing has to be reduced by, say, a third to get the deal done, it takes about half a nanosecond for that math to flow through to the deal offerings.

The most buoyant slant of the week's sickening collapse was possibly from VC leader Tim Draper, as he inferred that the Dot-Com value implosion now placed venture capitalists in a stronger bargaining position in their discussions with Net managers: "This now gives us a negotiating edge." That's one way of acknowledging that the pendulum swung quickly—some say that very week—from Dot-Com start-ups entrepreneurs dictating terms in the first week of April 2000, to being fortunate to have calls returned at all by the second week.

SPRING 2000, BROKEN

Warm weather beaconed on Easter weekend, 2000. But that year's Spring Break had absolutely nothing at all to do with Connie Francis

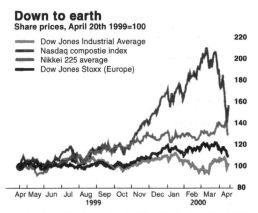

Down to earth
Share prices, April 20th 1999=100

- Dow Jones Industrial Average
- Nasdaq compostie index
- Nikkei 225 average
- Dow Jones Stoxx (Europe)

Apr May Jun Jul Aug Sep Oct Nov Dec Jan Feb Mar Apr
1999   2000

"After the Gold Rush,"*The Economist*, April 22, 2000, 69. Copyright © 2000, *The Economist* Newspaper Group, Inc. Reprinted with permission.

FIGURE 5.2. American leadership: Nasdaq leads the way down—Spring Break 2000.

songs, beach blanket bingo, or college hi-jinks. *This* break refers to the snapping of Nasdaq's spinal chord from March 10 to mid-April 2000. The beginning of the end for crazy, hazy netPhase I.

Change in Course

Spring Break 2000 forced radical changes in tactics for Internet companies already in the public marketplace as they struggled to deal with new, stark equity market conditions and depressed valuations. Along with imminent expulsion of many NIQs—those companies that never should have been brought public in the first place.

Post-Easter weekend 2000, *any* IPO is lucky to proceed. The owner-founder of the struggling B2B industrial auction company with initial promise but little more suddenly faces the prospect that his start-up may have already used up all the capital it will ever receive.

Latest Dot-Com Metric: Cash

After the Spring Break, Dot-Com prospects required a credible business plan that specified where and when positive cash flow would be achieved. A plan that made a convincing case for why this particular company will be a survivor in the coming consolidation.

Almost overnight, the financing picture changes from Too Much Cash to Capital Rationing. The B2Cs and some B2Bs that couldn't qualify for post-IPO institutional financing withered on the vine. Venture capitalists investment bankers and other stakeholders simply had too many cash-burn victims to shore up and had to by necessity make judgment calls about which staggering Dot-Com could win.

Valuation by faddish Dot-Com metrics were and are ignored by responsible financiers for the simple reason that they usually have nothing at all to do with that company's value and viability. But now, with firms such as PR-intensive Lastminute.com selling at a market value of only one-third of the March 2000 launch level, an all-new valuation question emerges: Who has the internal cash-generating capability to survive, without using outside cash as a crutch?

Valuation Fluff Offset by Viability Concerns

Implicit in even moderate valuation approaches is the going concern principle. This is the presumption that the corporation will continue to exist into the future. To pay debts and salaries, includ-

---

valueOUTPERFORMER
www.vbmresources.com

May 31, 2000

THE DOT-COM FLATLINER MAKEOVER

Stock price plunged so low that it's mistaken for a soccer score? Your original business plan gets the biggest laughs when read aloud at comedy clubs? Your share certificates are given away for free with a full tank? And then discarded half a mile down the road? Take heart, you Dot-Com flatliner. There's new hope for you and scores of other Internet companies staggering from the rubble of the Spring Break 2000 Dot-Com collapse with only three months' cash left, some torn-to-tatters business "modelz" filled with discredited Netenomics baffleprose (see *netValue's*, Chapter 4) and a dozen pocket protectors (used). For in true phoenix-style, the culling out of the e-dross has spawned the next full employment act for your pals, management consultants! You asked for it, you got it: it's the Dot-Com Flatliner Makeover, with generalists, box pushers, e-cubators, techies with concepts too bizarre for even netPhase I, and even some veterans of OTHER collapsed Dot-Coms promising to fix everything wrong with your business. We will fix those flagrantly wrong forecasts. We will crop those cascading costs. We will tweak that terminal-generation technology so that your Web site visitors are no longer sent to Yaks-R-US in Mongolia. We'll even imply (carefully, of course—we have great lawyers) that we "might" uncover some fresh financing sources for you. We can't, of course, unless we're an acquirer ourselves, but you don't know that and at this point you're desperate and will grasp at almost anything. Now you ask me how much this great service will cost. LemmeTellYa. Only 120% of your remaining survival cash. Don't have any actual chance of survival? WE DON'T CARE. Company offers a pedestrian service easily imitated by others around the globe, at lower cost, better effectiveness? WE DON'T CARE! Out of cash? WE CARE! You don't think we're stupid enough to take stock a second time, do you??

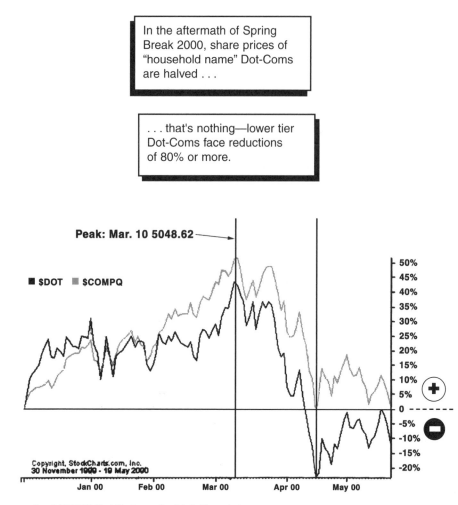

In the aftermath of Spring Break 2000, share prices of "household name" Dot-Coms are halved . . .

. . . that's nothing—lower tier Dot-Coms face reductions of 80% or more.

Peak: Mar. 10 5048.62

■ $DOT ■ $COMPQ

Copyright, StockCharts.com, Inc.
30 November 1999 - 19 May 2000

Jan 00   Feb 00   Mar 00   Apr 00   May 00

Copyright © 2000 StockCharts.com. Reprinted with permission.

LEGEND	
$DOT	TSC Internet Index
$COMPQ	Nasdaq Composite
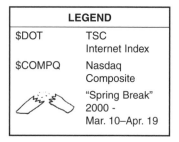	"Spring Break" 2000 - Mar. 10–Apr. 19

FIGURE 5.3. Nasdaq composite index versus TheStreet.com Internet index 120 days:11/30/99-5/19/00.

ing the superstar compensation packages that (should) distinguish possible Net champions and netPhase I compost.

Money to build an enduring franchise through advertising and other expenditures in the case of B2Cs. Funds for a variety of price, positioning and proprietary development strategies by B2Bs. Money to pay for support and logistics so that the Dot-Com company prospers from increased hits on its Web site, rather than plunging into operations crises.

But what happens if the going concern principle no longer applies? When it becomes plausible that the company lacks enough funds to survive, DCF valuation formulas are worthless. Salvage value becomes the only basis for practical valuation, as five- and ten-year cash flow projections are rendered worthless.

WHAT IF DOT-COM STOCK FALLS IN THE FOREST...

But no one hears?

Has that company's market price actually dropped?

---

valueOUTPERFORMER
www.vbmresources.com

June 8, 2000

DOT-COM DEATHWATCH

Think the Internet shakeout means an end to new business activity? Think again. The prospect of a continuous trickle-trickle of collapses as 70-plus percent of netPhase I Dot-Coms fail over the coming quarters provides a brand new feature area for business publications documenting the downs and ups of the Net. In its June 12 edition, *Fortune Magazine* (www.fortune.com) announces its Dot-Com Deathwatch (p. 12) with a cordial invitation to "Tune to this space as more croak." And don't forget *Upside Today*'s (www.upside.com) Dot-Com graveyard. From the same aces who broke the story about the untimely demise on June 6 of the quintessential Internet Phase I start-up. That's right, dude, Surfbuzz.com wiped out.

FINANCIAL TIMES
www.ft.com

April 28, 2000

@ IS THE SCARLET LETTER
by Andrew Hill

Dotcom (.com) fever is over. Companies have begun to shun the once-glamorous suffix, as investors dump Internet stocks. Says Martyn Straw, president of Interbrand, the branding consultancy, "People are beginning to recognize that the basic fundamentals are still true and just adding a dotcom [to the company name] is an indication of nothing."

The change coincides with growing efforts by listed Internet companies to focus investors' attention on potential profits, rather than just growing revenues. Last year, more than a quarter of initial public share offerings in the US were launched by companies with dotcom in their name. Now, the percentage of dotcom IPOs has declined to below 20 per cent, according to CommScan, the research group.

Writing in this week's *New York* magazine, James Cramer described the suffix as "the curse, the scarlet letter." He should know. Shares in TheStreet.com, the online financial news site that he founded, now trade at around $6-1/2 compared with a momentary peak on their first day of trading of $71.

US Internet stocks as a group have fallen by an average of more than 50 per cent since mid-March. Those carrying the dotcom tag have been hit slightly harder than their peers.

Within the last two months, a few companies have begun to shed the suffix. Infospace.com, a provider of commerce, information, and communication infrastructure services, dropped its ".com" on March 1, arguing that its strategy now incorporated the online and offline world. Gameplay.com, a UK-based interactive games company, took the same decision, reflecting the fact that it gets a larger share of its revenues from interactive television.

But Raghavendra Rau, a finance professor at Purdue University in Indiana, points out that more companies are adding the suffix than dropping it—25 small companies adopted a dotcom in March and April, in spite of the stock market fall-out. One place where the suffix's late 20th-century glamour lives on is Half.com, Oregon. The town changed its name from Halfway for a year, starting in January, in a publicity deal with the Web site of the same name.

Dick Crow, Half.com's mayor, said on Friday that the townsfolk now thought [townspeople] might even consider extending the name-change for another year. He has no intention of proposing a change to Quarter.com to reflect the slump in dotcom stock prices.

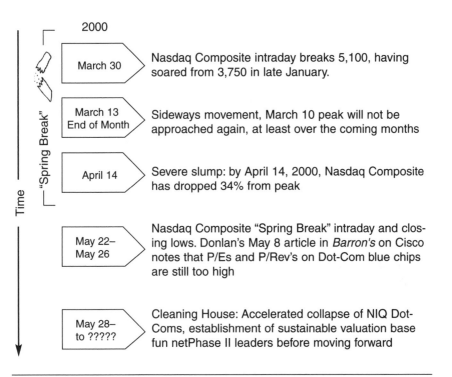

2000

| March 30 | Nasdaq Composite intraday breaks 5,100, having soared from 3,750 in late January. |

| March 13 End of Month | Sideways movement, March 10 peak will not be approached again, at least over the coming months |

| April 14 | Severe slump: by April 14, 2000, Nasdaq Composite has dropped 34% from peak |

| May 22– May 26 | Nasdaq Composite "Spring Break" intraday and closing lows. Donlan's May 8 article in *Barron's* on Cisco notes that P/Es and P/Rev's on Dot-Com blue chips are still too high |

| May 28– to ????? | Cleaning House: Accelerated collapse of NIQ Dot-Coms, establishment of sustainable valuation base fun netPhase II leaders before moving forward |

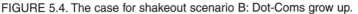

FIGURE 5.4. The case for shakeout scenario B: Dot-Coms grow up.

The Net era counterpart to the age-old philosophical question arises as Dot-Com companies both excellent and mediocre are forced toward lower market value tiers. This means not merely share price reductions directed at a single company, segment, or major sector, but rather a fundamental re-valuation of Internet companies and their market values.

In the aftermath of Spring Break 2000, every Dot-Com slips. Those B2Cs that have been sliding downward since mid-1999, when there were serious concerns about their revenue sources and other aspects of their business modelz, just keep slip slidin' away. Willoughby's "Burning Up!" lists victims such as CDNow and DrKoop and displays sickening "reverse hockey stick" share price patterns, along with warnings from their auditors.

B2B infomercials proclaiming the sector as the next Net champion group hype emerge with increasing frequency. Institutional

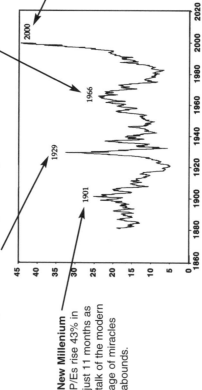

Price/earnings (P/E) ratios 1881-2000, S&P composite

Roaring 20s
The stock market will never go down; '20s, the last time that ordinary people though that securities speculation was a real job. P/Es reach 32.6 x at 1929 peak. S&P index drops 80.6% by June '82.

New Millenium
P/Es rise 43% in just 11 months as talk of the modern age of miracles abounds.

Growth Stock Mania
Guns & Butter. Johnson prosperity popped by Vietnam war, oil crisis "growth" stocks that stopped growing P/E peak in '66 of 24.1x. 56% slump by '74.

netPhase I Surge
"I never met a Dot-Com I didn't like" — unbridled enthusiasm creates runaway momentum markets, first overall and then "Hot" sectors (B2B, Infrastructure). Speculation becomes an ordinary B2B again. Nasdaq Composite falls 34% in March 10 through April 14 Spring Break, eliminating individual speculators.

Real (inflation-corrected) S&P Composite Stock Price Index, monthly, January 1871 through January 2000 (upper series), and real S&P Composite earnings (lower series), January 1871 to September 1999.

Source: Shiller's calculations using data from S&P Statistical Service, U.S. Bureau of Labor Statistics; Cowles and Associates, Common Stock Indexes; and Warren and Pearson, *Gold and Prices*.

Price-earnings ratio, monthly, January 1881 to January 2000. Numerator: real (inflation-corrected) S&P Composite Stock Price Index, January. Denominator: moving average over preceding ten years of real S&P Composite earnings. Years of peaks are indicated.

From Robert J. Shiller, *Irrational Exuberance* (Princeton, New Jersey: University Press, 2000) 8, Figures 1.2. Copyright © by Princeton University Press. Reprinted by permission. Other P/E format suggested by Faisal Islam, "Wall Street's Party Pooper," *Observer*, May 28, 2000, B5.

FIGURE 5.5. The case for a shakeout scenario A: Crash and burn (Shiller's graph).

investor Safeguard Scientific announces its withdrawal from B2Bs on April 10, 2000, in favor of e-infrastructure.

Even some of the new Can't Miss companies are brought low. An article regarding Cisco in *Barron's* on May 8 affects the company for days afterwards. In boom times, the Donlan article would have been easily shrugged off. In scorched earth post-Spring Break 2000 times, such articles send share prices reeling, causing the evening business press to speculate about a domino impact going forward.

But these are the falling "trees" that everyone hears. There are many, many other more unseen, unheard Dot-Com Spring Break victims that are effectively invisible to the markets.

These victims include the IPOs that are not strong enough to go to the marketplace for secondary financing: the Dot-Com walking dead. The clock is ticking as scarce remaining funds run out. Their only chance for the future is a savior merger.

Then there are the B2Cs and some B2Bs in vulnerable segments (see Chapter 7), that find their initial public offerings cancelled, raising serious doubts about survival.

That's never the language used, of course. In best Net-spin style, the words as publicly released merely refer to "waiting for market conditions to improve."

Hey, has to be better than the truth. The truth is that even if the IPO market *does* manage to rebound, a new set of fresh Can't Miss Dot-Coms will crowd the market for available funds, lowering the prospects of survival for all. If the "old" Dot-Com has encountered new competition that renders its business model obsolete, financiers may be inclined to simply dump the "old" Dot-Com company beset by problems in favor of the fresh, new Internet wannabe without any hubris.

The Dot-Com that proceeds with an offering at half the target IPO price set just a few weeks looks either desperate or unsure of its worth. On May 16, 2000, Chello Broadband NV agreed to cut the market value of its coming flotation in half, to Euro 400 million. Other stories are much the same.

But there's still one more explanation for the plunge in valuations, and why some companies figured that it makes sense to proceed with an IPO in May 2000 that reflected half the valuation of just eight to ten weeks earlier.

Truth is, the nosebleed "values" were never real to begin with.

Goldman Sachs investment analyst and one of the Big Three Dot-Com Stars, Abby Joseph Cohen, forsees a continuation of the tech-driven multiple year bull market in May 2000 . . .

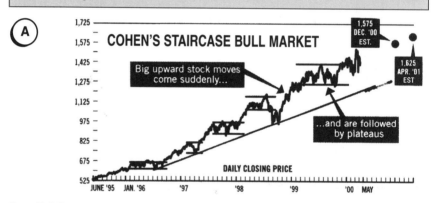

Source: Emily Thornton, "Rising Step by Volatile Step,"*Business Week*, May 22, 2000, 67-68. Data: Goldman Sachs, Co., Abby Joseph Cohen.

But compare the generalist S&P 500 with the far more Internet relevant Nasdaq 100, and (1) the "Staircase" appears flat while (2) the slump in the deteriorating Nasdaq 100 is disquieting.

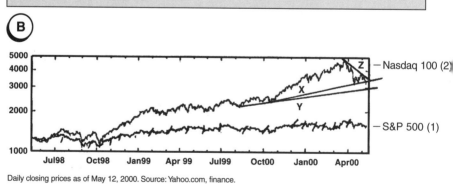

Daily closing prices as of May 12, 2000. Source: Yahoo.com, finance.

FIGURE 5.6. The case against fundamental Dot-Com re-valuation: Cohen's "staircase."

POST-SPRING BREAK 2000:
IN SEARCH OF FINANCING AND
SUSTAINABLE VALUATION LEVELS

Where does netPhase II lead next?

The Seventy Percenters Begin to Waver

There had been announcements before March 10, 2000, about troubled Dot-Coms, but before the Nasdaq Composite peak and Willoughby's March 20 article, such developments were infrequent enough to be spin-managed by the many groups with a vested interest in sustaining the Dot-Com valuation fantasy persisting for all of netPhase I.

Suddenly, in late March, a few of the B2Cs on Willoughby's list began to implode. The *Barron's* senior editor received the customary greeting of the adult who comes down the stairs and tell the kids their party's over—go on home.

---

value OUTPERFORMER
vbmresources.com

May 9, 2000

THE POINT BEHIND DONLAN'S POINT

The degree of venom directed at Thomas Donlan for issues raised in his recent article ("Cisco's Bid's," *Barron's*, May 8, 2000, 31–34) suggests fears that the points may actually be true. Donlan questioned Cisco's merger-driven business strategy and some aspects of its accounting. But it is the third issue of greatest concern here. "These values are still very high, even with the recent tech sell-off," suggests Carrie Lee of WSJD, also owned by Dow Jones. The point behind Donlan's third point is that the whole Dot-Com sector may well be on an unstable valuation plateau, ready to collapse again. Just as no directly involved investment bank or venture cap firm was willing to publicly utter the "O" word (overvalued) as the Nasdaq March 10, 2000, exhaustion gap approached, there is similar eye-of-the hurricane misleading quiet as the market waits for Greenspan's 50 basis point rate hike on May 16. The second major adjustment in Dot-Com valuations towards more rational levels is imminent.

The follow-through to Spring Break means fast exit of the NIQs that should never have gone public in the first place during netPhase I. These companies have no chance of survival, and each day of fraudulent existence robs a possible survivor of funds critical to survival.

Toward Sustainable Valuation Levels

The way that this index came down, it's not a correction, but a blowout. A move that begins a (far greater) correction.

(This is) not a short-term matter. Far more important than that.

CNBC *Street Signs*, May 1, 2000
Philip Roth, Morgan Stanley Dean Witter

Where are Dot-Com prices headed next? To a lower plateau. Toward a stable new valuation range.

The weeks following the dramatic Spring Break 2000 period represented the eye of the Dot-Com re-evaluation hurricane. Deceptively quiet, as characterized by low volume. The mere trickle of sell orders following the five-week Spring Break period caused some permabulls to think that the netPhase I party still has a few months left.

NetPhase I is dead. Put aside all the charts and turn a deaf ear to all "the market is at a bottom" sales-baffleprose from the tethered analysts told to talk up the market. Self interest drives such drivel: *hurry up and buy or we're all fired.*

Jag Hoag, partner, Technology Crossover Ventures, an investor in both public and private companies, speaking of Dot-Com companies on May 19, 2000, following the Spring Break market action, epitomizes the sentiment: "Of course, a lot don't look attractive even 80% below their highs. That's a bit scary."[5]

The positive news is that even if the second down leg goes to a "super-tech" P/E range (such as hypothesized in Chapter 8, Figure 8.1), the emerging netPhase II champion companies—the developers of enduring Dot-Com value—still have the funds and the strategies and the acquisition currency to excel. The whole sector moves to a more sustainable level, and the leaders continue

SETTING SUN

Think that failure rate estimates of up to 75-plus percent for netPhase I B2Cs and up to 50% of B2Bs are too severe? Gartner Group says that the Asia collapse is destined to be worse.

About 85% of Asia-Pacific's pure e-business companies will either go bankrupt or be acquired by traditional companies or bigger dot-coms by 2003, predicted consulting and market-research firm Gartner Group Inc.

Many smaller dot-coms in the region lack the experienced staff and business skills to survive in the long term, said Joe Sweeney, Gartner's Asia Pacific research director. What is likely to happen in the next few years is that these companies will either be bought by traditional companies looking to build their online operation or be forced to merge or be acquired by other Internet companies.

Why the high failure rate? "It really comes down to one word: greed," said Mr. Sweeney. What has happened so far is that a large number of companies are simply riding on the Dot-Com frenzy trying to make a quick buck, he said, noting that many of these companies don't have a solid business plan or organization structure to make it in the marketplace.

This will be especially the case for Internet companies that rely solely on advertising revenue, he said, predicting that online ad revenue will slip by 30% to 40% in the next 18 months. As a result, by 2003, the Internet market in the region will be dominated mainly by what he calls "hybrid" companies—companies with both traditional and online businesses and channels. He cited America Online Inc.'s merger with Time Warner Inc. as an example of the hybrid model.

"The 15% of the pure Internet companies that will survive in Asia Pacific in the next few years will most likely be the ones that are already well-established, such as Chinadotcom Corp. and companies that have multiple revenue streams," said Mr. Sweeney. He also warned that global Internet leaders will be moving into the Asian market in a big way given the explosive online population growth and the high competitiveness in developed markets such as the United States.

---

valueOUTPERFORMER
www.vbmresources.com

June 3, 2000

AND WHICH WILL JUST BE SERIOUSLY INJURED?

Speculation over possible future coming "burn rate" victims becomes the stuff of biz-press competitive speculation, both in print and online. Arguably, the survey for readers in Jesse Berst's June 2, 2000, "Next Dot-Coms to Die" column for ZDNet's Anchor Desk (www.zdnet.com/anchordesk/) is the most direct we've encountered to date.

Suggests Mr. Berst: "Give me your nominations for the first Dot-Coms to die. . . And be sure to take our Quick Poll below:

Which of these companies will die first?

   __ **Ask Jeeves**

   __ **EarthWeb**

   __ **Buy.com**

   __ **FTD.com**

   __ **AutoWeb.com**

(vote)

---

to have their valuation advantage over other Dot-Coms, which is essential for the Internet consolidation wave coming next.

But netPhase I was just the warm-up.

Notes

1. From John H. Christy, "The Best Is Yet to Come," *Forbes Global*, July 3, 2000, 124.
2. From "The Dotcom Graveyard," *Upside Today* (www.upside.com), June 7, 2000.
3. CNBC *Europe Squawk Box*, May 24, 2000.
4. "Band-Aid Financing Keeps Dot-Coms Afloat," Anchor Desk, ZDNet (www.zdnet.com).
5. Suzanne McGee, "Dot-Coms Seek IPO Alternatives," *The Wall Street Journal*, 27.

Chapter 6

TRANSITION TO NETPHASE II: DOT-COMS GROW UP

We believe after the recent shake-out that only strong IPOs will come to market. Translation: I wonder if I can still make 18 pounds of fries per minute?

Peter G. Miller,
May 27, 2000, TheStreet.com[1]

The best of the first generation [Internet] companies will survive and regain every bit of their lost valuations.

Richard L. Brandt,
Upside Today, June 10, 2000[2]

Crash and burn of the seventy percenters ensures many months of carnage as netPhase I excesses are reversed. In a historical context, this is to be expected. In any change market of importance, there's a reaction—almost a depression—that invariably follows five-to-seven years after the initial period of runaway exuberance.

In 1849, prospectors discovered that the streets of Sutter's Mill were not paved with gold nuggets. After all, car makers at the turn of the last century learned the Good Industry- Bad Company

"Alex" reprinted with permission by www.telegraph.co.uk alex-cartoon@etgate.co.uk.

lesson that entrepreneurs deliberately forget at every boom: it matters nothing that the new economic era represents the next great thing. That has little to do with individual company prospects or performance.

A turnkey company launched during netPhase I doesn't become a world-beater just because everyone's excited about the Internet. To the contrary, there is unbridled enthusiasm about the new era's promise.

Where to next? To realizing the *full* promise of the Net. To putting juvenile illusions aside for the very serious work of building champion Net companies out of the best of the survivors from netPhase I.

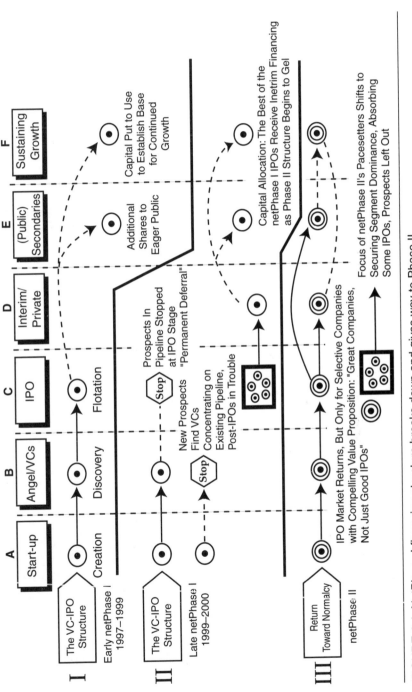

FIGURE 6.1. NetPhase I financing structure breaks down and gives way to Phase II.

The best is yet to come, but only for those Dot-Coms that can move forward. Only for those Internet entrepreneurs, managers, and financiers who can shape the second major phase of the Commercial Internet revolution.

Tears for the passing of netPhase I? No. Instead, cheers for the promise that can be achieved in netPhase II.

DOT-COMS' FINANCING ODYSSEY: FROM IPO ASSEMBLY LINE TO MAINSTREAM

> *External markets' financing emphasis will shift away from premature IPOs, and towards accelerated development of those few Dot-Coms with the greatest promise of excelling and dominating in the Net's second phase.*
>
> Peter Pervere, CFO,
> Commerce One, May 2000[3]

Nonsense Nasdaq valuations of netPhase I are history. They're not coming back. Nor is the financing structure that created that fiction.

During netPhase I, the venture capital-dominated IPO structure shown in Figure 6.1 was designed to churn out as many Dot-Com IPOs as possible, and fast. While allowing some investors with an early stake in the company to cash out early, at least partially. That temporary structure now gives way to something else, something more familiar.

NetPhase I's VC-IPO Financing Structure: Designed to Meet Extraordinary Retail Demand

Measured on the basis of the sheer volume of Dot-Com IPOs brought to market, the netPhase I VC-IPO financing structure (I and II in Figure 6.1) was extraordinarily effective.

Before such a financial assembly line existed, venture capitalists faced the prospect that their occasional stellar discoveries might yield far less than expected.

For the venture capitalist, all the work of helping developing, say, the next Yahoo!, could disappear in an instant if the timing was wrong, or if the environment in the financing community was not exactly right for that type of deal.

But a new Dot-Com deal financing mechanism *did* emerge, providing relatively easy IPO access to both the Dot-Com great and the mediocre. As Perkins & Perkins describe in their insightful *The Internet Bubble*, threshold events such as amazon.com's initial financing established pre-conditions that permitted the structure shown in Figure 6.1 to emerge.

One Dot-Com financing shock success led to six more, and then to twenty-six. Pretty soon, the financing miracles became everyday magic. Venture capitalists invaded Wall Street, with Net IPOs crowding out the financings of all those boring non-Net firms.

As a consequence, the Internet became the modern equivalent of the 1849 California Gold Rush, capturing the imaginations of retail stock market speculators in a way rarely seen.

Most technologies have a limited shelf life. Either customer benefits are overhyped by marketeers who don't understand that the functionality is unmarketable, or burdened with some technical feature that excites the engineers but is irrelevant to end-user customers. But the Commercial Internet was—and is—different. Instead of an isolated high tech company launch in Year One followed by one competitor in Year Three, the Net's financing structure inspired a *swarm* of provocative investment propositions.

Rather than a few, narrowly-defined technologies brought to market, scores of overlapping inventions and combinations emerged. The frantic, festive result was scarcely controlled chaos, with each IPO entrepreneur dreaming of becoming the next Cisco. All this despite the screaming warnings in all prospectuses that the chances were far greater that the company would instead follow the Dark Model path of Digital Entertainment Network, Toysmart.com, or Boo.com, than succeed.

Equally if not more important, many of these early Dot-Com companies were rendered *understandable* for newly empowered online BubbaGreaterFool investors.

It is no fluke that the *least* promising of the three primary Net sectors—business to consumer—was nonetheless pushed to the forefront as the early Dot-Com showcase sector. Bubba GreaterFool may think that an Internet Protocol router is a hog that's good at finding potatoes under dirt. But through careful spin doctor explanation, Bubba at least can understand the general principle of ordering his favorite brand of beer online.

Roaring retail demand from BubbaGreaterFool and his pals created the imperative for a share delivery system for almost any Dot-Com IPO. This was a delivery mechanism featuring a three-part formula of (1) this quarter's fad sector; (2) highlighting a slick story that makes Bubba's blood boil; and (3) suitable rent-a-management for the Dot-Com that makes the whole thing seem viable, at least temporarily.

After netPhase I:
The Assembly Line Is Dismantled

> *External markets' financing emphasis will shift away from premature IPOs, and towards accelerated development of those few Dot-Coms with the greatest promise of excelling and dominating in the Net's second phase.*
>
> Interview with Peter Pervere,
> CFO, Commerce One, May 24, 2000

With the Net now a part of the new way that almost all of us do everything, expectations that the VC-IPO structure might continue indefinitely are not as extreme today as they appeared in the somber days following March-April Spring Break 2000.

The Dot-Com churn 'em out production line shown as I and II in Figure 6.1 was a financing fast track for the value creators driving America's future. Year-to-year revenue percentage growth rates of the early Net companies were in the *hundreds*, even the *thousands*.

But then the aging assembly line began to throw some gears and eventually broke down entirely (III, in the figure). Two factors were central to the end of too-easy Dot-Com financing in the 1996-to-Quarter 1, 2000 period: quality breakdown and venture capital's retreat back towards its more traditional set-up role.

Quality Breakdown

While the VC-IPO structure might be ideal for churning out the greatest volume of Net IPOs over the shortest period of time, venture capital is no stack-'em-up proposition where anyone can magically triple the number of viable companies just because demand for Dot-Com shares triples.

Before the mid-1990s, a top venture capitalist thanked his lucky stars for three or so blockbuster discoveries per decade. Then all of a sudden, the Corporate Internet arrived for real, and the old success probabilities were supposed to disappear. Even assuming the debatable proposition that the Net means a somewhat higher success "hit" rate than pre-90s venture capital, the rush of excess entrants lured by nosebleed valuations partially cancelled any such benefit.

HTML generation search engines, online buying services, generic Internet Services Providers (ISPs) that provide little more than Web access, lookalike second-tier B2B and B2C 'community' sites. Even assuming that success probabilities for Dot-Com businesses may later prove to be a full ten percentage points above the level of pre-Net era, the surge of excess rivals, all using price as their primary differentiation, cancels out any such percentage edge.

Nosebleed valuations turn out to be the Achilles' heel of the entire VC-IPO financing structure of netPhase I. Sure, the magic mix of thin floats and factoids instead of facts caused share values for e-Bankruptcy2001.com to triple in the first week after its trumpeted IPO. But stratospheric share prices also ensured high supply. Within two quarters, e-Bankruptcy's oh-so-unique proposition to the marketplace was drowned out by competing claims from twenty companies that looked alike, and sounded alike.

E-Bankruptcy.com? No, no, no. What you really, really would rather have is something that looks alike, sounds alike, yet is faster/ better/cheaper. What you need is e-Insolvency.com instead.

Advertising-dependent B2Cs face a killer combination. An absolute requirement to pay three times their original budgeted amount for ads to grow the business, that generate only half of the expected market results.

	netPhase I	netPhase II
Ideal company	Thin float IPO, all-new online standalone start up	Second generation bricks 'n clicks hybrid with compelling market proposition
Fundation investor/ shareholders	Individual online investor, buying anything in current Cant Miss sector on dips	Institution, adapting value investment principles to volatile internets
Key player	Startup originators, early stage angles, VC, top IPO investment bankers	Killer model developers, secondary (mainstream) financiers
Primary management focus	Positioning: Being in the right sector	Viable business plan that ensures survival today, segment leadership tomorrow
Presence [Paraphrase]	Participation: "It is a massive market with opportunities for many. We will be one of those to thrive"	Domnation: "Don't even bother entering without 40/40 critical mass"*
Market share capture approach	Bottom up: "Sustain triple-digit growth long enough, and market dominance is unavoidable"	Top down, approchable market: "Incremental conversion to online too slow, too risky. Establish the hybrid approach that converts the whole category, first and best"
Sector emphasis	(1) Early infrastructure pioneers and B2C-stand-alones	(1) Second wave infrastrure and B2B companies that avoid Dark Model pitfalls
	(2) B2Bs	(2) Selective B2Cs with credible cash positive dates, limited post-IPO financing requirements

* Note: 40/40 critical mass refers to penetration of (i) overall market share as well as (ii) Dot-Com portion of total demand. Explained in greater depth elsewhere in this chapter.

FIGURE 6.2. Transition to netPhase II.

	netPhase I	netPhase III
Positive cash flow in the future	Communicated via "perceptions management," CFO's role is to sustain credibility with financial markets	Through specific forecasts and commitments, tracked more closely than EPs, cash flow per shares
netBrand development	Reliance on high risk, low-yield, high-cost traditional media—not because it works, but because of absence of alternatives	(1) Extending the few highly successful key Net nameplates (2) Bricks 'n clicks hybrid nameplates leveraging on traditional market presence
Mergers and acquisitions emphasis	Cross-Dot-Com commercial contracts with spin as special alliances	Industry group strategic alliance announcements: overpromise Next: Killer model clicks 'n bricks combinations despite Dot-Com deep discounts
Market share capture strategy	Bottom Up: Sustain Triple-digit growth long enough, and market dominance is unavoidable	Top Down: Approachable market: Incremental conversion to online too slow, too risky. Establish the hybrid approach that converts the whole category, first and best

FIGURE 6.2. Transition to netPhase II (continued).

The B2B sector's fragile pricing structure succumbs to excess entry. The e-procurement firm that once commanded high margin per-seat and per-transaction fees in the marketplace is forced to beat a hasty retreat, as too many Me-Too competitors undercut prices that already cover only a small portion of the e-businesses' operating costs.

As Infobank CEO Graham Sadd suggests, the B2B e-procurement firm that lacks distinctive multiple market software effectively excludes itself from global customers that require a world platform.[4]

The Dot-Com companies that came public during netPhase I with high hopes but a fatally flawed business plan are now poised to be driven out of business before January 1, 2002. Sometimes even sooner. The broken Dot-Com rushes to bankruptcy or—more likely—is absorbed in a face-saving takeover. Assuming there's something to salvage, that is.

Early on in the Commercial Internet boom, this quality problem was not widely recognized. Some hype-fueled optimists actually thought that all 17 losers out of the 20 coming to market might somehow succeed in a crowded market. Such was the fractured "logic" of Dot-Com's new math.

Everyone knew of the 70%-plus failure estimates. But everyone assumed that those percentages applied to some-one else.

Gradually, the realization dawned: many Dot-Coms were brought public without any chance of survival. *Just because the company is publicly traded doesn't mean it will succeed much less survive.*[5]

Pressed for answers about how *their* specific online businesses will beat the long odds, for survival, pre-Spring Break responses start with mantras about "trusting the Net." The first hope: early unquenchable demand for shares of Dot-Com companies will continue forever. The second hope: that roaring IPO demand today ensures ample post-IPO funds tomorrow, as well.

But no post-IPO financing structure was developed during netPhase I, with the result that some Dot-Coms heralded in mid-

What they SAY	What they really MEAN
"We have decided to temporarily defer our IPO until market conditions improve."	Actually, the IPO was chancy at the best of times, but now we have no chance at all. The bankers have disappeared, so we're on our own.
"We are exploring relationships with strategic investment partners."	Maybe there's someone out there who hasn't heard we've been dropped by our banker and who will still invest mindlessly, based only on our five-minute elevator pitch.
"We have engaged investment advisers to explore a full range of strategic options."	We're out of cash within six months but can't let the investment community out there know we're hurting, or you can kiss our equity goodbye.
"The IPO market is not the only path to financing, and investors are not just looking to get in and get out."	We're excluded from IPO sales at any price, and also from secondaries and private interm financing. We hope that our spin about "long-term prospects" cancels concerns about our near-term reality.
"We are carefully reassessing our position forward financial projections, with a view to both maximizing growth and shareholder value."	Our original projection of becoming profitable by Qtr 2 2001 must be pushed forward a year if we are going to receive any more financing from our bankers. However, true projections show that profitability will not be achieved until later than first hoped. We're toast.
"We have more than sixty million in cash as well as other substantial financing arrangements."	You're right to be concerned about our cash position. Please don't ask whether we can survive on internal cash generation alone.

FIGURE 6.3. New lexicon of the Dot-Com cash poor.

1999 as the next great things in their segment suddenly began to encounter the marketplace's concerns about viability just six months later. We know of nothing else that can explain changes in share prices of relatively stable businesses from more than $100/share at its peak in April 1999 to less than $13 per share one year later.

As Kambiz Foroohar, ex-TheStreet.com business editor now working on his own Net start-up (hey, what else) suggests, "Imperative is to create an aura of activity, of prosperity for six months after the IPO. All those 'alliances' and 'announcements'

---

valueOUTPERFORMER
www.vbmresources.com

April 19, 2000

Adapted From
BITTERSWEET SPRING FOR DOT-COM BANKERS

For investment bankers who have been bringing a range of different quality Internet companies to IPOs for years, the present watershed Internet re-valuation period (the Nasdaq Composite slumped 34% on April 14 2000, from highs) brings a bittersweet season to an end. The market's sharp fall obliterates the bankers' fantasy components and contaminated discounted cash flow models designed first and foremost to bring viable companies to market. The risk (r) and term (t) components in bankers' contaminated DCF models are now business cartoon parody.

As long as nosebleed valuations went unchallenged, no one ever told the Emperor that he had no clothes. But now the world has changed. Assuming ten- to fifteen-year lives for companies in segments where the companies last for three or less on average is obscene. So is the practice of developing Betas based on an unrelated portfolio of companies and then slapping that risk factor onto a completely different company.

The post-hallucinatory period's consequence (besides the fact that advocates of contaminated DCF analyses are now laughingstocks): far fewer IPO fees for the bankers as the market suddenly regains its quality consciousness. But don't shed a tear quite yet. The forced Internet re-valuation period means that the pace of Dot-Com industry consolidation will pick up in the months ahead. So although the banker's IPO group suffers, there's new M&A activity in a different department.

made in the first three months after the launch are pre-planned. As long as share price stays relatively stable for six months or so after the [IPO] launch, the packagers figure they're home free."[6]

So when some early 1999 B2C champions became chumps by mid-year, the stage was set for the crushing March-April break in the market in spring 2000. Spring Break 2000 probably would have occurred six-nine months earlier, in the fall of 1999, except for excess liquidity pumped into markets by a Federal Reserve scared about the end-of-century Y2K threat.

By September 1999, sector lemmings had already jumped from B2C to B2B. There were few problems with Net valuations, with the highly visible exception of weaker B2Cs. But that had nothing to do with B2Bs in autumn 1999, the real essence of the Net promise.

Or at least that was the fairy tale at the time.

Venture Capital Financing Reverts to Role

Eventually, the limitations of a financing structure designed to deal with only one part of Dot-Coms' total, ongoing financing requirements became painfully apparent.

One of the key reasons why a star chief financial officer is such an essential member of the pre- and post-IPO Dot-Com's team is because he or she guides financial community expectations about future cash flow and that all-important date when the company might become cash flow positive. Personal influence is critical, and Dot-Com "solid" projections are often based on marketing and operations metrics that are at best tangential to cash flow.

A far more important role for the Dot-Com CFO is to develop the corporation's sustaining financing after the emotional high of the IPO. Because until (and unless) the day arrives that Dot-Com secondary financing is as prolific as Dot-Com IPOs were during 1999, the CFO must somehow devise a one-off financing plan from pieces.

This is like trying to put together a mountain bike present from tiny parts on Christmas Eve, when you're not even sure that all the parts are even enclosed in the carton.

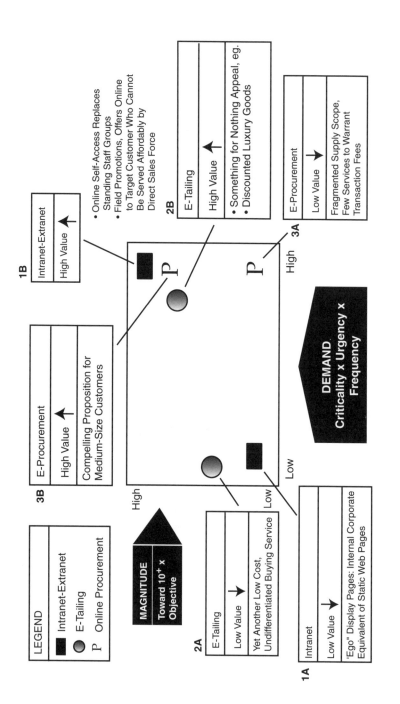

FIGURE 6.4. Beyond the single sector decision: Three sectors, high/low value alternatives.

Better still, some CFO-banker combination is needed to help create the all-new secondary financing structure for Dot-Coms in the future.

More than 40 publicly-held Internet companies issued nearly $20 billion in secondary stock offerings. That's more than five times the amount of the comparable period of the year before.

But that doesn't necessarily lessen the threat of funding shortages. Most of the financings described above involved sales to insiders and sales by previously restricted shareholders directly to the public.[7]

The EToys Precedent

The netPhase I companies in the best position to qualify for post-IPO era private funding are those firms that can make a convincing case for a future Number One role in a high margin segment.

In June 2000, EToys.com received recognition that it would be a dominant player in any future online toys sector, along with the savior financing that comes with such recognition. But EToys' new, tough private financing terms in mid-2000 bear little resemblance to the relatively easy IPO money of netPhase I.

A PIPE for EToys:
There's No Going Back to 1999

The good news on June 13, 2000 for embattled etailer EToys was that it received a $100 million PIPE (Private Investment in Public Equity) cash infusion from a consortium lead by Promethean Asset Management.

Not every post-IPO that experiences a plunge in its share price from a high of $86/share to single digits (Figure 1.7, Chapter 1) can reasonably expect any new funding at all, much less an extra cash infusion of $100 million.

The bad news was manifested in shareholders' reactions to the savior arrangement. Share price slumped 2.5% on the first day following the announcement, 6% on the next. A curious reaction, as the alternative could have meant no financing at all.

valueOUTPERFORMER
www.vbmresources.com

April 5, 2000

DOT-COM TALENT AND OPTIONS REPRICING

The US Financial Accounting Standards Board (FASB) has to date permitted the most lenient accounting treatment of stock options possible. Value of the options are not even included in the issuing firm's compensation costs, even when the employee cashes in. But there's not much exercising of options going on theses days, at least not Dot-Com company options issued after Q4-98, which are now mostly deep "underwater"—that is, far below their stated exercise prices.

Adding to the problem is that the FASB recently introduced a new rule specifying far less lenient treatment of REPRICED options. Dot-Com mouth-pieces insist that repriced options are critical to retaining present value-creating star employees. But now, if a company reprices its options, any appreciation over the exercise level must be subtracted from corporate earnings. Reaction? Many Dot-Com managers see the new rule as flatly eliminating ANY possibility of repricing, especially in the prevailing post-Willoughby List environment of increased emphasis on positive cash flow and earnings.

The never admitted, but always suspected, stance is that Dot-Com management figures that everyone's in the same boat, so What Me Worry? Company value-creating stars will just have to stay put. Or will they? Brand new start-ups care almost nothing about any financial statements but ARE obsessed with grabbing the top value talent needed to outflank those already in the e-marketplaces. If those netPhase II raw start-ups can convince Corporate Key Contributor holders of underwater options that THEIR new, new share options may actually be worth something in the future, then these late Dot-Coms stand to live off some key talent.

Another prospect: some companies deliberately collapse and reappear as all-new firms, rather than pressure their original capital sources for savior financing. By combining with other burn rate victims among the new Dot-Com cash poor, company management helps disguise the fact that it is essentially reorganizing primarily to "reset" the original options price. The reborn "Phoenix.com" then establishes a "new" options price, in line with new, far lower, more rational Dot-Com valuations, and benefits from the more favorable treatment granted to originally-issued options as contrasted with treatment of repriced options. At least until the US FASB decides to change treatment of ORIGINALLY issued share options, too.

No EToys under the Christmas tree in 2000 or any other year, for that matter.

Sure, the amount is right, says Jonathan Cunningham, head of convertible securities at Jeffries Co., but EToys "probably wouldn't have done a transaction like this if there were any alternatives."[8] Thus ends the hazy, lazy crazy financing days of netPhase I, when almost any Dot-Com with a pulse left the IPO party with bags of cash.

NetPhase I is over. In the aftermath, only those companies projected as "number one in their space" (description by Promethean's James O'Brien) can expect to be first in line to receive post-Spring Break 2000 funds.

Implications for Dot-Com Valuations

"Across the board there has been a substantial revaluation in the private sector paralleling what's happened in the public sector over the past six weeks."

Doug Smith is head of H&Q Chase's Internet investment team. He concedes that the type of revaluation implicit in Promethean-EToys deal is already being reflected in B2B and even e-infrastructure sectors. Tough terms for today's favored sectors, not just for beleaguered B2C.[9]

DOT-COM IPOs, REDONE

> *It's as if a screen has been placed over the IPO window, and it allows only the fittest companies—or those in hot new sectors—like optical networking and wireless communications equipment—to pass through.*
>
> Jonathan Rabinovitz and Mark Mowrey,
> *The Industry Standard*[10]

Yes Virginia, there will be a return of the general Dot-Com IPO marketplace. But nothing like 1996–1999.

Friday, April 14, 2000, was not a happy day in Manhattan. The Nasdaq Composite index slumped another 4.2% and once again closed well below support levels at 3,500. Over the weekend, announcements of Dot-Com initial public offerings cancelled, scaled down, or deferred dominated the evening TV business news. Boo.com, the London-based global-scale clothing e-tailer, collapsed and went into receivership.

But there was at least *one* silver lining: the New Focus IPO. The Santa Clara manufacturer of fiber-optic parts ended its first day as a public company at more than double its offering price of $20. In percentage terms, that's nothing compared to the routine tripling or quadrupling of launch-day share prices during netPhase I's heydays. But the buzz was that the old days of IPO excess had returned, stronger than ever.

Not a chance. As the closest thing to a hot sector in the first half of 2000, optical networking received special attention. But that elite group represents the exception. Practically speaking, IPOs remained improbable to impossible for all other Net startups.

Different, Not Dead

But this drastic narrowing of the IPO field doesn't mean that there will be no more new Internet IPOs.

People didn't stop using electricity just because a high percentage of the early competitors were blown away. And when we last looked, there are still a lot of cars around, even though the first twenty years of the 20th century saw the collapse of hundreds of automakers.

Predictions of the untimely death of Internet IPOs are similarly exaggerated. Even though venture capitalists have relinquished their control of the Nasdaq Tower and retreated back toward a more traditional financing role, vencap will continue to exert tremendous influence when it comes to the Net.

You don't expect VC celebrities such as Tim Duncan to be fazed by something as minor as a 70% collapse in market values, do you? Entrepreneurs and their handlers eat market optimism for breakfast. Even if the failure rate was a disastrous 99%, we suspect that the first thought is that *they* are in that one percent. *Gee, I wonder how all those other guys are going to cope?*

The dream of launching another Yahoo! remains vivid until and unless the companies that inspire such dreams also disappear. Post-Spring Break headlines may not ooze about Infobank's expansion into the US or Commerce One's new opportunities in

---

valueOUTPERFORMER
www.vbmresources.com

May 28, 2000

TELL THE FRIDGE TO STOP TALKING TO ME

As spring 2000 staggers toward summer after the first bloody leg of the Internet re-valuation, there's a fresh message for all those Gen-XYZs devising billion dollar online databases for birdwatchers and vertical industry catalogues for sand manufacturers.

That message: future financing will be limited to only the most important new Dot-Com company developments, those that can quickly become dominant in high profit, major segments of the Net's next phase. No more "free" services that have never figured out how to survive and won't. No more backing the seventeenth search engine, the twelfth auction site, the tenth vertical industrial community site based on nothing better than "there's enough room for everyone" failing logic. In fact no more Losers.com at all. So what—if anything—attracts the newly smart Dot-Com money?

Why, the Net-enabled home of the future, of course. Broadband that hooks my garbage bin up to the grocery store via high speed link and orders whatever I'm throwing away. Refrigerators that examine the contents on my shelves and use cellular Internet link to consult with a variety of recipe sites and then prepare a written exotic-'n-fast recipe for me in printout form, with a verbal reminder every ten minutes or so. WHAT ARE YOU DOING, DAVE?

Never mind, HAL. And then there's my washing machine that examines every stain on my clothes and consults with the right home cleanliness site online to automatically apply the right stain remover. How did I ever live without these essentials of life itself! For sure, this is the high value path of the Net future! Ah, but then it all went terribly, terribly wrong. The washing machine shredded my precious bleeding madras patch preppy slacks. I thought I turned the "taste" instruction OFF. And the neigborhood problem kid threw something into my garbage can outside and something has been automatically ordered online and the police want me to stop over "just for a little talk." Then, my refrigerator's modem blew up trying to find recipes for Guinness Stout plus chocolate ice cream. And the darn thing won't stop talking to me. THIS IS HIGHLY IRREGULAR, DAVE.

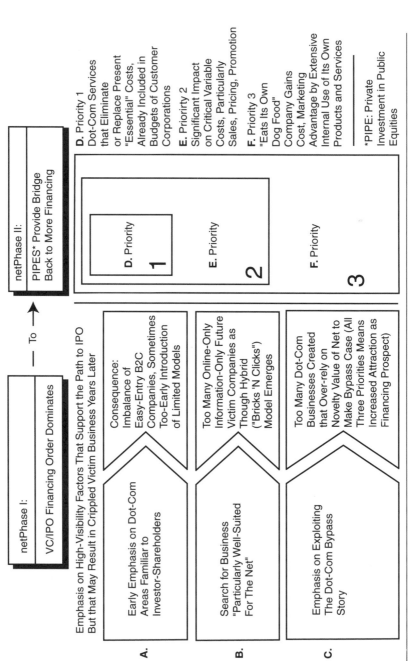

FIGURE 6.5. "E-Camelot" fluke financing causes marketplace distortions.

China. But such growth continues to inspire new Dot-Com company formation by sustaining the dream of IPO riches.

The netPhase I IPO Is Dead, Long Live the netPhase II IPO

The hot, hot Dot-Com darling category of the time will always be able to get IPOs placed. Next in line are companies that are high-priority targets of Net consolidators.

Chasing the Next Dot-Com Darling Sector

E-infrastructure has been proclaimed as the next great sector. Reality is that only one small sub-part of that sector is hot: optical networking. In similar manner, look for high-growth subsets of B2B to emerge as pacesetters, not the whole sector.

Business-to-government (B2G) emerges as an underexploited sector to date, and it is possible that an abbreviated version of the second half 1999 B2B surge could recur. While some B2Bs will argue that they also possess special expertise for this emerging market as well, deep understanding of government RFP procedures is critical. The most successful new IPO candidates will be those Dot-Com companies designed expressly for the B2G marketplace.

Attractive Targets

Aging communications infrastructure equipment manufacturers will seek out niche companies that help increase speed and capacity, buying time for their internal development effort. To the extent that B2B vertical industry marketplace leaders act to exploit their marketing strengths (see Chapter 7), next generation sales presentation tools and automatic reorder software loom as targets of opportunity.

Small to medium business B2B sites—designated by size of cutomers' enterprises—also emerge as targets for e-procurement stand-alone companies.

"Sponsored IPOs"

The tracking share offering for AT&T Wireless was not technically an IPO, but it was *perceived* by many as such, which is all that matters.

The draw of the AT&T name was unmistakable. No more anonymous companies with zany cyber names. This was a household name, marking the entrance of Dot-Coms into mainstream US business.

Assume that existing sectors are rationalized into smaller groups in terms of total competitors worldwide, not market potential: net II groups paced by one or possibly two clear leaders. The stage is then set for these emergent champion companies to become prime spin-off sources of future IPOs, as they continually expand and refine their business portfolios.

Such "sponsored IPOs" come to market with the Dot-Com legacy plus developed profitable companies in the past.

PATH TO PROFIT (P2P)

> *"When you strip away the sexy dot-com aspect and the technology out of it, these are still businesses that need the fundamentals— budgeting, planning and execution."*
>
> Jim Rose, chief executive of QXL.com,
> European online auctioneer.[11]

P2P? Oh no, not another Netstylish combination: B2C, B2B, B2G.

No, not at all. Path to Profit (P2P) is an altogether *different* catch-phrase, designed for a completely different purpose.

The CEO of the post-IPO Dot-Com now nursing his final three months of cash for as long as possible cites "P2P" as part of the campaign to try to convince the private money sources that *his* Dot-Com will thrive. That his e-Bankruptcy2001.com is nothing at all like those other companies you see crashing every day.

The Dot-Com leader who missed the April 2000 netPhase I final window for IPOs shouts "P2P" even louder. In just ten short weeks, the phrase "burn rate" was transformed from a cheeky boast of Net success to an expression of unconscionable waste.

But this time around, there is no slick sound byte that can save the Dot-Com company encountering difficulties. In February 1999, almost all the e-Bankruptcy2001.com's CEO had to do was to make sure he cited at least three of the top five Netenomics (Chapter 4) buzz-phrases. *Make that one First Mover Advantage, one Scaleabilities, and a Metcalfe's Law for measure.*

Such snappy patter used to impress Bubba GreaterFool. But Bubba is long gone. And glib phrases such as P2P may even exert the exact opposite of the intended effect on no-nonsense private financing syndicates that expect a far better return than they settled for in 1999 IPOs.

---

valueOUTPERFORMER
www.vbmresources.com

June 9, 2000

LATE-TO-THE-PARTY ECUBATORS' DILEMMA

The sea change in Dot-Com financing structure causes the odd-man-out dilemma for small- and medium-sized Internet incubators, or 'ecubators.' Many late entrant ecubators (formed after mid-98) now find their portfolios packed with a high percentage of non-investment-quality dross (ask them to prove otherwise). These are the "living dead" (*Red Herring's* term) Dot-Coms poised to make those 70-plus percent failure rates appear plausible, maybe even conservative. But those failures in the portfolio are not declared quite yet. The independent mid- to small-sized ecubators are effectively financial intermediaries, companies highly dependent on periodic infusions of capital lifeblood from larger ecubators and traditional sources. The dilemma, especially for the late and the small: choosing which of their living dead will be propped up for a couple more months to prevent a damaging hit to that investor's portfolio statistics. This is a losing game as the "70-percenter" Dot-Coms will never be viable. Those companies might have lingered a while under loose Phase I conditions, but only grown-up businesses thrive in netPhase II. Some of the late 'n small ecubators with the time and the spin doctors to repackage their facade proclaim a new specialty concentration. Endgame: the big ecubators and more mainstream financing sources are now looking instead to the champion Dot-Coms themselves as their venture conduit. Because when a Dot-Com leader is the venture partner, a revenue stream often comes with the deal.

Mouthing the Mantra of the New Profit Religion

Old practices die hard, and there's always the suspicion that Dot-Com executives who have converted to managing for profit will say anything, just to buy another six months. But they lack profit experience and sometimes, good intent.

To be fair, *everyone* lacks in-depth experience at achieving profitability in fast-changing markets that morph every three months. The Dot-Com in the dynamic sector faces the practical reality of re-calibrating share, liquidity, and target profitability dates every 90 days or so, or risk having its share price shrink to that of a worthless piece of paper.

Dot-Com managers and their financiers need forecasts built the way a workout specialist constructs them, not the unachievable numbers of the optimistic futurist. They need cash projects built upwards from solid commitments from existing identifiable sources, not guesses based on ol' Rings O' Saturn Research's trillion dollar-plus projections.

And then there's the matter of intent. Given a choice, there's no doubt that netPhase I Dot-Com management would prefer to board a time capsule and go back to those idyllic days of too-easy Dot-Com IPO money.

Can "Net-Lite"—the Internet business developed during hazy, crazy netPhase I—suddenly grow up and act like a netPhase II commercial warrior, complete with fully credible cash flow forecasts, a business plan built from facts, not hopes or hype, and a clear strategy for becoming a leader of that segment? The response is always "yes." Reality is something else again.

Asked to describe what is different in the post-Spring Break financing environment, E-steel's Michael Levin suggested that the markets are no longer tolerant of B2Bs "with no revenues." [12]

Slip of the tongue? Maybe, but even the most ephemeral of Net business models generates *some* revenue—heck, until the mispractice gained wide attention from the SEC, merely swapping advertising credits between sites might generate some illusory sales, out of thin air.

The critical principle is of course *profits*, rather than revenues, which might have been Levin's intended word. But maybe Levin's choice of words was correct, after all. In some B2C and B2B sectors, the famous steep demand curves into the trillions from "Rings O' Saturn" and other such respected research groups appear to be flattening. Triple digit growth rates in Net portal services slow to double digits or less. A post-Spring Break fluke soon to be reversed. Only time will tell.

Earlier Profitability Announcements

If P2P is today's trendy post-Spring Break 2000 buzz-term, then the announcement of earlier profits than expected is the implementing device.

The logic is straightforward. If analysts are now bombing the company's market value because of liquidity concerns, then it

---

valueOUTPERFORMER
www.vbmresources.com

June 5, 2000

LSMFT.COM LOOKS FOR EARLIER MOVE INTO THE BLACK

Just coincidentally after its investment bankers used the words "pigs" and "fly," in assessing post-IPO financing prospects, astonishing portal-auction-biznews-shopbot sliver leader LSMFT.com announced that it was anticipating an earlier than expected move to profitability. Savings include compensation for the Dot-Com's "name" CFO as well as salaries for several other senior officers, all of whom left when their options plunged underwater. And, after CEO Dude Spinwell pondered aloud about whether future salary payments might be made in the form of credits towards time on the company's premium access content areas.

Advertising is being dramatically slashed, and yet there are no planned reductions in projected revenues. Asked to explain the basis for this revised projection, EVP of Marketing Dude Spinwell responded, "Sure, like someone is going to try to check THIS data. . . ." In a separate announcement, VP of Customer Support Service Dude Spinwell announced that the company's help desk was being temporarily discontinued. The company's auditors have scheduled a press conference for tomorrow.

takes direct actions to counteract those concerns. *We've just amassed a huge pile of back-up cash—see how big it is?*

They continue: *We know we said before that we wouldn't be profitable until the last quarter of 2002. Now we are proud to say that profitability will be reached on exactly December 8, 2001.*

Truth is, investors facing boasts about cash levels are likely to view such proclamations as those of desperation. Up to six weeks before, management was insisting that any retreat from its plans to burn five million dollars a month (in operating costs and ads) would fatally injure the company. Today, management is agreeable to a lower burn rate of four million. Three if you insist.

Does that now mean that management is willing to risk creating a lifeless Dot-Com shell in exchange for more financing? Maybe. The seasoned Dot-Com manager is already a master at brinkmanship, and he'll worry about what has to be said to obtain the next injection of funds when that time rolls around 18 months from now. But there's evidence of a clear path to future dominance in a profitable sector despite reduced financing, then any extra financing is just wasted.

The first thought when e-Bankruptcy2001.com's management is so agreeable to a cut in the burn rate is that the original budget was padded. Second thought is that it is concealing key data. But it is the third thought that is truly jarring: that management never has had sufficient understanding control of its budget in the first place.

Budgets? They're so twentieth century.

"THERE ARE A COUPLE OF PROBLEMS WITH THE NUMBERS"

During netPhase I, Dot-Com revenue and other forecast numbers were viewed as important only as a potential obstacle toward IPO. No credible numbers at all? No problem, just make 'em up. This is the Internet after all, where the rate of demand growth is limited only by your dreams. Disneyesque research bureau guesses will support almost any rate of growth you wish to show.

That is not to suggest that all of the outlandish numbers are intended to deceive. Sometimes, overly-optimistic numbers are just reflections of justifiable confidence in the business, as when Juniper Networks' chief executive Scott Kriens suggested that formal estimates that Net backbone browser use would increase to two billion people were far too conservative. But ten billion? The world's total population is only around six billion.[13]

But in netPhase II, "the numbers" are no longer just prospectus guesswork, but indications of Dot-Com management's competence and credibility. Companies lacking bottom-up achievable numbers based on solid projections—actual accounts and achievable demand—find their financing spigot shut off.

Ring O' Saturn Research
Forecasts a Ten Trillion Dollar Market for B2B by 2005

It's the late 1990s. Do you know where your Net forecast data is?

Certainly not here. There are NO reliable forecast numbers to help anchor the business cases of the hundreds of Dot-Com gold diggers all trying to take advantage of the once per generation financing fluke before it disappears. Massive financing is available, regardless of whether the company is a survivor or not.

Following is never outwardly said, yet it is clearly communicated: *Just develop a story line that touts the promise of the Net, dig up some numbers from somewhere, and ensure that there are dire warnings throughout all the formal registration documents. As long as the Dot-Com doesn't collapse six months after the IPO, we can get away with shoveling pre-bankruptcies to the public.*

No top-down numbers at all for developing even rough future estimates? Don't worry—our friends at one of the now numerous New Economy research organizations will churn out a plausible surrogate for systematic research. Who cares if their ten trillion dollar number could just as easily have been eight, or twelve? No one can even *imagine* a trillion, much less debate it.

Next step is to apply a small, small percentage penetration assumption factor to Rings O' Saturn Research's finger-in-the-air forecast.

The smaller that percentage the better (looks more conservative). Multiply the two "bad" numbers together, and what do you have. Right: a third bad number.

But you may also have a number that might masquerade as "data" long enough to get the IPO planned and completed.

Remember, just like the five-minute elevator pitch for the Dot-Com itself, the objective is *not* necessarily to develop something that is thorough and correct. In order to get the IPO done, just make sure that neither the facade story nor the projection number is so fanciful as to delay the financing.

The Allocators

Today, the contest for funding is between scores of post-IPO Dot-Coms, all of which will run out of funds in the coming quarters. The financing community's arduous task is to somehow extract the few winners from all the rest. To allocate scarce capital to some companies and not others.

This also means picking losers. Letting some non-investment quality (NIQ) companies starve for lack of cash. After all, these are firms that should never have come public in the first place.

It means making some necessary judgment calls about which Dot-Coms will be cut from further funding, as they will merely tread water for a couple of years before disappearing. Only the clear market leaders are likely to enjoy the premier valuations in the future (Chapter 8).

Accessible Market Penetration, Not Available Market Penetration

Forecasts based on the *available* market assumptions can look as shaky as Ring O' Saturn's hallucinatory trillion dollar macro forecasts.

During the IPO talk-up stage, the objective was to make it appear as if the company's revenues were based on the largest demand possible. The online toy business claims that its potential available market is based on demand for *all* toys, regardless of channel.

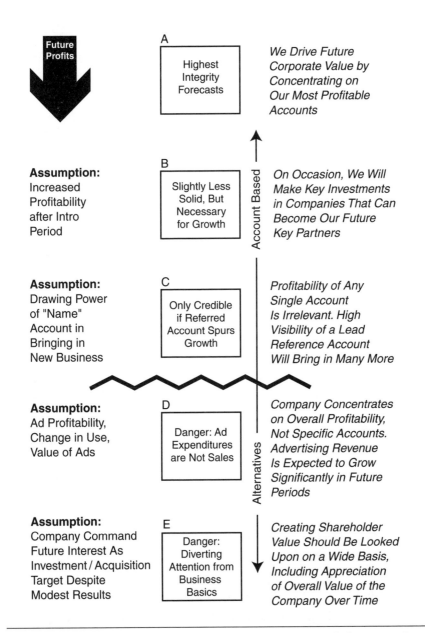

FIGURE 6.6. Back to Dot-Com basics: Survivors challenge their assumptions about future profit sources.

But some analysts point out that such an online company demand forecast is wrong. Only a small percentage of toy sales will ever be made online. *Accessible market* shrinks still further depending upon two factors. First, the scope of product range and distribution, second, numbers and range of competitors.

We are continually amazed when online industries experience significant additions to the number of competitors and yet individual company financial forecasts remain unchanged. For analysis purposes, the market is zero sum in nature, at least over the intermediate term. There's only so much demand to go around, and only one or two Dot-Com rivals secure enough to survive.

One Account at a Time

But there's far more to forecast integrity than just cutting some of the obvious fluff out of the top-down projections. The new financing order of netPhase II means a departure from unreliable trickle-down analyses altogether.

Only solid sales at full margin cover the company's costs and repay financing. The result is intensified scrutiny of customer data, not just incidental data tangential to profit-creation: Web site hit rates and costs of new account acquisition and old account retention.

Figure 6.6 illuminates the issue of the consistency and reliability of that customer sales data.

Low-quality revenues can be developed easily for a while; some Dot-Coms even tried to manufacture various top-line numbers by swapping ad credits with other online companies.

That bottom-quality revenue contrasts starkly with highest-quality revenue from sales at full margin.

But few companies conduct the kind of split analysis shown in the figure. Why? In some instances because the financier is still fooled by the Dot-Com label and doesn't insist on exacting analysis to separate enduring sources of value from those that can easily be blown away by the competition.

SECTOR LEMMINGS

When the stocks of online retailers crumbled, business-to-business became the rage. B2B, they said, has a "better, more substantial and sustainable" business model. When the B2B stocks crashed, "infrastructure" was the place to be. . . . Now infrastructure stocks have tanked. What to do?

David Simons,
Managing Director of institutional research firm
Digital Video Investments, commenting in *Forbes* [14]

The world shook on April 10, 2000 when Pennsylvania-based ecubator Safeguard Scientifics made an announcement widely interpreted as indicating that the institutional investor was abandoning B2B and jumping with both feet into the latest Can't Miss Net sector, e-infrastructure.

In an interview conducted by *The Wall Street Journal's* reporter William M. Bulkeley, Safeguard's president Henry Wallaesa plumped Internet infrastructure as "the next big thing, with market promise far greater than B2B." [15]

As if a switch had been turned on, a dozen business publications suddenly proclaimed "Here's What's Terribly, Terribly Wrong With B2B." Even though most of those same publications led the way in the B2Bs-as-juggernaut hype just a few months earlier.

The Game Changes in netPhase II

"Pick the Winning Sector" was the name of the game during the Commercial Internet's wild initial period. But that game is over in netPhase II, when the Dot-Coms have to grow up.

No more Dot-Com darlings touted as Buys based not on business fundamentals, but rather on whether Happybang.com is in today's "right" Net category. No more sector lemmings at all.

The sector lemming approach includes the preposterous notion that someone can choose a select category of companies and then get rich by buying almost anything in that group. This might almost sound reasonable during runaway momentum markets or with daytraders hypnotized by prize action alone. But for the real world, it is the differences between competing companies within the group that make all the difference between accumulating a position in that company's shares versus dumping the turk-e, pronto.

The problem isn't just that one fad sector gives way to another. It is also that the sector lemmings who jump to the newly crowned "hot" sector quickly discover to their dismay that they have no reliable means for separating the wheat from the chaff within that e-category.

When B2C was hot, hot, sector lemmings didn't want to know about the critical differences between, say, an amazon.com with a viable business purpose and approach, versus pre-bankrupt terrestrial consumer business merely slapped online. When sector lemming thinking prevails, weak Me-Too copies of the real thing are often mistaken for viable competitors. The netPhase I spin goes something like this: *this is a massive Net segment with opportunities and profits for many in the future.*

The Lemming Mindset Unwinds

OK, perhaps several leaders *might* survive and even thrive in a particularly strong sector, but *all*? Combine sector lemming mindset with too-easy entry, and the result is a debacle such as occurred in B2C in early to mid-1999.

With everyone and their cousin seemingly launching a retail Internet business whose success would depend on Christmas 1999, advertising was so excessive that almost no one's message penetrated that fog.

Even if some of the Dot-Com advertising mega-modelz described in Chapter 4 *might have* worked, overcrowding made sure they *couldn't* succeed.

The poison combination of lemming mentality plus excessive entry of too many competitors alters basic sector economics. Forget the Rings O' Saturn's study stating that B2C represents an explosive category with massive future profit potential. Even if those top-level revenue and profitability guesses for 2005 *are* credible, so many rivals compete for a piece of the action that almost no one survives. Conditions are rife for a shakeout, if only for the reason that without the elimination of weak players, the otherwise strong sector is pummeled to the status of a profitless Dark Model, as described in Chapter 4.

The sector lemmings have a real problem with groups that fall out of favor on one date only to fall back *in*, at some future date, at least in part. B2B's star began to fade in early 2000, as pundits proclaimed the era of end-user customers establishing their *own* online buyer cartels, bypassing the independents.

But now, as it becomes apparent that the Do-It-Yourselfers face tougher operations, technical, and even regulatory challenges than first thought, the sector lemming's nightmare becomes true: the out-of-favor group begins to rebound.

---

valueOUTPERFORMER
www.vbmresources.com

June 12, 2000

"I'VE BEEN MARKED DOWN!!"

Bette Midler's anguished wail in *Ruthless People* occurred when she discovered that her ransom price was plunging, fast. Markdown now takes on new meaning, as imploding online-only (O2) e-tailers discover that they sometimes aren't even merger targets, as there's almost nothing to salvage. A key part of the appeal of B2C "e-tailers" in the emotion-over-analysis years of 1997-98 was that these companies could operate "virtually"—with almost no standing inventory or ugly downtown building. The flip side is that when the collapse occurs, there's nothing but air and unpaid bills. Inventory? Back with the manufacturer. Logistics system and software? Property of the developers—all the O2 possesses is a license. Logo and "Web presence" (today's ten-dollar phrase for passable interactive Web site)? Pennies. After all, in high style fashion circles, front-running is mandatory. No wants to remember the oh-so-chic format of Loser.com. After going through more than $120 million in investors' funds, fashion leader Boo.com turns out to be effectively ineligible as a merger target and worth less than $400,000 on a salvage basis.

Focus Shifts to Individual Companies, Away from Categories

Even languishing B2C faces a partial rebound in the quarters after the severe Spring Break 2000. But only after elimination of most of the seventy percenters. These are the companies that make predictions that 70-plus percent of netPhase I start-ups will fail seem believable, even conservative.

The importance of individual company analysis emerges for other reasons, as well. Examine the in-favor fad sector closely, and what you actually find is that there are one or two key seventy percenters driving the future. And only one or two prime mover companies within that subset.

Optical networking breaks away from e-infrastructure. Is that an all-new fad sector, or subgroup of an existing hot sector? Doesn't matter—only specific companies make a value difference. The sector lemming mindset was dead on arrival. The true challenges in netPhase II: first, discover the champion companies; then, accelerate their growth.

NEEDS VERSUS WANTS

Transition away from emotion-driven netPhase I and toward analysis-guided netPhase II means dealing with the problem of distinguishing essential Dot-Com customer needs from deferrable wants.

Search for an e-Business Sorting Mechanism: Learning by Doing As Default Option

In most markets, at most times, at least a few guidelines exist to help separate probable successful future businesses from the others. To help ensure that a respectable percentage of companies that advance to public ownership actually can survive for a couple years after the IPO. To direct scarce capital to those Dot-Coms with the best chances for future success.

Occasionally, a major paradigm market emerges, such as the US automotive industry at the turn of the last century. Then, there was NO reliable forecast data to point to future success. Any information could easily be blasted by the entrenched incumbents as irrelevant, possibly misleading.

Dual issues are *how much* the new paradigm market must rely only on learning by market trial and error, and for *how long*. In the first quarter of the last century, more than 3,000 separate automobile companies were started by pioneers. The companies with at least a fighting chance of surviving long enough to become part of the permanent industry structure learned early that most of the weak competitors were doomed to disappear.[16]

Gradually, that general sense of what separated winners from losers became codified and — far more importantly — adopted by financiers to the fledgling industry. No marginal start-up could receive the financing necessary to survive.

But such learning is incredibly inefficient, and during netPhase I, it meant that many companies without any credible chance of survival were brought public anyway. Not because they were outstanding businesses with tremendous prospects and high probability for future success, but merely because there was unbelievable demand for such stocks. Little advance data suggested that the underlying companies might fail.

"Invest in What You Know"

Some of the early netPhase I deal packagers emphasized easily understandable B2C online businesses. The first reason was that an online version of an existing retail business is a lot easier for Bubba GreaterFool to understand. *This* paradigm market would be marked by an unusual role of Bubba leading the netPhase I Dot-Com buying frenzy. It is always difficult to generate a great deal of grass roots enthusiasm for obtuse technologies such as bubble memories and optical networking. A simple merchandising concept such as flowers or books or electronic gear sold online plays a lot better on Main Street.

Reason two was that the familiar B2C business fits well with the tonier individual investors who hear something akin to "invest in something that you know" and think that advice is terrific.

Invest in What You Know started to crash around everyone's ears as early as mid-1999. Too many lightweight concept B2Cs emerged in every retail category imaginable, thus canceling the ad effect and market shares of each participant.

From demand-push marketing to online banking, incomplete B2C packages rushed to market before their time sometimes had the opposite of the intended impact. Receptive customers were forced to endure a hurry-up Web site that failed to live up to even a fraction of the hype that preceded the launch. When that initial online experience ended in disappointment, some prime customer targets were lost for years.[17]

"Businesses Particularly Well Suited to the Internet"

Say hello to scores of site-bite Net pundit columnists in sports, business, and investing—with one caveat: they must make their point in seven words because that's the maximum attention span of the cyber-customer.

Application of the "well suited" bromide led to disastrous experimentation with online only approaches to Net merchandising, even though hybrid alternatives quickly proved more effective in fields from toys to wine, pet goods to drug store over-the-counter merchandise.

Exploiting the Dot-Com Bypass Story

"Getting rid of the middleman" is a simple message. Literally hundreds of Dot-Com businesses have been started and financed based on the disintermediation imperative.

But is that message always true? One of the tough points landed by CNBC's Kate Bulkley, when talking to management of online travel and reservations business Lastminute.com in March 2000, was that they were essentially middlemen operating on the

Net. The comment wasn't directly denied—the spin response made reference to the term "aggregator."

That reporter's point applies equally well to a variety of other online service businesses, where developers seem to take advantage of the fact that observers sometimes presume, automatically, that they are cutting out the middleman by going online. In some instances, all they are doing is replacing the terrestrial middleman with his online counterpart.

Value-Based Net Shakeouts:
Or, Is This Online Product/ Service Really Needed?

The Dot-Com value shakeouts started even before Spring Break 2000 was over, if Safeguard Scientifics' change in investment emphasis is any indication.

Every value shakeout period in every field means that some visionary but unproven (and largely unwanted) products and services are jettisoned. During easier times, when cash was flush and novelty rewarded, devices such as home online garbage cans that communicate back to stores or exotic new methods for organizing bookmark data when the existing answers are totally satisfactory are nonetheless hyped as the next Can't Miss online sure things.

The hard sell was there for a reason. Without such artificial momentum, it is questionable whether the future "wired household" or navigational tools have much built-in demand at all. Do you *really* want your fridge to talk to you in a voice like that of HAL from *2001: A Space Odyssey*.

Eager marketeers in the Dot-Com firms argue that continual promotion and reinforcement were necessary to "educate" buyers. To tell customers what they *should* desire, whether they do or not. This is a self-correcting situation. In tougher financial times — such as today's interim period between initial boom period netPhase I and maturing sector period netPhase II — dollars for hype promotions and the extra marketeers that push them are both eliminated.

Dot-Coms try to strengthen their case for additional financing by cutting back on expenses so they can announce that they will achieve profitability one or two quarters sooner than expected.

Outlays for marginal projects are embarrassing reminders of the "profits don't matter" period of netPhase I, an embarrassment ever since the fall of e-Camelot

Then there's the good sector/bad company situation. This refers to the marginal Dot-Com firm in a hot Net sector. When funding decisions are made on the basis of sector rather than company (see "Sector Lemmings" earlier on in this chapter), some firms with little real chance of survival nonetheless slip through. Such as the lightweight B2B marketplace "community" comprised of little more than some trade news and some generic procurement software, but nothing to draw key accounts away from the existing market leaders.

This type of company faces an end to the financing as soon as financiers realize that this "Not-Com" is already dead. Too many other Internet companies offer the prospect of solid industry leadership, and that's where the funding goes.

While a "new-new" label on a Dot-Com concept likely suggested dynamism and originality in 1997 and 1998, the same description in 2000 causes the prospective financiers to roll their

---

valueOUTPERFORMER
www.vbmresources.com

MERGERS OF THE DOT-COM LIVING DEAD

June 5, 2000

The post-netPhase I clean-out accelerates as burn rate victims announce mergers of necessity in droves. CDNow was one of the first companies in Jack Willoughby's Mar. 20 trigger article ("Burning Up!," *Barron's*, Mar. 20, 2000) to announce difficulties. On June 2, management indicate that they will announce a merger partner by the end of the month. Share prices soar from a bottom-trawling 2 9/16ths to 4 7/8ths, for a 111% increase rise. But such massive percentage jumps should be viewed for what they are: bounces of the Dot-Com living dead (acknowledgments to *Red Herring*). Temporary merger blips are never to be confused with underlying value creation.

eyes back into their heads. Unproven suggests losses, at a time when portfolio strategy calls for the opposite emphasis.

Excessive Entry:
When Participation Becomes
Detached from Base Demand

> *Just like the 1849 Gold Rush, there was a mentality that anyone could participate. . . . A lot of bad ideas were funded.*
>
> John Backus,
> affiliated with Tim Draper's venture capital firm
> Draper Fisher Jurvetson,
> May 26, 2000[18]

Another characteristic of the early part of the Net Boom was the illusion that mere participation is enough to ensure Dot-Com riches.

The unspoken message was that the Net is growing so fast in so many areas that even a moderately plausible business plan can work. Thus a thousand e-business concepts bloom, regardless of the fact that only three out of ten would survive a couple of years. Just as in the California Gold Rush 150 years earlier, one spectacular success prompted thousands of failures.

The quote by John Backus, above, hits the nail on the head. Dot-Com egalitarianism bubbled up, playing into the Horatio Alger mystique that lies just below the surface of the American psyche. Dangle the imagery of an open marketplace, where speed and guts are the most important requirements for success, and the door is broken down.

Problem is, the resulting excess entry threatens to strangle all businesses in the segment, sweeping out the good and the great along with mere temporary market participants. The essential difference? Proprietary demand, expressed from customers *on an unsolicited basis*.

Any fly-by-night Dot-Com, B2C, or B2B, can sustain a temporary illusion of business need by generating some near-term activity. The business is only sustained by the *unsolicited* responses— the customer revenue that comes without excessive, expensive ads and promotions.

Some netPhase I financiers fell on their face when it came to this aspect of online advertising. At best, high impact fluff ads create awareness, they don't build the brand," as the self-interested Dot-Com manager insists. When the ad budget was first dialed back 2% and demand plunged 20%, the indications were clear for that specific business: it is a fad, sustained only by continuous, unaffordable advertising hype, a Black Hole business that will never make money.

Even after Spring Break, a couple of dozen me-too secondary "specialist" search engines still endure, even though most demand is directed toward those few engines affixed to the major portals, particularly Yahoo! Eight to ten B2B "communities" persist in some commodities and industry fields, even though customers say they would be well-served by half that number.

Excess choice—alternatives far beyond those indicated by customers themselves—persists in fields as diverse as financial market information and commentary, online brokerage, insurance selling sites, and consumer electronics buying sites. Excess choice absorbed funds during netPhase I that could have been directed to segment champions.

THE DOT-COM CONSOLIDATION IMPERATIVE

Dot-Com pundits are in almost universal agreement about one thing: that the post-Spring Break 2000 period would be followed by months of frenetic Net-to-Net consolidation, in almost every Dot-Com segment and category.

After VC-IPO Financing Structure Winds Down

A key factor was the unwinding of the original VC-IPO financing structure, as depicted in Figure 6.1. That structure was primarily designed to get prospects to IPO early while permitting some of the earliest investors to cash out. There is little if any attention to the issue of ongoing financing after the initial public money is all used up.

But if the IPO doesn't plan beyond six months after the launch and if management of the typical profitless Dot-Com says that its firm will still be cash negative for a couple of years, how is that firm to survive?

The question that few investors asked (and that even fewer Dot-Com executives and handlers answered) was what the company would do for cash during this interim. When a response was offered, it was typically the sort of Netspin that today makes even the most bombastic Net zealot wince:

The IPO funds were intended to help the company implement its business plan and develop its Net brand and market presence. As more and more people come to understand the great advantages that we offer, we expect a corresponding increase in customers and revenues.

Or, in other words, we don't have the faintest idea what we are going to do after the minimal cash we received from the IPO is exhausted. We hope that a secondary market emerges that is as easily "guided" as the primary markets. But there's nothing to indicate that our Happybang.com will qualify, even if such a financing structure arises.

Endgame. It's one thing for exchanges to turn a blind eye to NIQ Dot-Com investments by settling for full disclosure (prospectuses that are three-quarters filled with warnings), instead of limiting exchange entry based on a minimum quality of the companies entrusted to the public market. But it is something else again to extend the same laissez-faire softness to secondary offerings on grown-up, first-tier exchanges.

Besides, the structural constraints against such mischief are solidly entrenched. An ecubator with little more than cash plus some spin sometimes sneaks into one of the new variety of junior league tech markets. But there's no Big Board secondary offering for Happybang.com.

Big Is Beautiful. Also, Financeable

Enter the BBS (Big Bag of . . . . . er, Stuff) theory of Dot-Com value disaster control, as literally hundreds of seventy percenters fulfill their destinies and collapse.

Groups far and wide with a strong interest in preventing an overall Dot-Com market rout sit up and take notice. *Can't have that: There's no way that the Nasdaq can rally with business news presenters proclaiming failue every day.* Today, the auditors of yet three more struggling Dot-Coms announced that the firms they examined may no longer be "going concerns, in their opinions. . . . "

Maybe, just maybe, the various piece parts can be combined to fill management, technical, and customer acquisition gaps. Of course, such megadeals will always be described as "marriages made in heaven" by participants and pliable members of the business press. In M&A parlance, that phrase means a transaction that we're pretty sure won't blow up in our faces over two years.

The other interesting notion about BBS is the notion that if we somehow make the asset pool big enough, we might even be able to attract some private funding from old-line capital sources easily impressed by a bloated balance sheet. Such early "fooled-em" financing could set up other commercial bank lending or convertible debentures in the future.

You see, to some lenders, *assets* still connotes downtown property grossly undervalued on the company's balance sheets or locomotives that can be sold in excess of book value. Back-up protection just in case they happen to grossly misjudge the transaction.

For BBS.com, one challenge is to redirect the spinners' lenders/private investors. The compelling message: the Dot-Com may possess few physical assets in the conventional sense, but many command massive intellectual property rights. Which are even better because such "rights" act as a continuous font of future profits.

Just don't tell those financiers the three truths about those intellectual property rights. First, that many of those 'assets' have worth only in the sugarplum dreams of their developers and of those consultants who pushed their clients into undertaking seven-figure intellectual asset development consulting projects in the first place. Everyone in Dot-Comland thinks they have their own amazon.com One Click™, but only amazon.com actually does. The patent filing was merely free advertising to underscore that point.

Second, that those assets tend to be readily imitated if not duplicated by competitors. Any differences are often irrelevant to customers. Third, that the resource may be controlled and sometimes owned by another, unrelated firm. All that the Dot-Com actually has is a licensing arrangement and a bill for payment.

Boo.com, notorious for high burn-rate arrogance, added another surprise for receivers trying to salvage anything in spring 2000. The company's international order and logistics system was much admired, quite the opposite of opinions about that Dot-Com's curious notions of selling clothing online at even higher prices than retail stores. But when receivers KPMG found out who actually owned the software and systems, they discovered that the logistics outsourcers were the owners. And that they were creditors of the collapsed Dot-Com. Boo.

Ensuring the Acquisition Currency

Key to being the acquirer rather than lunch (the target)—in the post-Spring Break consolidation contest—is a price-to-revenue (PTR) nosebleed multiple and the cheap (Net2Net) acquisition currency that results.

Of course, we would never, ever imply that numerous bankers are now directing private capital first and foremost to those post-IPO netPhase I survivors that still—for now—have nosebleed faux-valuations in order to make those firms into acquisition magnets, regardless of the basic viability of the firms.

But just suppose that some renegade bankers are using some post-IPO e-Bankruptcy2001.com as their BBS magnet to clean up the books while others become netPhase II champions.

Just as an illustration, if, say, B2B e-procurement is threatened by Do-It-Yourself customers, then consolidation could help redress the situation. If the top five independent third-party firms just happen to someday become two, then the competitive landscape changes, dramatically.

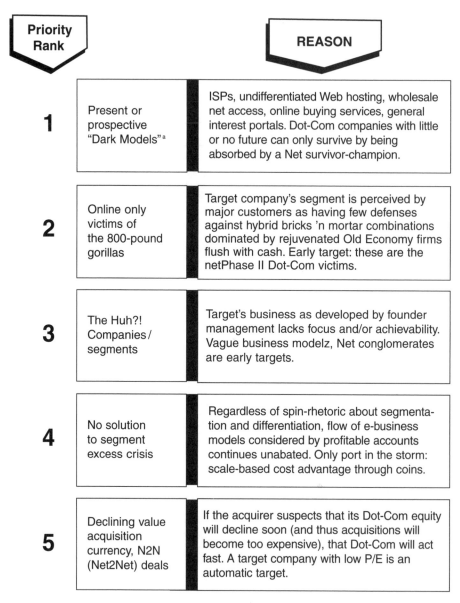

Priority Rank		REASON
1	Present or prospective "Dark Models"[a]	ISPs, undifferentiated Web hosting, wholesale net access, online buying services, general interest portals. Dot-Com companies with little or no future can only survive by being absorbed by a Net survivor-champion.
2	Online only victims of the 800-pound gorillas	Target company's segment is perceived by major customers as having few defenses against hybrid bricks 'n mortar combinations dominated by rejuvenated Old Economy firms flush with cash. Early target: these are the netPhase II Dot-Com victims.
3	The Huh?! Companies / segments	Target's business as developed by founder management lacks focus and/or achievability. Vague business modelz, Net conglomerates are early targets.
4	No solution to segment excess crisis	Regardless of spin-rhetoric about segmentation and differentiation, flow of e-business models considered by profitable accounts continues unabated. Only port in the storm: scale-based cost advantage through coins.
5	Declining value acquisition currency, N2N (Net2Net) deals	If the acquirer suspects that its Dot-Com equity will decline soon (and thus acquisitions will become too expensive), that Dot-Com will act fast. A target company with low P/E is an automatic target.

Note that some companies may be in more than one category.

FIGURE 6.7. Dot-Com consolidation: Top five target categories.

Dot-Com Target Types

Every surviving Dot-Com wants to be the acquirer rather than target, but wishing is never the same thing as getting. The desire is certainly understandable, if only because those attached to the acquirer are probably in a superior position in terms of preserving at least some equity stake.

But that desire on its own doesn't amount to anything. Figure 6.7, "Dot-Com consolidation: Top five target categories," suggests the types of companies that are more vulnerable to becoming lunch. The categories are non-exclusive: if the company is crippled by a business model that never worked anyway (category 3) and is also in the gun sights of powerful customers who just decided that they want to become your competitor instead (category 2), then the risk of disappearing increases.

"GET BIG FAST" UNDER ATTACK

> *In the broadest context of history, it's an aberration, but there is some logic to it.*
>
> Michael I. Barach,
> chief executive of MotherNature.com Inc.
> in May 2000.[19]

GBF— Get Big Fast—the slogan attributed to Jeff Bezos that is also the name of a book on the company—has inspired a hundred parallel tactics, mostly by B2Cs eager to match amazon.com's early success.[20]

During netPhase I, Get Big Fast communicated all the desirable things about the fledgling Dot-Com firm as superior Internet warrior: speed, responsiveness, pursuit of scale economies, continuous improvement. GBF became NetSpeak, with suspicions that those not chanting the mantra lacked the right Dot-Com stuff.

GBF Disappointments

In the end, the biggest problem with Get Big Fast is that the approach simply doesn't work. In the rubble of Spring Break 2000, few private financiers and no public investors-shareholders were willing to provide financing, just so expansion-minded management at a Dot-Com could play one more round of the GBF game.

For the company with marginal profitability to begin with, GBF only threatens to make things worse. Naive expansion initiatives based on flash promotions often disappoint, and/or are easily imitated by rivals. Even if the initiative does succeed, the extra sales can spell doom for the unprepared Dot-Com, as operation costs to support the increase in order volume spin the Dot-Com out of control.

Limitations of Sales at Any Cost

Whether individual or company, the "sales-at-any-cost" hard closer might somehow manage to force an initial sale, but this closer rarely repeats. Loud pitches that "we provide the total solution" quickly become tiresome. Costs to acquire new customers soar, reflecting the high churn.

The focus on revenues is certainly understandable. For most Dot-Coms, sales represent not just financial lifeblood but also the closest thing to a trackable figure for management and financial backers alike. Regardless of whether the young Dot-Com company is still in the early venture capital development stage or further along, the revenue figure is often the most consistent number— sometimes the only company statistic—exhibiting at least *some* pattern from period to period.

Price-to-revenue multiples are used not out of choice, but rather, necessity. No profits or positive cash flow exist in many Net companies.[21] But implicit in GBF is an assumption of eventual profit. The bridge concepts include "Netenomics" as described earlier in Chapter 4. Say hello to "first mover advantage" and "scaleability."[21]

The theory: Weave the two concepts into the Dot-Com's pitch, and management's dreams of preference customers who help drive unit costs lower. The reality is very different. Both "modelz" have been in fast retreat since mid-1999. The CEO who makes the mistake of spouting these two bromides today risks being shut out of survival funds permanently.

According to MotherNature.com's Barach, defending the GBF path arguably contributed to the precipitous plunge in market cap to just $30 million (equal to the prior year's indicated marketing expenses). Says Barach, "Management's objective is to enhance shareholder value. Last year, companies that lost money had higher stock appreciation than companies that made money."

Necessity is the mother of invention, even at MotherNature. What about that ardent belief in GBF? Barach has seen a new light, just coincidentally as his survival funds trickle away. *The Wall Street Journals*'s Dodge quotes the CEO as saying, "We have a totally different mindset. We're going to spend as little money as possible to get it done."

MotherNature is hardly alone. Scores of other Dot-Coms (both pre- and post-IPO) face the same dilemma, along with their financiers.

In their heart of hearts, most managers at these companies still believe the 1996-1999 Dot-Com dream of wealth through juggernaut growth, with revenues and (hopefully, later) profits soaring as on one of those hockey stick charts from Rings O' Saturn Research. The company's operations are still directed to "doing an amazon" (the GBF poster child company), but always in a different way that avoids some of the criticism leveled at amazon from time to time about losing focus.

New perspective? Belief in the old religion of GBF dies hard. We suspect that many of these "conversions" are out of necessity, as financiers stress early profitability as paramount.

Perhaps Michael Barach expresses it best of all: "It's relatively easy to buy revenue. What's hard is to get profits."[22]

THE IMPORTANCE OF 5 TO 10 TIMES

One of the critical transitions from netPhase I to netPhase II is to ensure that the new and proposed (or the old and continuing) Dot-Com is perceived to be clearly superior to the other firms competing for scarce cash. First, other Dot-Coms with identical or similar business models. Secondly, comparable traditional ("terrestrial") businesses.

Five-to-ten times refers to that combination of price, performance, and functionality that makes all the spin about superiority credible. The critical goal: to beat the competition by 5:1, at least.

Is this threshold too high? In *Only the Paranoid Survive*, Intel chairman Andy Grove describes how he looked for a 10 times advantage, as over-estimations, delays, and just the high failure rates associated with new innovations made it critical that only the most promising prospects are pursued.[23]

Me Too? Not Any More

Insisting that the new Dot-Com prospect is both clearly better and different from companies that came before, undermines the Me Too modelz described in Chapter 4, first and most.

These are the companies created to take advantage of early enthusiasm for a particular, specific type of Dot-Com pitch. EToys initially soars and spawns a half-dozen imitators. The same happens for online pet stores, auction sites, search engines, and online brokerages.

The advantage of the Me Too approach is that it helps stamp out new Dot-Com startups in the shortest time: a critical factor during 1996-1999 periods of excess demand for nearly anything Dot-Com.

But that flexibility is also Me Too's Achilles' heel. For Me Too means little or no market differentiation. The dangerous combination of an easily copied model plus temporarily high market values assures that the markets are quickly swamped by excess entrants.

The Me Too model might work great with five competitors, and things are only OK with seven. But when there are ten entrants, everyone goes broke.

For the most part, the marketplace makes automatic adjustments for these Dot-Coms. The Me Too is like an insect that lives fast and furiously but only for a single day. When the temporary conditions of market imbalance that allowed imitation Dot-Coms to thrive disappears, so do the Me Toos.

Comparisons to Other, Similar Companies

The 5-10 times strategy relies on the opposite of Me Too: that is, meaningful, profitable differentiation. Price alone is never a sufficient differentiator.

The Dot-Com's distinctive difference is typically more in the eyes of management than the perceptions of the market. The B2B information business that hopes to command the industry is shocked to discover that key editors from that industry's trade press dismiss that company's offering out of hand, as they can obtain equal or better content from a dozen sources with more arriving daily.

Europe's auctioneers QXL.com in Qtr. 4 1999 included the story that the company was committed to organic growth and was confident that other companies (e.g., EBay) faced some problems in seeking to expand abroad because of the distinctive characteristics of separate European nation-markets. But EBay continued its march on Europe, while QXL merged with a German rival in mid-year 2000.

RELEVANT GROWTH: 40/40 CRITICAL MASS

Even following the Spring Break 2000 corporate carnage, one is hard pressed to find a Dot-Com word used more often than "growth." Advocates of PEG valuation (price/earnings multiple divided by revenue growth rate, Chapter 1) contend that given two comparable companies with the same P/E, the company with the higher annual revenue growth rate deserves the greater market valuation.

But a troubling problem with percentage growth rates is the small base/large base distortion. When online represents only a small portion of total demand and/or when the individual

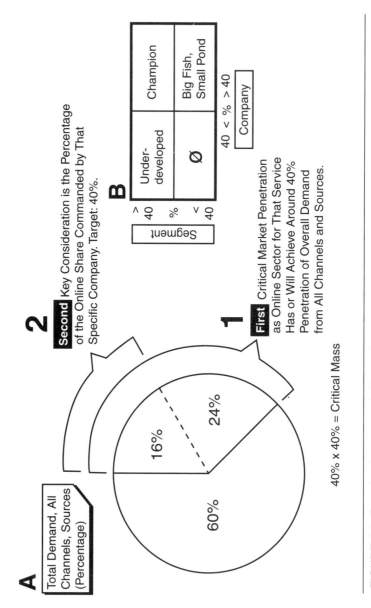

A Total Demand, All Channels, Sources (Percentage)

60%

16%

24%

2 Second Key Consideration is the Percentage of the Online Share Commanded by That Specific Company. Target: 40%.

B

	Under-developed	Champion
Segment > 40%		
	Ø	Big Fish, Small Pond
< 40		

40 < % > 40

Company

1 First Critical Market Penetration as Online Sector for That Service Has or Will Achieve Around 40% Penetration of Overall Demand from All Channels and Sources.

40% × 40% = Critical Mass

FIGURE 6.8. Focusing future growth: The 40/40 share guidelines.

Dot-Com company has a share less than, say, 40% of online sales, percentage gains come easily.

Too easily. On a percentage basis, the revenue gains on a tiny base can be astronomical and are often misleading. When the revenue base is $10 million, adding $2 million more means just a 20% growth rate. But increase that base revenue amount by $2 million, only, and the stated growth rate doubles to 40%.

Critical Mass:
Online as Percentage of Total Industry

Figure 6.8 (A) considers growth in the context of dominant market share. That means share from all channels, from all sources.

Below 40% market share penetration or so, reality is that online is "just another channel," and nothing special. "Terrestrial," that is, bricks 'n mortar competitors don't believe that they are at a disadvantage if they lack a major online operation. A nominal facade service or stories about possible future action will suffice.

Beyond 40% penetration, everything changes. Even if target customers in that segment foresee a multiple channel approach today with both terrestrial and Dot-Com participants, crossing the 40% threshold probably changes that mindset, and some begin to foresee the day when online takes over.

With cost per transaction advantage as much as 10:1, majority penetration doesn't have to occur online to start the rush of customers. Just enough penetration to provide opinion-setting customers with a glance at the future. Enough to make a convincing case for online's inevitable dominance. [24]

Why 40% as the critical mass threshold? It could be lower but should probably never be less than a third of total demand—33%. Key question in determining whether the threshold is 40% or 35% or less is: *What is the minimum online penetration at which online is perceived as the future dominant path to market?*

When that barrier is shattered, customers who before were content to do nothing suddenly scramble to catch up. Online market share of total demand soars. So do the market shares of those firms positioned to be the netPhase II leaders.

Multiple channel approaches give way to *online-first* approaches with critical pricing, billing, terms, and support arrangements changing in anticipation of the further changes ahead. There is anticipation of that day in the near future when *everyone* suddenly acts to take advantage of online's transaction compelling cost advantage.

Despite all the news surrounding B2B online procurement, e-purchasing still represents a miniscule percentage of total pur-chases as of Spring Break 2000. Until and unless e-procurement is perceived as critical in order to be competitive, the pace of *overall* adoption remains slow.

But if a major competitor fully adopts online purchasing and then applies most of that advantage to destroying competitors' prof-itability while grabbing their market shares (by passing the cost sav-ings onto customers), the race is on. That is when conversion to online ways of doing business becomes mandatory, not optional.

Critical Mass:
Company's Share of Online

The combination of one high online share as a percentage of total industry revenue with two high Dot-Com company shares sets the condition to become that segment's champion (refer to Figure 6.8B).

Individual company growth rates are irrelevant unless that growth results in a dominant share in a segment where online is posed to take command. But where that combination is emerging, that's where you will find tomorrow's Dot-Com champion com-panies.

Think back to amazon.com in the books portion of their busi-ness, Charles Schwab in the US online brokerage portion of their industry, Cisco in infrastructure, and possibly, ELoan in mort-gages. The company is positioned to be a netPhase II Dot-Com blue chip only when the online advantage is successful in achiev-ing major market penetration.

How? By increasing the sense of online urgency among customers. If the epitome of netPhase I was the retail share purchaser in a buying frenzy afraid of being left behind, then the symbol for netPhase II is the online business that faces a terrifying but necessary prospect of either commanding segment demand or disappearing.

ATTACK OF THE KILLER DOT-COM BUSINESS MODELS

> *In highly competitive markets, it's very difficult to know which new technology is going to leapfrog you next.*
>
> Ron Insana, CNBC,
> June 7, 2000, questioning a developer
> of a Net-related switching device

Full transition from netPhase I to netPhase II requires a dynamic approach to Dot-Com business model development. The stagnant but underperforming business model is almost worse than no model at all.

The good news is that you've perfected a viable business model that can pave the way for future success. The bad news is that the sucessful Dot-Com business model will be effective in the marketplace for half as long as you hope. Today's champion models become tomorrow's chump modelz, just six months later.

When developing a viable Net business course for the future, the first major challenge is avoiding the stylish but fatally flawed "modelz," as described in Chapter 4. Modelz with provocative names that are sometimes even initially convincing—so long as you don't probe too deeply.

The Dot-Com company executive implements a powerful Net business and value model that works in actual practice, not just because a spin doctor claims it does.

So, the Net warrior company is set for future accelerated growth, right?

Not yet. Dot-Com juggernaut or Old Economy dinosaur, there's the constant possibility that there's a successor model just around the corner that can easily eliminate yours.

In terrestrial industries, major model transitions are reflected in product/service generations, each of which generally lasts around two to five years these days, depending on industry and segment. But in Net time, no sooner is a model established than its killer model successor is born and begins to grow. Sometimes the Internet generations become so compressed that technologies overlap, as when Wireless Application Protocol (WAP) phones lurch into the marketplace, only to be almost immediately outflanked by far more advanced Net-to-cellular technologies.[25]

Not every new Net technology spawns its own successor, but many do. Year 2005-6 search engines will be based on an entirely

---

valueOUTPERFORMER
www.vbmresources.com

May 13, 2000

BOO-YAHOO!—SCHIZOPHRENIA.COM

As the Dot-Com era of IPO plenty gives way to the successor period of rationed financing, more and more one-time hot-shot Internet companies find they must consider Net-to-Net acquisitions just to survive. With catchy eye-candy names mandatory for netPhase I's flash Internet IPOs, a number of provocative merger combinations emerge.

One example: if imploding fashion e-tailer Boo.com is acquired by the Net's leading portal, Yahoo!, the result is something that sounds like an expression from an escapee from your local mental institution: Boo-Yahoo.com. Or consider if a leading women's community site (iVillage) was forced to combine with GoTo.com, the specialized online search engine. Yes, the result would be suitable instructions to a NYC taxi cab driver: GoTo-iVillage.com.

And then there's the embattled UK online travel site parodied for its high profile PR and pedestrian business plan, www.lastminute.com. Combine this struggling site with another major portal in a last gasp attempt to generate some momentum through tabloid-caliber hype, and the result is last-minute2excite.com.

different technology from that in use today, creating new opportunities for those that can take full commercial advantage of the new capabilities, leaving others in their wakes. New forms of secure, very fast e-mail are already starting to re-segment what was considered to be the foundation of Net service in the 1990s.

In other situations, the critical differences in new "killer models" has more to do with competing tactics for capturing the market (Figure 6.9). Even here, technology plays an important gatekeeper role. Neither the third-party nor the major customer DIY approach to business-to-business online procurement is going to prevail entirely, which suggests that the successor model will combine the two, possibly with new software tools pioneered by existing majors or new start-ups absorbed by those companies.

Keeping ahead of the killer model curve means that "destroying your existing model" is now mandatory.

Management might kid itself into thinking that it is taking bold maverick action in "killing off our models before the competition does it." Forget the illusion: self-destruction of business models is now standard practice for Dot-Coms.

Extend the same change-when-forced-to-do-so to Net businesses with life cycles that are measured in months rather than years, and the result is a business that never gets untracked. Alternatively, when the successor business model is already in place and ready to go at the date of the launch of the first, it removes the tendency to hold onto the legacy approach past its time because the replacement successor is not yet available.

Since the successor model is immediately available, management has nothing to lose but everything to gain to see how much, how fast Model 1 can be deployed in the market, with internal rewards within the firm for doing the best job of squeezing the most from that model, in the fastest time. That's a 180-degree difference in mindset compared to embattled executives clutching desperately to an obsolete incumbent model as if it were a life raft. It's a dead weight instead.

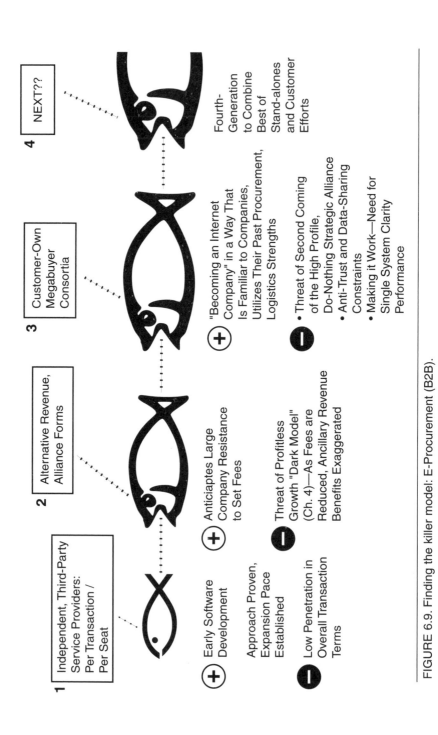

FIGURE 6.9. Finding the killer model: E-Procurement (B2B).

IN SEARCH OF THE "TWENTY OR THIRTY" DOT-COM CHAMPIONS

> *The final conclusion cannot be replaced till the Dot-Com companies are transformed from visions into tangible and sustainable businesses.*
>
> Steven Bakovljev
> Previously Invesco's chief investment officer,
> "Thanks for the Dot-Com Sanity,"
> *Financial News*, May 1-7, 2000

No more sector-chasing. No more listening to those momentum voices in your head, because the momentum's back is broken and Mo's fiercest zealots got wiped out in a margin call (Chapter 3).

Not for the first time, James J. Cramer captures the sense of the Dot-Com change. On May 22, a few weeks after Spring Break 2000, TheStreet.com's founder-columnist concedes that most Dot-Coms will flounder. But, "Twenty or thirty won't. In the coming months, we'll find those 20 or 30." [26]

Individual company analysis. No shortcuts—looking for the companies that will drive growth in netPhase II. These champion companies of the future have a plan for simultaneous internal and external growth. *They* are the high valuation leader—consolidators in their segments, not the competition.

They have tough-minded plans for achieving 40/40 critical mass, as described earlier in this chapter. These companies preference platforms (Figures 6.11 and 6.12): deep-seated sources of intrinsic value as reflected in customers' purchases.

Taking all these considerations into account, we refer to these as companies that have hard-wired their future success with present and future customers and partners. Theoretical penetration rates may have been good enough during frothy, fluffy netPhase I. No longer.

Three companies and their preference platforms are described in the pages that follow. Juniper Networks' market base exploded from two major accounts to twenty-two over one quarter. Amazon established itself as the resilient epitome of Dot-Com's future B2C promise despite bumps in that journey. Psion

WHEAT

CHAFF

A • Business Plan

• Business Plan

– Avoids future Black Hole (Chapter 1) and Dark Model (Chapter 4) areas

– Anticipates liquidity issues, 12 months-18 months forward

– Clear path to No. 1 or No. 2 dominance in future profitable market segments

– Automatic adjustment for excess entry

 What happens to forecasts if revenue must be spread over 20-50% more competitors

– Non-price deterrents erected against competitor's entry

∴ Avoidance of FMA-first market mover advantage—because it doesn't work

∴ The roster of early deterrents varies over time as rivals adjust Competitors continually put on the defensive adjust with times

– Value plan merged with business plan
Pivotal question is fully addressed: How does this business model translate into maximum value for sharesholders?

– Obsession with growth, unable to translate that growth into clear sector dominance (40/40) critical mass

– Numbers calculated from loose "top down" macro numbers, almost never adjusted for new entrants and other fundamental changes in marketplace conditions

– Market penetration assumptions based on possible (theorhetical) levels rather than achievable accounts

– Participation bias-business approach: hopeful management relies on being one of several survivors, rather than single dominant pacesetter

Continued . . .

FIGURE 6.10. Separating the cyber-wheat from the chaff.

WHEAT

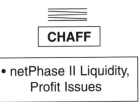

CHAFF

B | • netPhase II Liquidity, Profit Issues

• netPhase II Liquidity, Profit Issues

– Avoidance of short-term mindset (re-financing every six months) as volatile Dot-Com markets dramatically increase the risk of this hand-to-mouth expedient non-approach

– Profitability
Assumptions anticipate disaster scenarios, with contingencies

∴ Reality of excess entry remains—how will it be confronted

∴ Anticipates major structural change in industry, basis of competition

– Explicit strategies to develop company's equity as acquisition currency, for possible use in both for Net2Net and Net-to-Terrestrial acquisitions

– Myopic emphasis on cash level announcements instead, raising concerns about why such proclamations are necessary

– Inadequate answers to tough questions about the fat in prior period burn rates

Why wasn't it deleted before now? How much fat remains?

– Brinkmanship approach to liquidity: announce earlier cash flow positive date to secure funds, even if it decreases probability of survival

– Participation bias-business plan relies being one of the survivors, not sector share 2 business dominance

∴ Do financial re-engineering tactics disguise the reality that there is no 40/40 critical mass strategy?

Continued . . .

FIGURE 6.10. Separating the cyber-wheat from the chaff (continued).

WHEAT

CHAFF

C • Management	• Management
– Clear, deeply-held netPhase II mind-set throughout—no burn mentality – Top financial management with multi-year contract, capable, experienced with private financing, converting into public/private coordinated schedule – Fully capable marketing/sales management able to win the zero sum contests separating Dot-Com dominants from laggards – Executive/strategic/financial management experienced, capable of designing combination internal (organic), external (acquisition) growth together	– Bad omen: Executive exodus doesn't stop even with radical options repricing – From frying pan into fire—netPhase I visionary (poorly focused) management replaced with even worse alternative caretakers – Inability to attract, retain top mid-level technical talent, even with accelerated options, vesting – Departure of the Net-savvy respected CFO .˙. No one to manage expectations that future profit plans are credible .˙. During netPhase I, loss of heavyweight CFO foretells imminent collapse

FIGURE 6.10. Separating the cyber-wheat from the chaff (continued).

linked with Sony in an arrangement that has implications from California to Finland.

Juniper Networks:
Early Adoptions Create an Infrastructure Challenger

Cisco Systems' CEO John Chambers describes his competitors as good people, worthy rivals. And in the case of Scott Kriens, CEO of Juniper Networks, the description appears to mean more than just another example of Chambers friendly disposition.

For Juniper now challenges Cisco in the core Internet Protocol (IP) backbone marketplace, the foundation of the Internet, literally. Well into 1999, Cisco management claimed that almost all Net traffic ran on their IP backbones. E-infrastructure scale means take-all type contracts and market share.

But Juniper's arrival cut into that dominance. Most analysts said that as of mid-2000, Juniper had around 20% of the core routers market, mostly drawn away from Cisco, although it is true the market was expanding rapidly as management of both companies concedes.

It is *how* Kriens built Juniper's $30 billion market valuation (based on April 13, 2000, share price) that is important in terms of identifying tomorrow's Net champions. The number of Juniper major accounts leaped from 2 in the first quarter of 1998 to 22 in the first quarter of 1999.

By closing early strategic sales with Wordcom's UUNet business, with Cable & Wireless (which runs one of the largest backbone networks within the US), and also Verio, Juniper instantly established its credentials with buyers worldwide. Revenues per account increased in each quarter during 1999, supporting management's statements that the company was well-positioned to perform even better in the future.[27]

Amazon.com:
Preference Platform of One
(or Rather *Thousands* of Ones)

> *We think that the sort of discrimination that causes investors to differentiate between companies that are just creating short-term value versus those that are creating something of sustained value is good for amazon.com.*
>
> Jeff Bezos,
> April 4, 2000,
> *The Wall Street Journal*'s Steve Frank on CNBC

The world's best-known Internet company had to create its segment first, before trying to establish any knock-out preference with customers.

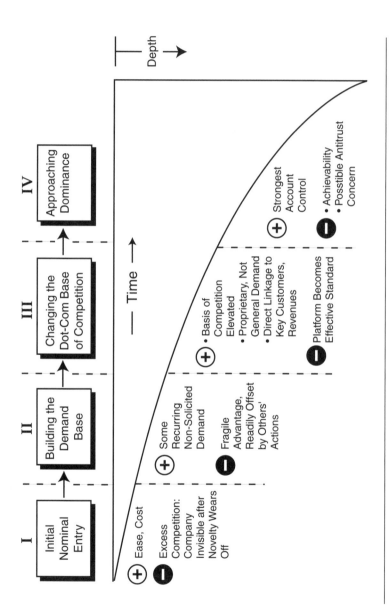

FIGURE 6.11. Depth of critical account, customer control.

The logic of initially focusing on books as the ideal vehicle for an early netPhase I B2C company was not apparent to many except the amazon CEO. The new, new Net was designed for far flashier stuff in the opinion of many.

But Bezos stuck to his instincts and tried to radically alter the buying habits of customers purchasing products they might buy anywhere.

With some degree of luck (Barnes & Nobles's awkward response left the e-book field open to Amazon longer than expected), the likeable chief executive had the opportunity to actually achieve what the push-marketing types could only imagine: massive selection as vendor of choice by millions of individual customers.

Sector	B2C	B2B	E-Infrastructure
Company (business)	amazon.com (books, other retail)	Psion (PDAs, 3G smart devices)	JUNIPER Networks (servers)
Platform	"One-step" ™ perceived price leadership	Symbian (28% owned by Psion) EPOC	Advanced generation Internet protocol (IP) backbones: MI60 core, M10 regional router
Preference Basis	Broad adoption, ad hoc standard takes hold because of rivals' late start	Sony embraces Symbian's EPOC software, further validating that platform as the one to beat	Early market acceptance and successful installations at UUNET (Worldcom), C&W, establishes reference sale momentum for Juniper in 1999
	PDA—Personal Digital Assistant		
	3G: Third-Generation Intelligent Cellular-Net Technology		

FIGURE 6.12. Preference platforms, across the Dot-Com spectrum.

How? The One-Click™ feature is well known, but we believe that it has been the perception of low price leadership that is key to broad adoption of amazon's approach, with emphasis on *perceived*.

Chasing the lowest price down is a loser's game in etailing. Yet, online customers insist on a 10-30% price break compared to terrestrial services as they, too, read those statistics about far lower transaction costs online. Shopping robot (shopbot) technologies are improving all the time, making it easier and easier to compare deals online.

In both consumer and business markets, low prices are no longer a differentiator, but rather, a requirement for market entry. Gomez.com confirms that Amazon is often outdone in terms of prices by two or three e-booksellers, based on their sampling methodology.[28] Doesn't matter. Amazon is frequently *perceived* as the practical lowest price combination, nonetheless. Bezos's tactics are diverse, including a combination of specials, discounts "up to XX%," and are continually changing. The combination seems to yield the desired result as thousands perceive that the prices are low enough that it doesn't make great sense to switch. [29]

Psion's Terrific, Terrible Opportunity

> *The market now wants . . . to make the next step, from a concept—play validated by big deals—to a real-world phenomenon validated by people increasingly adopting it for everyday use.*
>
> Author Geoffrey Moore [30]

Being a company in the gunsights of Microsoft and competing in one of Lord Gates's future target markets probably doesn't strike you as the best rationale for arguing that a company is poised to prosper in the Commercial Internet's second phase. But in our judgment, both descriptions applied to Psion and its chief executive, David Levin, as of mid-2000.

Even with Department of Justice distractions and looming break-up prospects, no one *ever* underestimates the 800-pound gorilla from Redmond, Washington, except at their own expense. The world is littered with competitors' that developed superior software compared to Microsoft's offerings, only to later be blown away in the marketplace because of Microsoft's massive embedded user base and effective tactics.

As if firing a warning shot across Psion's bow, Microsoft attracted/hired/lured away/poached (choose one, depending on your perspective) Juha Christensen, EVP of Symbian, to become Microsoft's new vice president of sales and marketing for product server software development. That move is fiercely contested. On May 9, 2000, London Chancery Court ruled that the Danish scientist could not move to Microsoft until after his contract with Symbian expired on September 16, 2000. [31]

That's the terrible part for Levin and company. Here's the terrific part:

Psion owns 28% of software pioneer Symbian, also based in the UK Symbian's EPOC operating software (OS) is critical to Psion's future. Arguably, EPOC enjoys a clear preference advantage among independent assessors compared to both past and present versions of Microsoft's competing OS for personal digital assistant (PDA) devices.

Symbian's EPOC and the recently updated version of Microsoft's CE software are OS combatants in the coming future of portable, Net-enabled communications and computing devices. If that sounds like a collision of engineering baffle-jargon, that's because PDAs such as Psion's Revo, the Handspring Visor, and the Palm III and "smart" cellular phones are converging. Fast. Enthusiasm for this new series of Net-enabled devices is reflected in record fees paid for 3G (third-generation) cellular fees in auctions worldwide.

Despite EPOC's preference advantage among engineers and many end-users, Symbian arguably lost some forward market momentum after the 1997 announcement by Psion to form that software company, with partner-customers Nokia, Motorola, and Ericsson.

Never a company to let a technical disadvantage get in the way of aggressive marketing, Microsoft's Steve Ballmer barnstormed Psion's Symbian partners in a style described by Americans as "aggressive" and derisively by Europeans as "cowboy."

Before April 2000, minor battles characterized the EPOC-Window CE warfare. No big losses by Symbian to Microsoft, but limited forward momentum. Left to a variety of alternative operating and technical platforms, the engineering mentality of customers is often to "qualify" ALL platforms, so as not to be excluded from any, ever. OK for the engineer's sense of closure but not so great for market development, which requires action on a specific platform.

But then, Levin and Symbian management captured their *own* 800-pound gorilla: Sony.

Then in April 2000, Sony Corp. announced that it was licensing EPOC for use in smart phones, starting with a projected model for sale in Japan in 2001. *The Wall Street Journal's* David Pringle proclaimed a new phase in the battle between the two camps.[32]

With tomorrow's third-generation applications and uses unknown and/or poorly understood today, branding and marketing is critical. Nokia set the pace in transforming boring cellular phones into consumer fashion items that also communicate. No company has ever come close to accomplishing that in consumer electronics-communications except . . . ah, Sony.

Sony's decision to go with EPOC and its action on an EPOC-based phone in 2001 now makes Symbian's software the one to beat (Figure 6.12 and Moore quote, above). Yeah, but that was also proclaimed back in 1997. What's different this time?

Only everything. Carriers' "winning" 3G licenses in auctions these days understand that they can quickly become losers struggling to pay monumental license fees if the applications are unpopular, over-reaching, or both.

Psion's Levin understands the carriers' opportunity/threat dilemma. He emphasizes the importance of adapting all aspects of his marketing and technical co-operation with carriers and next-generation cellular phone makers to those needs. Just that orientation is a stark contrast to take-it-or-else "encouragement" found elsewhere.[33]

The prospect of Sony achieving in third-generation C&C devices what it did for consumer electronics doesn't merely re-credentialize Psion-Symbian, it reduces the risk of 3G devices becoming like the initial version of the Apple Newton: interesting, but neither useful nor usable for prime customer functions. Arguably, it was Psion that transformed the struggling "organizer" segment into a high function/high demand Personal Digital Assistant with its first Psion Series 3 handhelds.

Also, Sony's entry is interpreted by us as providing a subtle but unmistakable signal to Symbian partner-customer-shareholders: get off the fence regarding EPOC.

As long as there was no plausible challenger to Nokia's hegemony, cellular phone manufacturers played a political game, accumulating extra non-exclusive operating system arrangements like the high-demand football star gathers non-committal offer sheets from various different bidders. Never know when you might want to play one against another.

But Sony's recent reorganization reportedly places that firm's championing of the Psion-Symbian arrangement in an even better position to implement their aggressive marketing plans. Just coincidentally, of course, Ericsson's R380 using EPOC was introduced to market in June 2000.

DOT-COMS' MISSING MANAGEMENT

In the weeks immediately following Spring Break 2000, the phrase above suggests the Internet company CEO who bolts because his options plunged underwater and backers could/would do nothing to fix the problem, or the Net CFO who bolts.

The latter knows full well that his skills and Dot-Com experience are pure platinum in the interim period, before any systematic Dot-Com secondaries market emerges that can compare to the VC-IPO netPhase I structure shown in Figure 6.1.

Real Value Exodus

The departures above are the management gaps that are the most visible in the biz-press, but they represent only the part of the ice-

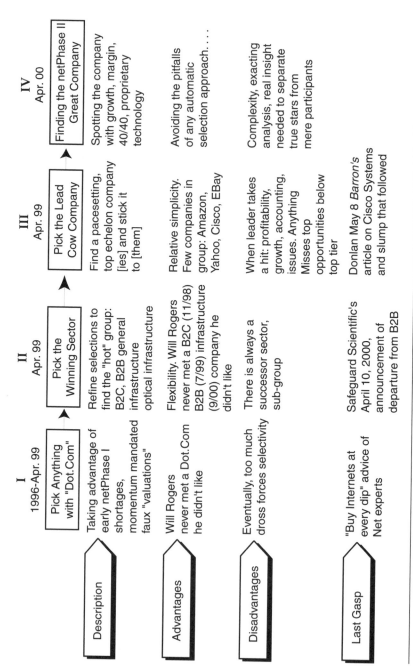

	I 1996-Apr. 99 Pick Anything with "Dot.Com"	II Apr. 99 Pick the Winning Sector	III Apr. 99 Pick the Lead Cow Company	IV Apr. 00 Finding the netPhase II Great Company
Description	Taking advantage of early netPhase I shortages, momentum mandated faux "valuations"	Refine selections to find the "hot" group: B2C, B2B general infrastructure optical infrastructure	Find a pacesetting, top echelon company [ies] and stick it to [them]	Spotting the company with growth, margin, 40/40, proprietary technology
Advantages	Will Rogers never met a Dot.Com he didn't like	Flexibility. Will Rogers never met a B2C (11/98) B2B (7/99) infrastructure (9/00) company he didn't like	Relative simplicity. Few companies in group: Amazon, Yahoo, Cisco, EBay	Avoiding the pitfalls of any automatic selection approach....
Disadvantages	Eventually, too much dross forces selectivity	There is always a successor sector, sub-group	When leader takes a hit: profitability, growth, accounting, issues. Anything Misses top opportunities below top tier	Complexity, exacting analysis, real insight needed to separate true stars from mere participants
Last Gasp	"Buy Internets at every dip" advice of Net experts	Safeguard Scientific's April 10, 2000, announcement of departure from B2B	Donlan May 8 *Barron's* article on Cisco Systems and slump that followed	

FIGURE 6.13. Defensive strategy transition as the Net boom matures.

berg that is visible. If the board and bankers have not been able to solve the problem of underwater options for the execs, then you can be sure that the top technical talent has bolted long ago.

Our anecdotal evidence suggests that many of the top tech types—the ones who can make the difference between just being on the short list and a continuing contract with (gasp) advance cash—tend to be very careful about diversifying their *personal* portfolios. We were curious about whether changes in vesting ratios would increase loyalty of the very top talent that is the ultimate lifeblood of all these Dot-Coms.

The customary vesting formula calls for a quarter of the total options package total over four years. We were curious to see what might arise if a client in the future skewed the weighing more toward the front-end in recognition of continuously accelerating Internet time.

One half the first year and total vesting in three, rather than four years? Not interested. Probing a bit, we discovered that some of the top techies also have the 70+% netPhase I failure rate in the back of their minds. And because of that expectation, some deliberately seek out four separate stints in four different aspiring Dot-Com companies. One per year.

The logic: they can never tell which might beat the odds and make the 30% success group. So ensuring a portfolio of at least three top prospects increases the expected economic return on a very personal basis.

Implications for PIPE Investors

So if the top technical talent leaves either one, their underwater options are not being re-priced, or two, they know something about the firm's or the segment's true prospects that the spinners will never reveal, a big bright danger red flag is raised.

In either situation, management that fails to re-price underwater options of its top talent is effectively saying that it is willing to become a valueless shell. Just keep those pay checks flowing a few more months, please.

Hey, here's a fellow who has gotten the message about the new importance of profitability; think we'll put him at the front of the line for Dot-Com private investment in public equity funds.

Big mistake if it turns out that to advance that schedule, management said no to pulling the options packages of the top marketing do-ers and top technical talent out of the drink.

For financiers-investors thinking that they can swing a good deal by taking advantage of a switch in advantage from entrepreneurs in Dot-Com prospects to lenders-investors, beware. *Start* the due diligence with a talent audit, both in absolute terms and relative to the competition. If you find out that all the talent who pioneered all the key innovations to date are elsewhere, contact them and find out why they left.

Notes, Chapter 6

1. "An End-to-End Paradigm Shift of Powerful Dynamics: A Guide to Press Release Hyperbole," www.TheStreet.com, May 27, 2000.

2. "Three-wheeled Business Plans," www.upside.com. Brandt is senior contributing editor of *Upside*.

3. Two interviews with VBM Consulting, May 2000.

4. VBM Consulting's discussions with Infobank chief executive Graham Sadd, May 2000. Chapter 7 describes attempts by independent, third-party e-procurement and vertical industry communities to develop new value in the Net's second major phase.

5. Chapter 1, Figure 1.1, "Bringing the non-investment quality" (NIQ) company public." The figure shows how Dot-Com companies were brought public prematurely to meet hype-stoked over demand for Internet companies. But just because a company is publicly traded doesn't necessarily mean it is.

6. Interview with VBM Consulting, March 30, 2000.

7. Statistics from Alexander, Garth, "Dotcon Burnout," April 9, 2000, *The Sunday Times* (London), 3.5.

8. Lisa Bannon and Suzanne McGee, "EToys Raises $100 Million, But Terms Are Unfavorable," *The Wall Street Journal Interactive Edition* (www.wsj.com), June 14, 2000.

9. CNBC's "Internet Investor" segment, hosted by *The Wall Street Journal*'s Steve Frank. Frank asked Smith whether the "haircut" implicit in the EToys June 2000 private financing would be limited to B2Cs only, or extended to other Dot-Coms in major Net sectors seeking post-Spring Break financing, in addition.

10. "IPO Market Unravels," www.thestandard.com, May 29, 2000, 58.

11. Rose quote from Stephanie Gruner, "Trendy Online Retailer Is Reduced to a Cautionary Tale for Investors," *The Wall Street Journal Interactive Edition*, www.wsj.com, May 19, 2000.

12. CNBC, June 7, 2000

13. David Parsley, "The Man Who Would Take On Cisco," *The Sunday Times* (London), June 4, 2000, 3.11. Parsley goes on to explain that the Juniper Networks CEO anticipates that prime users will have more than one route to the Web, just as many active Net users employ more than one ISP, just in case their primary one goes down.

14. "If Infrastructure Is Out, What's In?," www.forbes.com, June 7, 2000.

15. William M. Bulkeley, "Safeguard to Shift Investments Out of B-to-B Companies," *The Wall Street Journal*, April 10, 2000, 4. Some, such as VerticalNet chairman Mark Walsh, contend that the ecubator's action was widely misinterpreted. More on this in the next chapter.

16. "Three-wheeled Business Plans." Brandt acknowledges Steve Lohr of *The New York Times* as the ultimate source of the statistics about auto industry start-up in the early 20th century.

17. Authors, *The Value Mandate*, Chapter 7, describes the critical value role of earliest adopters as the opinion setters that enlist others in the new company and its services. A poorly

designed online banking site that doesn't permit the trans-actions promised risks generating massive *negative* word-of-mouth.

18. Quote from David Streitfield, "Valley Welcomes Internet Bubble Burst," *The Washington Post*, May 27, 2000, A01. Backus was speaking at Schmoozefest, San Francisco.

19. John Dodge, "MotherNature.com's CEO Defends Dot-Com's Get-Big-Fast Strategy," *The Wall Street Journal Interactive Edition*, http://interactive.wsj.com, May 16, 2000. According to the article, MotherNature's share price reached a high of $14.565 in December 1999, the month the company went public. By mid-May 2000, the reported stock price was around $2/share.

20. "GBF" is also part of the title of Robert Spector's book *Amazon.com: Get Big Fast, Inside the Revolutionary Business Model That Changed the World* (New York: Random House, 2000).

21. Because of financiers' over-reliance on the revenue data, Dot-Com managements who adopt acceptable-yet-controversial accounting practices shouldn't be surprised when their stock price plunges, relative to rivals. Even the slightest hint of "managed numbers" can have a devastating effect on company value. A key focus area: merchandisers, market-markers and e-procurement firms that treat the full value of the goods sold as their revenue, even though they are essentially performing a go-between role. No implication of any wrong-doing or inappropriate treatment by anyone is expressed or implied here.

22. Dodge, "MotherNature.com's CEO." See note 19.

23. *Only the Paranoid* (New York: Currency Doubleday 1996), 55–71.

24. One example: Larry Downes and Chunka Mui, *Unleashing the Killer App: Digital Strategies for Market Dominance* (Boston: Harvard Business School Press, 1998), 45, Fig. 2.1.

25. The issue of staying ahead under conditions of imploding product/service life cycles is addressed further in *The Value Mandate*, Chapter 7.

26. "State of the Web: The Wheat and the Chaff," www.TheStreet.com.

27. David Parsley, "The Man Who Would Take On Cisco," *The Sunday Times* (London), June 4, 2000, 3.11. Customer statistics from Robertson Stephens' research report on Juniper Networks of April 14, 2000, Paul Johnson CFA (paul_johnson@ rsco.com), and Ara Mizrakjian, ara_mizrakjian@rsco.com).

28. Gomez Advisors (www.gomezadvisors.com) Online booksellers rankings, as of December 12, 1998. An overall score is based on multiple criteria including ease of use, customer confidence, on-site resources, relationship services, overall cost, and gift box.

29. "We will be competitive on prices . . . [but] our goal is to give customers the best possible shopping experience" amazon.com spokesperson quoted in George Anders, "Amazon.com Leads in Appeal But Not Price," *The Wall Street Journal Interactive Edition* (www.wsj.com), December 11, 1998.

30. "Approaching the Chasm," *The Industry Standard*, www.thestandard.com, May 15, 2000, 88. Moore is the managing director of the Chasm Group, a consulting firm, and a partner with Mohr Davidow. His books include *Crossing the Chasm* (1991), *The Gorilla Game* (1998—other authors are Paul Johnson and Tom Kippola), and *Living on the Faultline* (2000).

31. Richard Heller, "Defector!," *Forbes Global*, May 29, 2000, 23.

32. David Pringle, "Two Camps Pitch Themselves As Sites for Mobile Devices," *The Wall Street Journal*, April 28, 2000, 1.

33. VBM Consulting interview with Psion chief executive David Levin, May 11, 2000.

Chapter 7

REDISCOVERING THE B2B VALUE LEADERS, SELECTIVELY

It's not a craze, and it's not a mania. Forget the Tulip Mania stuff, this is very real.

Jim Seymour, TheStreet.com,
in "Don't Write Off B2B As a Craze"[1]

We believe that the rediscovery of B2B is key to the Internet's second phase. The fact that well-run companies can improve their corporate value by 20 to 25-plus% through implementation of a mix of Net cost and marketing initiatives is solid value creation bedrock. To those few who still contend that the Net isn't real 'cause it doesn't create anything, our answer is that it creates profits and value, although not always in the Dot-Com provider companies themselves.

Emphasis here on B2B doesn't mean that there aren't also individual Net company opportunities in infrastructure, B2G, and yes, even B2C. But there, as in B2B, the key opportunities following the Net shakeout will be found not by throwing darts at this month's fad sector, but by analyzing the source of enduring future cash flow the individual companies themselves.

Put aside those picks 'n shovels analogies for e-infrastructure. There *will* be some losers in e-infrastructure, starting first with traditional hardware manufacturers, impacted first and worst by optical networking. First-generation wireless technologies promised in 1999 as the next great thing have been overtaken by successors as of mid-2000.

Our spotlight is on selective opportunities in B2B. Despite a September 1999 to April 2000 roller-coaster ride that left the markets in tatters, the basic message of value for B2B end-user customers survives intact.

Figure 7.1 illustrates what we're talking about. (A) shows a corporation's traditional cost structure and elements. Variable expenses are stacked on top of fixed costs. While there may be opportunities for minor tweaks to both, unit cost changes tend to be minor and exceedingly difficult to achieve. Minimum price for goods and products sold is based on variable costs plus some contribution to fixed costs.

But then everything changes with (B), thanks to Net-based efficiencies. Numerous cost categories long treated as fixed as a practical matter (such as some costs for salaries and partial costs for procurement, marketing, and general administration) are transformed to variable.

As a consequence, end-user company management can address *its* maximum shareholder value mandate in a whole new way. Instead of starting with fixed costs, the cost foundation and planning for everything *starts* with variable costs. User company management that tries to apply the power of the Net first and best focuses on simultaneously slashing fixed costs while converting them to variable costs.

An example occurs when management replaces its mini-fiefdom for expense-report filing and reimbursement with online self-service. Costs per report are slashed. Reimbursement occurs much faster. The corporation's expensive bureaucracy shrinks, and more money is invested in growth.[2]

Fundamental benefits for Internet-adopting companies never went away. But somehow that value message faded away during the dramatic share price run-ups in Autumn of 1999 (Figure 7.2).

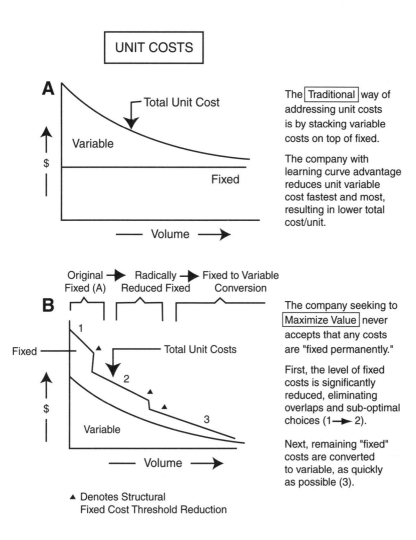

The Traditional way of addressing unit costs is by stacking variable costs on top of fixed.

The company with learning curve advantage reduces unit variable cost fastest and most, resulting in lower total cost/unit.

The company seeking to Maximize Value never accepts that any costs are "fixed permanently."

First, the level of fixed costs is significantly reduced, eliminating overlaps and sub-optimal choices (1➔2).

Next, remaining "fixed" costs are converted to variable, as quickly as possible (3).

FIGURE 7.1. The B2B value case: Fundamental reconstruction of corporate unit costs.

Nasdaq Composite slumped to a new year 2000 intraday low on May 22, raising concerns of a repeat of the March-April 2000 Spring Break period, further re-valuing all Dot-Coms.

Leaders in each of their respective B2B sectors, VerticalNet (Vert) and Commerce One (CMRC) merely gave up most of their netPhase I-froth after March 10, 2000.

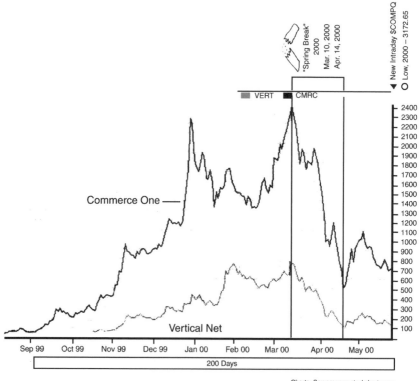

Charts, Source: www.stockcharts.com

FIGURE 7.2. Relative performance—200 days ending May 22, 2000: VerticalNet vs. Commerce One.

SELECTIVE B2B

> *The problem is that 90% of the B2B stocks are overvalued and ten percent are ridiculously undervalued—and the challenge is to figure out which is which. . . . There's an opportunity here to build a $100 billion company. Those that do are ridiculously cheap today. The others are worth zero.*
>
> David Perry,
> CEO of vertical marketplace firm
> Ventro Corp., in *Forbes*, May 1, 2000

Selective is part of this chapter's title to reinforce the message that magic sector selection is dead. The tough truth is that the stock picking based on Net category alone never worked except for a few momentum players with the instinct to know when Mo was finished and it was time to move on to the next Dot-Com darling category.

As with B2C, business to business lacks tight boundaries. In the hands of spin doctors who will be stuck with valueless B2C shares unless they can alter perceptions of their Happybang.coms., B2B is an eroded catch-all term that refers to any online sale involving any selling company.

B2B was always too broad a category to be useful for classification purposes—sorry, no more Shakespeare jokes. If "B2B" falls on its face when it comes to defining a precise category, just imagine the pratfalls when someone uses it as a lemming investment guide.

B2B spans a wide range of quite different sub-categories, each with its own value potential, its own cost and competitive structures. One B2B business, wholesale broadband capacity for businesses, is already becoming a commodity Dark Model business.

Contrast that with high margin, specific industry-adapted re-order software that checks the customer's stock of that supply, investigates suppliers' sources and availability, and automatically makes the purchase. A high-value function performed in moments rather than days.

Rediscovery of business-to-business as a prime high value sector during the netPhase II will be bittersweet to some B2B pretenders who "re-invented" their business descriptions and sometimes even their names in 1999 to bask in the glow of that periods hot, hot Net sector.

There were consumer online auction sites where some manager discovered that a couple of accounts were actually businesses swapping distressed inventory. Voila: the company is transformed into a B2B, for spin purposes, at least. Company spin doctors proclaim that not only is the company a business-to-business enterprise NOW, but also that it has always been one. Or at least since the spinners checked out those charts for Commerce One and Infobank from June-December 1999.

The sun stopped shining on B2B for a while—but it is peeking through the clouds once again as the flight to Net quality means far less emphasis on selling sneakers and Pokémon online, and far more on Net services with solid business worth. But does this value resurrection also extend to those that are B2B in name only? Not at all.[3] Not to b2bstores.com, spotted by Upside.com's Adam Feuerstein as a particularly extraordinary example of "Hide Behind the Impressive Sector Name" tactics.

The b2bstores.com Web site claims that the firm is in the business of selling janitorial services to corporations. Thanks in part to an accommodating exchange, the well-named Web site went public in February 2000. According to Feuerstein, this giant enterprise company generated all of $6,383 in revenue (there's no missing "M" or "B"), from the time of the company's inception in June 1999 to the end of March 2000.[4]

NEXT TIME, WITH ANALYSIS

Myriad promoters cite a Forrester Research report predicting that online commerce will hit $2.7 trillion in four years. . . . (but) hundreds of independent B2B sites may share as little as $1.4 billion in fees. . . .

Daniel Lyons, "B2Bluster," *Forbes*[5]

It isn't just that some of B2B demand figures devised during netPhase I were little more than finger-in-the-air guesstimates. What makes it worse is that the figures were (and are) often misapplied and are sometimes still referred to today.

Lost in the Forrester

Lyons's even-handed analysis of B2B prospects offsets some of the extreme anti-B2B attacks, which started shortly after Safeguard Scientifics' alleged abandonment of B2B sector on April 10, 2000.[6]

---

valueOUTPERFORMER
www.vbmresources.com

May 13, 2000

Adapted from
THE KEYS TO THE DOT-COM KINGDOM ARE YOURS

A favored theme of one of this season's set of seminar consultant-lecturers is to "Bring Dot-Com" inside traditional bricks 'n mortar companies.

Bring in the innovation mindsets, the 24/7 work ethic and most importantly, the cash.

Bring it all inside Old Economy companies eager to prove they are now the Dot-Com age's victors, rather than the victims.

Preaching to the choir. Any suggestion that it is now the Old Economy's turn to bask in the valuation warmth of the Dot-Com sun is gratefully welcomed from those execs made to feel in the past that they're down with their ship, old underperforming RustBelt International.

But now there's new hope for the laggards. See? The consultant said it's so, so it must be true: **the keys to the Dot-Com kingdom are ours for the taking.** How is this miracle possible? Well, for one thing it is clear from the March 10-April 14, 2000, drop. The Dot-Coms have lost the momentum, often finding it more difficult to achieve profitable growth than first thought. Which means that the momentum swings back to the companies like RustBelt International (RI). Right?

Not necessarily. Fact that the online warriors sometimes find the going tougher in 2000 than a year earlier doesn't automatically mean that momentum reverts back to the laggards.

Another factor is that the critical talent necessary to pull off a workable Dot-Com strategy left RI years ago in the tight labor market. No one in their right mind believes that the stellar programmer capable of converting RI into a Dot-Com superpower like the consultant said stayed around for four years and one tenth the expected compensation.

Nor was the Forrester number the highest research house B2B projection. Gartner Group announced that B2B transactions would hit $7.297 *trillion* by 2004, making the Forrester numbers seem like chump change by comparison.[7] "Many zeros indeed," comments *Fortune's* Mark Gimein, with the inference that the classic hockey stick-shaped demand curve is now dead.

Why issue research reports with telephone number demand guesses with little or nothing to back them? Because it sells research service subscriptions, Nasdaq breath. Somehow, we sense that report entitled "B2Bs to Show Moderate Growth for a Few, But Crushing Disappointments for Many" is not what our friends the IPO packagers are looking for to help substantiate their share pitch story.

Another consideration: who's going to check a projection for 2005, which is the 30th century in Internet time, after all? No one. *So might as well go back to the drawing board and make the slope of that demand curve even steeper. Do you actually imagine someone will try to check on something that won't happen for another five years?*

If the shape of that almost curve appears strangely familiar, you've got a good memory. Thin client, network computer, NC—call it whatever you want. *Those* hallucination-inducing projections were based on little more than manufacturers' bluster. Don't ask Rings O' Saturn Research to pull out its NC projections from 1997—it became cattle feed long ago.

Then as now, the trick is not to show that really, really steep part of the slope until at least two years into the future. That's long enough removed from today's data to avoid being discredited by near-term reasoned analysis. But far enough in the future to permit the chart to strut a pulse-quickening exponential shape. Most of the mini-research companies that perpetuated the NC folly disappeared years ago.

To be fair, there is no real comparability between the Forrester and Gartner B2B numbers, as the numbers are $4.6 *trillion* apart. Gartner Group's figures apparently reflect the full value of the goods and services sold, not just the revenue derived from buy-side (e-procurement) and/or sell-side (marketplace management, with sales emphasis) services.

It is important to note that some of the reports that avoid becoming ensnarled in these numbers—such as Gartner Group's "E-Procurement: A Blueprint for Revolution or Hype?"—are both carefully developed and thought-provoking.[8] But looking at the range of B2B "analyses," the simple truth is that the reports with the greatest shock impact tend to draw the most attention in the business press, Spring Break collapse or not.

The Real Problem:
How the Guesstimates are Used

But arguably, the real problem with the fantasy projections is how the $10 trillion B2B prediction issued from Rings O' Saturn Research is *interpreted.*

Never mind that *trillions* of dollars separate alternative guesstimates made under differing assumption sets. Or that demand numbers are worthless unless addressed in the context of fundamental factors including—but not limited to—timing, pace, and pattern of the Net boom's phases.

Forget all that. The financiers' babies need new shoes, which means that even the frothiest guesstimates are treated as solid bedrock for the purposes of trying bank vapor modelz. As explained in Chapter 6, the larger the starting number, the more conservative the market penetration assumption can be, yet still ensure a future revenue number that is guaranteed to lead the late nine TV biz-news.

There's always someone out there who thinks that Ariba or Ventro or one of those companies can capture "just" ten percent of the $2.7 trillion macro number in 2004. The resulting $270 billion dollar annualized revenue works out to an interesting market value sum when even the lowest of the price-to-sales numbers from Figure 7.3 are applied. Again, as we're so very conservative, the PTSs applied there are from April 6, 2000, that is, from deep into the Spring Break 2000 collapse.

Company	PRICE DATA Recent*	High	Market Value* (US$mil)	Sales** (US$mil)	Price/ Sales	Symbol	Business
Ariba	$105.38	$183.31	$20,255	$62.0	327	ARBA	E-procurement
Commerce One	64.44	165.50	9,974	33.6	297	CMRC	E-procurement
FreeMarkets	110.00	370.00	3,903	20.9	187	FMKT	Auction E-markets: Verticals
Internet Capital Group	73.88	212.00	19,524	16.5	1,181	ICGE	Ecubator
PurchasePro.com	57.63	175.00	1,804	5.2	345	PPRO	Communities/ Procurement Nets
SciQuest.com	24.06	91.63	637	3.9	164	SQST	E-market: Scientific, Educational
VerticalNet	59.75	148.38	4,255	20.8	205	VERT	Industry-Specific B2B Communities

*As of May 2000
**Latest 12 Months

FIGURE 7.3. B2B mainstream in May 2000: Shakeout is still to come.

Margins? Oops, negative for now, which means the more that is sold, the more the corporation loses. Sound familiar? But if you believe in concepts such as scalability (Chapter 4) and P2P (Chapter 6), then margins tend to improve. The bottom line: the hockey stick projection helps ensure that the netPhase I IPOs get priced, VCs receive their fees, and Bubba has reason to bid up the B2Bs until stratospheric share prices cause the inevitable collapse.

The Case for Foundation-Up, Not Guesstimate-Down

As noted in earlier chapters, post-Spring Break estimates of Dot-Com company collapses over the next couple of years tend to range upwards from 70%.

Our own guesstimate (that's all it is—can any such prediction ever be anything else?) at VBM Consulting is 75% for B2Cs, 50% for B2Bs. That puts us at the optimistic end of the range.

But just suppose that we're in the right vicinity when we all look back in 2004. That means that around *half* of the names on that long printout of B2Bs eCommerce companies dated Spring 2000, will be dead by January 1, 2000. Many of these "deaths" are disguised by face-saving mergers.

It's overtime for the spinners. Putting the best face on dying B2Bs is essential if early backers of the company are going to escape with anything at all. The most promising dying B2Bs are those with some proprietary software of note to sell. These cripples are absorbed by one of the blue chips in a "marriage made in heaven." Six months later, all the "acquired" staff are gone. Only software remains.

But if there's no software to shill, the sort of sickening euthanasia type situation seen first in March 2000 is the only possibility. The company lead by management with the dream of commanding vertical markets by becoming the ultimate information resource for scores of companies sounds OK on paper. But netPhase I was the era for trying to float unproven concepts—Phase II is for accelerating those that already work.

WHAT ARE THE REAL NUMBERS?

Unprofitable Dot-Coms in all sectors (including B2B) have created a quandary for themselves because of over-reliance on revenue numbers. For those accustomed to P/E multiples, price times revenue might be necessary, but isn't very satisfactory.[9]

When there are no earnings, scrutiny on revenue increases. In a company with ongoing profitability, management's selection of an alternative, acceptable GAAP approach usually creates few waves, if justified by the nature of the business, especially not if the bottom-line impact is visible and minimal. *No one cares about the top line? It's the bottom line that we track.*

But even though the "Profits Don't Count" mindset of netPhase I is disappearing faster than a middle-of-the-plate fastball to Sammy Sosa, that doesn't mean that there's something else available as a substitute. Not yet, at least. Until they become profitable and stay that way, individual B2Bs can expect continued tough scrutiny from value-determining analysts concerned with the *quality* of revenues, not just optimistic forecast amounts.

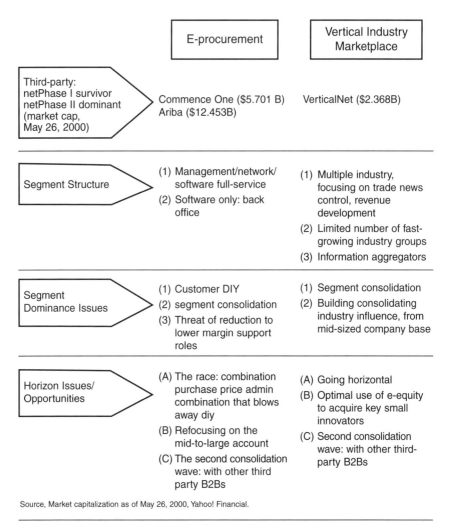

FIGURE 7.4. B2B key markets: NetPhase II challenges.

B2B gets special attention from the quality-of-numbers analysts because of some other practices by some of them. Some B2Bs still reason that since they take title to the property as a normal part of their market-making activity, they can express revenues on the basis of the full value of the goods and services being sold, not the far lower sum of transaction, software licensing, and service fees. Many analysts argue that although the practice may be permitted under GAAP, it is not the most conservative practice (as of this writing).[10]

A second area of concern surfaced in 1999, when analysts questioned the revenue mix of some companies that were treating advertising credits as revenue received on a market price basis, rather than based on the actual transaction amount. The upshot was that companies changed practices to reflect such revenue on the lower basis while actively working to decrease their percentages from that revenue source.

THE EMPIRE TRIPS ON A FAD

Investors have been treating independent B-to-B marketplaces like unsavory distant relatives because they believe that the indies will never be able to compete with coalitions of powerful industry players, more than 60 of which have announced plans to launch their own marketplaces.

Mark Roberti, *The Industry Standard*[11]

At issue is whether you need a separate B2B sector or whether companies can do it for themselves. I'm not sure you need standalone B2B players.

Scott Schermerhorn, Colonial Management
"Taking Stock" segment, CNBC, May 18, 2000

Even the most promising (Customer Do-It-Yourself) exchanges face huge obstacles. The first is understanding the technology and getting it to work. Beyond that, there are less tangible but more nettlesome considerations of antitrust and culture.

Clare Ansberry, *The Wall Street Journal*[12]

The latest fad of the Dot-Com soothsayers is the oh-so-comforting (to Old Economy dinosaurs) message that the keys to the B2B kingdom are theirs for the asking.

The dinosaurs are elated and rush out to form their own online buying cartel. Sound too good to be true? You're right.

A Question of Durability

Considering the requirements for a successful Net mania, see how Customers' Do-It-Yourself Business-to-Business (DIY B2B) schemes stack up.

On the NetTime calendar, precedent suggests that a fully successful Net fad must be capable of enduring at least nine months or so before it, too, is discredited and blown to smithereens (Killer Modelz, preceding chapter).[13]

Third-party (independent) B2B took off in autumn 1999, with the "Day of Reckoning" at the end of March of the following year, when the Prudential Securities analyst report warned about future revenue sources. As of late spring 2000, the two-month-old e-infrastructure mania was still going strong, with the possibility that *optical* networking infrastructure and services could split off and start their own three-quarter-long run.

Why do we believe that Customer DIY B2B might not have the same durability? To start with, some of the consortia announcements seem long on press-friendly sound-bite fluff. And very, very short on specifics about how they will work and how they will make money—little details like that.

Note that we say "some"—we refuse to be drawn into the one size fits all simplicity pitfall of the instant Net pundits who feel obliged to paint everything B2B all black or all white. Enron's highly successful online businesses have no similarity to Old Economy businesses scrambling into the DIY gold rush.

This Time, High Valuation
Only After It Works

There are some particularly vexing problems associated with many of the B2B DIY approaches by dinosaur firms:

1. Another Big Number Big Problem

    No, not the multi-trillion-dollar research house guesstimates described earlier in this chapter. Big number problem here refers to the (estimated) 20 to 25% or so savings that many of these consortia set unconsciously as savings objectives at the time of the buy-side consortia announcement.

Such optimism might seem to be fully justifiable from the perspective of financiers and deal packagers eager to generate some deal volume from the new, new concept.

But questions immediately arise. Are those targets based on realistic, achievable performance? At a minimum, check out for yourself whether the touted "savings" range is based on specific investigation for that industry group and also for the specific companies and people involved. Look at those operations as they exist today, not after some hypothetical step improvement to be achieved someday in the future.

If those answers are unsatisfactory, it is likely that "the numbers" may be momentarily persuasive, but wholly unachievable—Dot-Com fiction created by an analyst bolting one general ratio against total spending.

A 20 to 25% savings range looks rich to us. Merely combine purchase orders with your archrivals, and the maximum realistic savings look to be more like 7 to 10% tops. Even the smaller may be difficult to achieve. For carmakers, for example, a major supplier of multi-component assemblies such as Dana Corp. can and will argue convincingly that they are already pricing at the minimum level, and that paring back revenue to them merely jeopardizes the buyers themselves.

If an auto manufacturer needs to secure Dana's cooperation to help further reduce the new product development cycle to narrow that advantage still held by the Japanese, then depleting the suppliers' development funds is hardly the way to achieve that.[14]

If the initial 7 to 10% in the 25% savings goal is achieved through sheer market power directed at smaller suppliers, government action becomes a real threat. The remaining 15 to 18 points must result from a combination of internal efficiencies (read: staff firings and elimination of overhead and processes) and software-based improvements. Let's concentrate for now on the first. Without the discipline of a merger (impossible when major rivals are cooperating in the same online buying business), tough reality is that such savings are probably an impossibility.

2. Last Generation Operations

This problem is also near the top of the list, deliberately. Prudential Securities' Crook and Infobank's Sadd both describe B2B as software driven, which means that the massive procurement departments with maze-like flow charts and four-deep bureaucracies immediately find themselves to be like fish out of water.

Preferred supplier programs, administered through advance ordering software and other automation reduces the role of the procurement relationship manager to a near-irrelevant role. When supply can be boiled down to an ideal of, say, five key sources for 80% of all purchases, then the CEO is the relationship manager by choice and necessity, since he or she squares off against his or her counterpart.

Unless the DIY B2B procurement group has ignored its regular job for years and just concentrated on developing pacesetting market exchange and network software (they didn't, or they'd be fired), they awaken to the radically different situation where their skills don't match the goals ahead. Double-staffing by bringing in software pros from the independent third-party e-procurement firms jeopardizes the buy-side consortium's profit structure.

3. Deja Vu: Are Megabuyer Cartels the Next
    "Strategic Alliance" Illusion

> *At this point, they're only announcement-ware.*
> Net Market Maker (NMM) chief executive Kevin Jones,
> CNBC, June 7, 2000

Call us cynical, but we've seen the result too many times. The zingy and clever new business fad enthralls suits who are persuaded by ego rather than logic that it's that easy to create a new billion dollar high technology company from scratch.

Before netPhase I, the result was often the hollow celebration "strategic alliance." Tolerated as a PR event at best, the stylish underperformance of the strategic alliance is recognized by everyone in the corporation (except the CEO) almost instantly. But jobs are scarce and no one dares tell the Emperor that he has no clothes. Not until a plain talker like AT&T's C. Michael Armstrong cuts through all the fog and invites the visionaries who emphasize form over function to "explore other opportunities."

Guess what! The same mistake is happening all over again! Just replace the phrase "strategic alliance" with "industry supply group." For managers broadly viewed as Net victims awaiting elimination, the Empire strikes back. The senior manager of the dinosaur company can scarcely believe his luck. Not only is there now an instant answer to the board's insistence about "becoming an Internet company," but it's in a preferred Dot-Com darling sector.

For now, the demise of netPhase I proved that gravity does exist for the Dot-Coms. It sometimes just takes a while to burn off the fad's froth. Dinosaur managers are disappointed to discover that mere participation never ensures Net success.

4.   Regulatory and Antitrust

Finally, there's legitimate issue concern about regulator scrutiny. The spinners always insist that everything is on track for government agency fast approval, which is exactly what you'd expect them to say. But others oppose the view that regulatory approval or buy-side megacartels will be straightforward.[15] Some issues relating to regulation and antitrust are addressed further on in this chapter.

Amateur Night Ended with Phase I

Bottom line is that the do-it-yourself giant customer B2Bers had better enjoy their 15 minutes of fame because it only gets tougher after the announcement.

But the period immediately following the megacartel announcement now is the hiatus, before the requirements for specific performance begin to separate pretenders from the achievers. Before those who naively think that just acting together as a buying force but nothing more constitutes a viable business plan discover the awful truth.

It doesn't. Besides, *too* overt exercise of buying influence by traditional rivals invites regulatory scrutiny or worse.

It is also during this hiatus that some Old Economy Dot-Com dinosaurs out of their league discover unhappy truths. Their function is not competitive with the operations of the pure independents. They lack the focused emphasis on e-procurement software platforms and buying network management to sustain a viable e-business.

Amateur Night is over in cyberspace. That message was underscored with the termination of netPhase I in Spring 2000. Post-Spring Break 2000, living dead Dot-Coms are like children suddenly forced to compete with the grown-ups. Say so long to temporary Net companies. And their cash.

ISSUES, CHALLENGES ON THE B2B "BUY" SIDE

The emerging regulatory environment for independent B2B third-party companies affect the "buy" side B2B—online procurement—first and worst.

But it isn't just Fed concern about bitter rivals becoming too chummy that threatens to pop this bubble. Price-based competition is tough and getting tougher daily. The ideal of preferential customer access to the lowest price from many competing online sellers is alive and well in the dreams of the developers of new wraparound software. But whether such industrial shopbots present a major threat to the e-procurement leaders in the foreseeable future remains to be seen.

Don't Say the "R" Word,
(And Don't Even Think the "A" Word)

> cartel 1. Also called *trust*. A collusive international association of independent enterprises formed to monopolize production of a product or service, control prices, etc.
>
> —The Dictionary

Regulation. So there, we've said it. The "A" word is even more onerous: *antitrust.*

Both *R* and *A* are e-procurement issues. Says VerticalNet's chairman Mark Walsh, "*That's* a concern to the [e-procurement] "buy-side" businesses. Not us—we're the 'selling side,' helping companies in vertical industries to grow their sales revenues."[16]

He has a point. Customer DIY enthusiasm is directed first and foremost at e-procurement. It is of course just a coincidence that US antitrust laws tend to be highly specific (and punitive) when it comes to sell-side collusion: When a group of major market participants get together to fix prices in the marketplace, one or more of them are invariably asked to change their address to Kansas for ten years, five with good behavior.

We're certainly not lawyers. But some of those who are suggest that antitrust guidelines are far less developed on the "buy side" than "sell side" around the globe but particularly in the US. Combine that with the misperception among enrolling DIYers that they can achieve 7 to 20% purchase savings just by starting a buy-side business with archenemies, and the emphasis on e-procurement is no surprise.

Getting together with your archrivals to collaboratively cut purchase costs for the mutual benefit of all is the stated thrust of most of the DIY buy-side approach, although never expressed in quite that manner. So if there is any future action to try to limit large companies' potential to exert market power by acting together as purchasers, it is the independents who would expectedly benefit the most.

Mark Hoffman at Commerce One, Keith Krach at Ariba, and Jim Conning at Infobank are all well-positioned to step into the breach should authorities act to significantly limit the market clout operations of customer-DIY megabuyer cartels.

Peter Pervere, CFO of Commerce One, stresses the importance of Big, as in developing the biggest, most extensive buyers' networks possible, or working with the largest partner companies. No withering in the face of DIY competition here.

But as the pace of global consolidation accelerates, the percentage of buying controlled by leaders in key industries also increases, raising concerns from some about the exercise of market power.

In a megabuyer cartel, the possible problem arises that exercise of extra buying power normally occurs only if the leaders in that industry companies merged. Management doesn't even try that, as it knows that a turndown would be instant. Question: so why is it suddenly permissible for the same two companies to conduct their coordinated procurement programs, just as if the prohibited merger occurred?

We suspect that these are among the questions being asked now, and that the need for clear answers about this new form of multi-company cooperation will be required soon.

In the early days of these megabuyer cartels, the new organizations are still in the congratulations-all-around stage, with impolite issues such as those cited here still far enough beyond the hazy horizon to be ignored for now. But circumstances can change, particularly if smaller suppliers can make a convincing case that their businesses were driven to the wall by an exercise of concentrated buying power that would be dismissed as impossible just one decade ago.

Industrial Shopbots for E-procurement: the Ideal, the Reality

Internet shopping robots ("shopbots") have inflamed imaginations ever since the concept first emerged as a commercial prospect in the mid-1990s. The ideal is that each buyer secures the best possible price and terms for the item desired. Worldwide and automatically via software, without human intervention.

In its ideal, the shopbot is the much fantasized Market-of-One made real. A single purchaser acting with the speed advantage and scale of an entire marketplace.

But shopbots become commercially viable only when an accessible markets exist. When sellers permit probing software to determine whether that consumer or industrial seller is first, third, or worst. Great for the leader, fiercely opposed by those with higher prices.

Shopbot threatens to disrupt traditional seller-buyer relationships by raising the prospect of lower prices from somewhere else, easily accessed. But if the buyer goes to the shopbot first, then it is the shopbot software company that controls the relationship with the end-buyer. Which helps to explain why retail sites such as AuctionWatch find themselves under pressure and consistent blockage attempts from firms such as EBay.

It isn't merely the prospect of losing a customer to a competitor site that has the lawyers working overtime. The threat is far worse, at least in the "losing" Dot-Com's views. For if retail or B2B customers become accustomed to making the shopbot their first stop, every purchase is effectively subject to competitive bidding. Even if the threatened Dot-Com prevails, prices are slashed and thus margins. The control of the account is significantly reduced, even if the traditional seller somehow manages to maintain control of the key account. For other industrial sellers gazing at B2B as a bright opportunity, shobots represent a rude awakening.

Softbank Venture Capital's Bill Burnham predicts that the B2B shopbots will eventually blow open the doors to industrial exchanges of all types. E-procurement tends to get the lion's share of the attention because of size and relative maturity. Burnham contends that B2B shopbots are also poised to have a major impact on B2B "sell-side" exchanges, as well. The former Piper, Jaffray analyst admits that there are numerous B2B shopbot companies in his company's portfolio.[19]

Burnham's prediction of an early and imminent death for organized exchanges clashes with the facts: growth of both (1) independent e-procurement exchanges served by third-party companies and (2) consortia B2B e-procurement exchanges. The movement toward e-exchanges is accelerating, not decelerating.

Far from being expendable, the exchanges perform an essential role: identifying, qualifying, and collecting the various supply sources worldwide.

Burnham's point about the future importance of online to "sell-side" transactions is well taken, however, particularly online services that help find the special supply source that otherwise eludes "terrestrial" sources.

Finding and securing the hard-to-find sources that are better/cheaper/faster than participating buyers' normal supply is the key to the entire exchange, regardless of operator.

Without these new special sources, the usefulness of the exchange declines. There is little reason for the new participants to join the exchange, as the familiar "good old boy" network operates just as well for that purchaser, with superior privacy. One thing leads to another. As buyers begin to trickle out, so do the sources in a continuing downward spiral.

Underestimating the importance of this sourcing function in the e-procurement exchange is as great a mistake as underestimating the importance of editorial control and influence of key opinion setters in vertical marketplaces.

Yes, some decades in the future a wired world will emerge with all supply sources linked, analyzed, qualified, and fully participating following a standardized format. With an equally robust set of ubiquitous buyers armed with tools that permit them to navigate the complex purchase of different items, amounts, and quality as easily as buying single item purchase from a local source.

Someday, but only in the distant future. If the extreme claims and subsequent crash of netPhase I teaches anything, it is to be wary of overreaching technologies that suggest a utopia that seems too good to be true. It is.

ISSUES AND CHALLENGES ON B2B's "SELL" SIDE

Two prime challenges will help separate the Phase II leaders from the others just struggling to maintain minimal funding and P/Es: First, effectiveness in creating new barriers against entry. Second, success at extending momentum into Web-based sales and marketing.

Building New Barriers

Excessive entry is the value poison that can render the otherwise highly effective Net business worthless. Excess entry means fragmented market shares too small to sustain anyone. The characteristic winner-takes-all pattern that epitomizes revenue-poor markets emerges, again and again, where chronic conditions of excess entry persist.

Excessive entry reduces the effectiveness of advertising and promotion spending on which both B2Cs and B2Bs business case often relies. Even if the pursuing firm "wins" the business, excessive entry means that far more had to be spent on marketing and sales than originally budgeted. The major account has been won, but so what? Factor in all the costs, and the previously profitable account has been transformed into a money-loser.

Excessive Entry and the B2Bs
(Third-Party Vertical Marketplace Operators)

Once viewed to be a problem primarily limited to B2Cs, excessive entry also emerges as a key challenge for B2B vertical industry market makers as well, where entry by two different groups of entrants multiplies the degree of crowding in this market.

First, there are the single industry experts with the personal reputations and visibility to bring those groups along with them. Chemdex (original name of Ventro) was among the most visible of these special expertise verticals, focusing on the chemicals sector. That success spawns a variety of single-industry verticals in almost every field. The allure is undeniable. Scientists and managers possessing arcane, in-depth knowledge and contacts (which they sometimes share for no payment) suddenly learn that this data may be stupendously valuable.

Then, some of the single industry companies expand, as investment bankers and others advise that a too-narrow B2B community may lack enough appeal and future to go public. Never mind that the one industry specialist may go beyond its expertise and competence by moving into unfamiliar verticals. Analysts are likely to miss that point, choosing to see only the extra revenues from opening new verticals.

Still one more source of unchecked market entry is from groups organized around the concept of *community*. Although they pursue vertical industry targets, the perspective is that of a general market formula applied regardless of the vertical market. Process prevails over specific expertise and trade experts, who are added later.

Independent, third-party vertical industry market makers fall into all three categories. VerticalNet's 55 trade communities fall into 12 industry categories, including many of prime interest to rivals, such as advance technologies, communications, food and packaging, healthcare, manufacturing, and metals.[20]

The Best Defense Is . . .

How best to defend existing vertical market positions? Whether a 12-categories leader or a single industry specialist, the key strategy is the same: remove as many market entry points for prospective rivals as possible.

Tactic 1: Further Enforcing the Trade Expertise Advantage

Not surprisingly, some of the smoothest operating vertical markets mimic that industry's leading trade publications, with separate departments for editorials, classifieds (requests for proposals), news, key indices, new developments, even classifieds.

Of these, actions to inspire and gain the active cooperation of industry opinion-setters and respected editors are the most important. If an old bricks 'n mortar trade publication editor still lives in the world of yellow legal pads and one-to-one secretaries and even dictation, VerticalNet's implementation teams do whatever is necessary to ensure that the editor is comfortable first, prolific and productive next. Sometimes that means scribes furiously transferring the expert's thoughts and transcribing the data online, if the old cigar-chomping pro is not yet Net facile.

Capturing—and maintaining—that center helps lower costs considerably. Chairman Walsh contends that he can open an all-new vertical for as little as $300,000, a fraction of the level of his rivals. How? Standardized structure where possible. But far more importantly are the shortcuts to market instinctively known and protected by just a few insiders in that industry. These are the knowledge-bearers. They can become market developers as well, effectively cultivated.

Tactic 2: Going Horizontal

The sell-side online market operator who helps companies in that vertical approach to win business that was previously just a dream gains massive good will with companies eager to spend to expand their business and its profits.

But if the client sees the marketplace operator as someone primarily to help accelerate sales and nothing more, the result is lost opportunity along with lost revenue, cashflow, and value. The independent B2B firm has earned an opportunity to pursue existing clients on other bases. The message is clear: "We helped you with this area, we can help you in others." If that opportunity for a favorable audience is not being fully exploited in other areas (procurement, logistics, internal processes, online self-service replacements for staff costs), then value is being underachieved. Which means that opportunities are missed and left for rivals to exploit.

The Independent Verticals' Marketing Opportunity

Besides filling in that X by Y grid of horizontal services for today's and tomorrow's vertical industry groups, further development of the marketing center aspect of vertical communities screams out as a development opportunity, as value missed if not actively exploited.

Leaders such as Walsh become absolutely evangelical when it comes to their "sell-side" combination of tools for accounts within key verticals, offering proven services for hard-charging middle-sized industry warrior companies seeking to grow much, much bigger. These are client companies that are often run by an ex-salesman who just instinctively knows the difference between a solid leads-contacts-key arguments-close sequence that's going to work, and the canned package or naive positioning that will *not*.

On the Net, everyone is instantly aware that your marketing pitch is lousy. But even the pre-bankrupt online B2B service can cloak its limitations to fool some of the customers some of the time, at least. As a consequence, cyberspace overflows with marketing software and other services and tools, directed at mid-sized companies, the bread-and-butter of the vertical industrial community pacesetters.

There are the catch-all "office on a Web site" services that purport to satisfy every need of every business, everywhere, regardless of need or the existence of far superior "terrestrial" alternatives. From archival storage of company data and online fax services to finding risk management expertise. From back o' the envelope M&A analysis to master database lists for prospecting purposes.

There are the field sales force support programs, designed by sales pros. Packages claiming to help the top producers steal time and customers from the competition. Product description downloads, online expense report services, routing services for that saleperson with the impossible task of accomplishing ten priority calls in a single day.

And then there are the software and services that even displace some of the business-to-business sales force, especially when it comes to high cost-to-serve accounts. As in all online services aimed at the middle market, the challenge for survivors is to establish solid credentials before also-rans' services crush the image of the sector. Pedestrian M&A advice delivered online is still poor service. The "office on a Web site" survivor faces the challenge of ensuring that it is separated from the e-dress in the minds of key accounts. The press is already savaging the online office sites that pump out garbage business advice and services, just faster than their terrestrial bucket shop competitors.

WHAT'S NEXT?

There are 600 sites to link buyers and sellers. But two per industry are plenty.

Robert D. Hof,
"E-Marketplaces a Bloodbath, "
Business Week E.Biz, April 3, 2000, EB, 72

Consolidation, for a start. The post-netPhase I reality of allocated private funding means that the Number Ones or Number Twos in their respective B2B segments can expect over-investment, as long as agreed market measures and of course progress toward future profitability remain on track.

Over-investment because the financiers must be able to demonstrate that their own top-tier investments are viable to prevent the possibility of being closed down by *their* financing sources.

Challenge 1:
Developing New Approaches to Deal with the
DIY vs. Independent Marketplace Tug-of-War

Take the Independents versus Customers/DIY B2B war with a grain of salt. That Old Economy versus New Economy slant alone ensures massive biz-press coverage. Instant issues require instant answers, so such articles invariably proclaim an absolute winner, even when the answer is more complex.

The actual marketplace is less convenient. BOTH groups, DIY and independent leaders, will survive, as lesser companies unable to secure 40/40 critical mass disappear.

Never mind that the DIY business models for some of the consortia are seriously flawed. Earlier in this chapter we describe why the 20 to 25% expectations of savings that many of these groups announce may well be overreaching. But the stronger DIY groups are here to stay (regulators permitting). Management of these units faces a clear mandate from its boards to secure a privileged position in e-commerce for its firms.

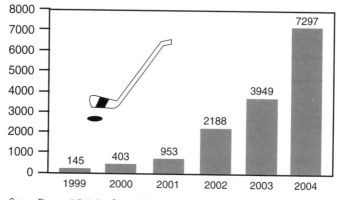

Source: Figures attributed to Gartner Group, Jan. 2000, from Wachovia Securities, Inc. equity research report of May 10, 2000 by Rogert G. Fontana (bob.fontana@wachoviasecurities.com), p. 3, Figure 1, Business-to-Business EC Forecast.

FIGURE 7.5. B2B e-commence, 99-04: The Gartner Group, Jan. 2000 estimates ($ billions).

Even if the buy-side cartel of the top three to four competitors commands, say, 60% of all the purchases in that industry, that still leaves a significant market share to be pursued by independent B2B companies that approach software as their first business, rather than as a sidebar.

The smart third-party B2B actually helps the DIY out of its dilemma because it is in the independent firm's self-interest. Since retreat will be slow for the reasons cited, the choice is either to work with these new combinations or be excluded from massive volumes of future accessible business.

One possible framework for DIY-independent integration is shown in Figure 7.6. In the rosy days immediately following the DIY's announcement (item 1), expectations soar. There is not yet any hard data to suggest that the ambitious savings objections are total fiction. At MegaBuyer's grand announcement ceremony, a principal confides that the eventual goal is to "go IPO."

Months pass (item 2), and the dreams of 20 to 25% savings begin to fade. That, in turn, endangers the ultimate objective of windfall wealth from an IPO. This isn't 1999 anymore, when profit-less Dot-Com wannabe businesses lacking the basic requirements for future success nonetheless won public market financing.

Aha, the possible structure suggested by one of the independents and its financial sources offers at least a partial answer to some of the struggling DIYs. The big three in that industry all effectively outsource their entire procurement departments to "New Co." (item 3), a separate, industry-specific e-procurement unit wholly managed by a capable B2B independent.

The third-party organization combines the three separate, battling archrival procurement organizations into a single operation, adding or deleting staff, procedures, network structure. The three "parents" effectively get out of the unfamiliar online business with at least some face saved.

Challenge 2:
Expansion by Acquisition:
B2B Indies Become Venture Capitalists

For unproven business-to-business independent (third-party) companies, the IPO door is closing or has already closed. But that

---

valueOUTPERFORMER
www.vbmresources.com

June 8, 2000

After the glad hands and smiles-all-round biz-press photos, some of the Customer Do-It-Yourself e-procurement megabuyer cartels find that actually implementing a Dot-Com business plan is far, far more difficult than the deal packagers told them it would be.

In computer equipment, steel, insurance, and several basic commodities, the DIY megabuyer cartel reality does NOT mean a leisurely sidebar business in which one confederation of bricks 'n mortar competitors reels in all the virtual trade profits that would otherwise revert to third-party firms. Rather, the reality is a future of market share wars of attrition with two to five other competing DIY consortia.

Problem is, the software and efficiencies required to prevail largely reside with those few companies that actually know how to run these complex, Netspeed e-procurement networks—not just how to churn out press-worthy announcements. These are the "indies": the leaders in the third-party, independent e-procurement B2B sector.

Welcome back, indie?

doesn't mean that the best of the post-April 2000 start-ups are automatically excluded from financing as netPhase II approaches. Remaining independent is another matter, however.

As Commerce One CFO Peter Pervere suggested in Chapter 6, financing sources have already started to change priorities: moving away from unproven speculative-investment caliber IPO candidates; and toward Phase II's projected champions. Picking winners instead of throwing a wide range of companies to the market wolves and hoping your portfolio contains enough of the 30% that will survive the *next* shakeout.

In the B2B sector, the established leaders become the financing conduits for many of these new companies seeking funds. NetPhase II markets have no tolerance for stratospheric valuations of companies that may not last two years. For the start-up, alignment with the more established B2B company from the start provides a built-in customer, plus central services and management help. There's the comfort factor of a company with established equity and analyst following.

The established B2B survivor-leader has already anchored its business model and is eager to cherry pick from the best of the new entrants in order to further differentiate their market offerings, and to further strengthen their argument to industrial customers that they lose a lot by going DIY.

The form of these netPhase II B2B combinations is still in the future. The B2B leaders' equity serves as the primary acquisition currency, which in turn underscores the importance of achieving profit commitments to sustain valuations. Slip the critical profit date forward and P/Es plunge and cost of acquisition equity soars.

But the netPhase II neophyte B2Bs needs cash, also. The established but still adolescent B2B is not usually a good source—not by itself. With burn rate awareness high and weakling Dot-Coms crashing daily, the netPhase I survivor must keep its cash and near-cash levels high to minimize any solvency concerns. Even before the Nasdaq peak, markets acted to destroy the valuations of companies suspected of being a viability risk.

All of which suggests a pivotal role for financiers to provide the extra liquidity for both new and established Dot-Coms. A no-more-financing-till-profitable policy sounds conservative but actually risks turning tomorrow's champion Dot-Coms into early bankruptcies. Not because their business models didn't work (they do). But because private financing sources lost their nerve.

Loans, converts, other vehicles directed at both the parent and the acquired company, initially treated as a subsidiary. Some creative structures emerge out of necessity, such as joint ownership of the acquired start-up by both the more established B2B and a pool of financiers. But don't confuse such a structure with ecubators: In this case, the equity vehicle is future shares in the more established B2B.

Some financiers who will be burned by netPhase I infernos will decide to sit out the next wave. This is understandable, as it takes many months for the 70%+ of Dot-Com failures to progress through the system. Daily news about the next Net collapse

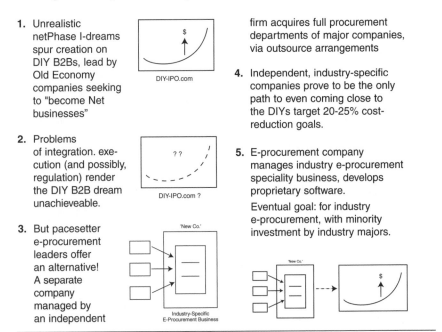

1. Unrealistic netPhase I-dreams spur creation on DIY B2Bs, lead by Old Economy companies seeking to "become Net businesses"

2. Problems of integration. execution (and possibly, regulation) render the DIY B2B dream unachieveable.

3. But pacesetter e-procurement leaders offer an alternative! A separate company managed by an independent

firm acquires full procurement departments of major companies, via outsource arrangements

4. Independent, industry-specific companies prove to be the only path to even coming close to the DIYs target 20-25% cost-reduction goals.

5. E-procurement company manages industry e-procurement speciality business, develops proprietary software.
   Eventual goal: for industry e-procurement, with minority investment by industry majors.

FIGURE 7.6. Helping achieve the procurement online dream: One approach.

hardly makes for a conducive environment for massive new financing.

But "Netspeed" also means responding to the new reality. The financiers who prosper the most will turn off the dead-and-dying stories of imploding Phase I companies and get down to the business of making sure that Phase II's potential champion companies have the means to excel.

Having been fooled by companies brought public before their time—some of which should never have come public at all—such caution is understandable. But standing pat can become the highest risk path during periods of dramatic change, rather than the lowest, as the wallflowers hope.

Challenge 3
B2B Buy Side / Sell Side Combinations?

Peter Pervere acknowledges that someday, even combinations involving buy-side (e-procurement) independents and their counterparts on the sell-side are inevitable. This is an opinion shared by Infobank's Graham Sadd.

Don't hold your breath. The sell-side leaders often seem to take delight in jabs at the "buy" side, and vice versa. Oversized egos tend to go with the territory.

But if the critical demarcation in B2B is between third-party firms and major customers who try to do it themselves, such eventual combinations make sense. The buy-side B2Bs try to strengthen themselves by diversifying their range and different revenue sources. On the sell-side, Ventro's CEO says that in order "to compete with horizontal exchanges, I knew I eventually needed to solve 100 percent of the buyer's needs."[21]

Notes, Chapter 7

1. Interview, April 18, 2000. Also, "Don't Write Off B2B as a Craze," TheStreet.com, April 22, 2000. Seymour (jim_seymour@zd.com) heads Seymour Group, an information-strategies consultancy.

2. From examples in authors' *The Value Mandate*, Chapter 8, "Unwinding the Crony Bureaucracy."

3. "Debunking the B2B Name Shell Game," valueOUTPERFORMER, www.vbmresources.com, VBM Consulting, June 6, 2000.

4. Adam Feuerstein, "Snookered by b2bstores.com," "Upshot," *Upside Today*, www.upside.com, May 26, 2000.

5. May 1, 2000, 50.

6. With emphasis on the word *interpreted*. In our discussion of May 22, 2000, VerticalNet chairman Mark Walsh was adamant that Safeguard Scientifics' departure from B2B was (i) grossly misinterpreted and (ii) irrelevant in any event because of the opinion-leading incubator's limited B2B holdings before the announcement. Regardless of whether Walsh's points are valid or not, the fact remains that the action was widely reported and interpreted as a flight from B2B. Refer to William M. Bulkeley, "Safeguard to Shift Investments Out of B-to-B Web Companies," *The Wall Street Journal*, April 10, 2000, 4.

7. "The B2B Boom: Memo from the Promise Land," *Fortune* (www.fortune.com), May 15, 2000. Refer to Figure 7.4. Also, Robert G. Fontana, bob.fontana@wachovia (securities.com), "Equity Research: Ariba, Inc," Wachovia Securities, Inc., May 10, 2000.

8. B. Reilly, D. Hope-Ross, J. Luebbers, E. Purchase, Gartner Advisory Group, February 9, 2000.

9. Figure 1.4 supports the use of DCF-valuation methods over either P/E or PTR (price-to-revenues). Nonetheless, we acknowledge that many investors and shareholders remain oriented toward the backwards-facing measures. Unfortunately for DCF supporters (VBM Consulting included), the disaster of discredited "Contaminated DCF" (Chapter 1) may dissuade companies from employing discounted cash flow methods using reasoned, defensible inputs, instead.

10. Greg Dalton (gregd@thestandard.com), "The B-to-B Math Problem, " *The Industry Standard*, www.thestandard.com, April 17, 2000, 61.

11. "B-to-B Ain't Dead Yet," www.thestandard.com, June 1, 2000.

12. "Hey, Let's Build a B-to-B Exchange!," April 18, 2000, 25.

13. B2C was still raging ahead as the quintessential Net category during late 1998, only to have its armor pierced around late spring of 1999. That's about the time that serious concerns first surfaced about some B2Cs' over-reliance on massive TV and billboard advertising in order to be heard above the competitive din.

14. Often lost in the DIY B2B instant business cases is the fact that key suppliers have often grown larger and more essential because of the combination of larger budgets, company preferred supplier programs, and component assembly. In more and more industries, the major source is closer to being a sub-manufacturer than a supplier based on old definitions.

15. Larry Dignan, "The Days Ahead: Why Some Consortia B2B Exchanges Won't Work," *ZDNet Interactive Investor*, www.zdii.com, May 15, 2000. At this writing, the Federal Trade Commission had not yet ruled whether GM, Ford, and Daimler-Chrysler could proceed with their consortia in the form planned. Dignan suggests that, "The auto honchos said that they expect approval from the [FTC] by September [2000]. Don't count on it."

    Even if approval does proceed, that doesn't mean the end of government scrutiny of megabuyer cartels online. The specter of cooperation by companies that normally duel to the death leaves a bad taste in the mouths of many. More to come.

16. Interview, May 22, 2000.

17. Interview, May 24, 2000.

18. One example: Bill Burnham, "Meta Networks Will Pull Apart B2B Exchanges," Burnham's Beat, *ZDNet, Interactive Investor* (www.zdii.com), June 1, 2000. Meta networks are the analyst-venture capitalist's term for what is referred to here as industrial or B2B shopbots.

19. "Meta Networks," (see note 18). Burnham, general partner of Softbank Venture Capital, just happens to note some companies that correspond to the meta networks (B2B shopbot) funded by SVC: Perfect.com, Syntra, and Hubstrom. Burnham is the author of *How to Invest in E-Commerce Stocks* (New York: McGraw-Hill, 1999).

20. Robert G. Fontana, (bob.fontana@wachoviasecurities.com), Equity Research, VerticalNet, Inc., May 5, 2000.

21. Quote from Rivka Tadjer, "The Trading Tango," *Red Herring* (www.redherring.com), June 2000, 427.

Chapter 8

AFTERMATH

The Commercial Internet's 1996 to first quarter 2000 period has been likened by some to "bubbles." If all the Dot-Coms were like Surfbuzz.com from the first chapter, we might agree. We might be willing to toss what we know about corporations being able to achieve solid value improvement by developing the right B2B applications as described in the preceding chapter.

But Surfbuzz is not the norm, as Alex and Brian Meshkin will tell you. One of the characteristics of this revolution that changes everything is that the same wave that sweeps in Cisco, Juniper, AOL, and Ariba also temporarily sustains pretend businesses such as Surfbuzz. And sometimes, sustains clones upon clones upon clones of e-commerce auction, books, urgent travel, jobs, and vertical B2B marketplace sites.

But the rubble of netPhase I does not detract from the emerging reality of Net champions. These are the companies that set the pace in their segments. The companies that are foundation members of all-new industry sub-groups that didn't even exist five years ago.

Bubble? The collapse of netPhase I was more like Dot-Com liposuction, with the unwanted fat finally being extracted forcefully by a market that had become tired of cyberbrats long before.

Bubble? Not quite. Geoffrey Moore suggests that "when a bubble pops, there is no residual substructure on which to build."[1]

All that's left at Surfbuzz are some empty pizza boxes. But lumping together Surfbuzz and other non-investment quality (NIQ) hubris with Dot-Com future champions and referring to them all together as part of a single bubble is dead wrong. When *this* bubble "popped," it was not a situation of nothing left afterwards. Rather, whole industries were formed.

Cisco created one server-based industry and is moving fast toward creating another. Firms such as Commerce One and Ariba transformed newsy stories about $150 dollar pencils into solid savings. And of course, amazon.com proved that it could all work, but not without bumps along the way.

For every wild-eyed investment banker who brought a pre-bankrupt Dot-Com to market, for every bizarre "Contaminated DCF" model used to foist e-dross on a gullible public, there were and are other financiers with the guts to confront conventional logic that says you only finance businesses that assuredly can become profitable in 18 to 24 months. But the financiers who lead the way into netPhase II rely on solid valuation methods, not just whatever homespun fractural math the back office dreamed up the night before.

PRECONDITION FOR RATIONAL DOT-COM VALUATION: Distinguishing the Black Hole Company from Tomorrow's Dot-Com Champion, at the Early Stages

The 43% March-May, 2000 slumps in major Dot-Com exchanges worldwide broke the back of netPhase I and shattered Disneyesque valuation described in Chapter 1.

The various types of valuation alchemy—"contaminated discounted cashflow," PEG ratios, operations metrics unrelated to financial performance—shared a single purpose. That goal was to make temporary price spikes caused by managed markets, short floats, and other machinations *appear* to be permanent. Fluff valuation methods for fluff value.

Emphasis is on the word "appear." Illusory values were broadly attacked for more than a year prior to the Nasdaq peak of March 10, 2000, by reasonable observers alarmed at the prospect of manic, soar-'n-crash market behavior that might kill off the Net boom entirely.

Then Spring Break 2000 arrived. A child spoke and everyone knew then that the Emperor had no clothes at all. So now the world has been made safe for rational valuation again, right? Conservative-realistic DCF comes back—or perhaps it never went away.

Not quite, at least not yet. While the nightmare period of Make It Up/Make Believe non-valuation of Internet companies is over, credible valuators still face the major challenge of ensuring that flexible DCF methods can somehow emerge to deal with the puzzle of accurately valuing companies with initial massive negative cash flow. And in doing so, to help analysts tell the difference between tomorrow's Net champions and Black Hole/Dark Model losers.

The answer to the problem of separating cyber-wheat from the e-chaff is *not* a matter of devising yet another improbable metric with no basis for credibility beyond the suspect "new" label. *Old* DCF works, but only when loaded with equally credible inputs. [2]

BACK TO EARTH—HOW FAR?

When these things get down to 65-70 times earnings, maybe then we'll be getting near a bottom.

Ned Riley,
StateStreet Global Investment, on CNBC [3]

How far? More importantly, how soon?

The 34% reduction in Nasdaq Composite on high volume over five weeks after March 10, 2000, signaled no mere correction. Assume that the five-week Spring Break alone didn't get the full revaluation job done. And, that many crippled netPhase I Dot-Coms remained to be cleaned out, and a second plunge to a lower tier beckoned.

Gone are the days when momentum factors mean everything and valuation is irrelevant. Post-April 14, 2000, every market tick down brought the same question: Are these Dot-Com companies really worth 300 times sales?

Just the fact that valuation has gone from afterthought to obsession suggests the inevitability of a second valuation leg down. When most companies in the segment can't even be measured on a P/E basis but must rely on price times revenue (PTR), fundamental questions about viability lurk in the shadows. That's the steep price movement down that occurs when company survival becomes doubtful. When future viability becomes a gamble, the market reverts to valuing the company as a Black Hole / Dark Model disaster rather than as a segment champion. Salvage value, at most.

Ned Riley's comment above reflects the sentiment held by many that maybe these Dot-Coms should someday settle back down at P/Es that are customary for high technology companies. Obviously, that range changes over time. In Figure 8.1, we refer to 70 times as an approximate top threshold (D) of historical high-tech P/E ranges.

But we suggest that a collapse down to those Legacy Technology P/Es may be too pessimistic. Thus in the figure we refer to a "Super-Tech" (C) eventual range of around 70-130 times. Pragmatic valuation compared to Dot-Com past, with at least some connection with market values, has been achieved historically by past high-tech leaders.

The argument in favor of the Super Tech premium shown here is that there has to be some extra valuation for the Net's commercial impact. In the Legacy Tech category (D), one finds everything from memory chip makers working on a new design to the next PC replacement. The point is that "regular tech" often faces an uphill battle in addressing the key question of "how can this create extraordinary value for customers?"

At least in part of the Dot-Com spectrum (see Chapter 7), there are some answers to that question, and thus an argument for an additional premium over yesterday's high tech company valuations, expressed in P/E form for illustration purposes here.

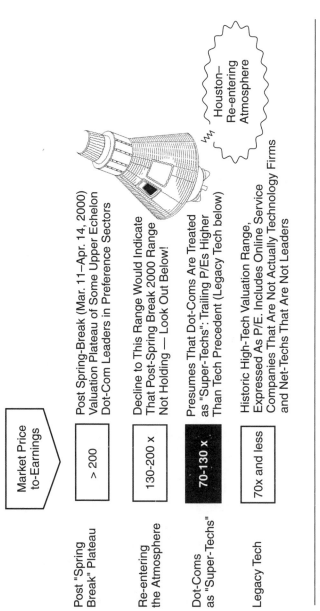

Market Price to-Earnings

Post "Spring Break" Plateau — > 200 — Post Spring-Break (Mar. 11–Apr. 14, 2000) Valuation Plateau of Some Upper Echelon Dot-Com Leaders in Preference Sectors

Re-entering the Atmosphere — 130-200 x — Decline to This Range Would Indicate That Post-Spring Break 2000 Range Not Holding — Look Out Below!

Dot-Coms as "Super-Techs" — 70-130 x — Presumes That Dot-Coms Are Treated as "Super-Techs": Trailing P/Es Higher Than Tech Precedent (Legacy Tech below)

Legacy Tech — 70x and less — Historic High-Tech Valuation Range, Expressed As P/E. Includes Online Service Companies That Are Not Actually Technology Firms and Net-Techs That Are Not Leaders

Houston—Re-entering Atmosphere

FIGURE 8.1. Back to earth: How far?

NETPHASE II VALUATION SPLITS: "DOING AN AMAZON" IS DISPLACED BY "DOING A CISCO"

> *The critical point for EBay and QXL is that only one of the survivors
> is likely to command a very high valuation.*
>
> *Financial Times*, May 5, 2000 [4]

Once broad valuation ranges for Dot-Com companies are set, key differences are expected to emerge between the recognized segment leaders and those stragglers just trying to survive.

The valuation differences are still to be determined in most Net segments, where both leaders and laggards are unprofitable and expected to stay that way until 2002 or later. But in Net infrastructure, Cisco System's reported P/E as of June 6, 2000, was 170 times, with Lucent Technologies at 54 times.[5]

In unstable markets where the pattern of dominance is not yet set, markets struggle to make the critical distinction between tomorrow's highly profitable Dot-Com segment leader and the Black Hole/Dark Model chaff at the other extreme, with a series of tiers in-between. As the segments stabilize that is, as at least some companies prove that they can operate profitably, ranges tend to narrow.

It is the *relative* valuation difference between the top tier of companies in a Dot-Com segment and other firms that is critical to future growth.

Even if overall Dot-Com valuations settle at "Super Tech" ranges (that are still a full tier lower than May-June post-Spring Break levels), the key factor is the leader's advantage in relative valuation. Higher P/Es mean cheaper equity—a potent weapon for consolidating the segment. The primary mechanism for growth through Net-to-Net acquisitions.

At this writing, Net-to-terrestrial acquisitions are still problematic because, first, there are so few historical reference points, and second, the effective forced reduction in Dot-Com value is so severe (see Chapter 1). AOL's effective 30% discount to acquire

Time Warner is not the only factor that makes such deals difficult to pull off. If the Net-terrestrial combination is imposing enough (such as AOL-TWX), the result can be prolonged regulatory delays and strategic drift. Whatever the reason, we expect the major emphasis to be on acquisitions within the Dot-Com segments.

Net companies fighting to establish credentials as top tier valuation leaders are now poised to acquire smaller competitors and even some Net start-ups that might have gone public during netPhase I.

Why? First, to accelerate the acquiring Dot-Com's rate of growth. Second, to fill voids, such as the third-party B2B vertical marketplace company that presently sells only two products to the industry it "owns" when there's the potential to sell six or eight. Leave that void open, and someone else fills it.

And finally, to prevent rivals in the same segment from winning the race to dominance. No one knows whether that particular Dot-Com segment will sustain one, two, or three global leaders— the companies clearly perceived and valued above all others in that segment.

The lowest risk assumption is that there will be only one King of the Hill. Remember past spin from late market entrants that the sector is growing fast enough to support many, many competitors? Forget it—netPhase II's champion acts as if its segment is a zero sum contest: acquire or be acquired.

If *"Doing an Amazon" was the war cry during the Net's B2C-dominated first phase, then "Doing a Cisco" is the wail during consolidation-oriented netPhase II.*

Donlan's May 8, 2000, article on Cisco Systems in *Barron's* focuses on the genius of the integrated internal/external expansion blueprint that helped put Cisco at the top of its segment. Instead of using acquisition as a fallback when internal growth strategies disappoint, growth slows, and Cisco's coordinated approach emerges as an alternative. Each acquisition is seen as a possible *alternative* for organic growth, and possibly the preferred path if market share and proprietary technology can be acquired in much less time than through internal development.[6]

NETSPEED AND THE FALLACY OF "OUR TURN NOW"

The pace of Net change is set by the swiftest and most effective worldwide. This undermines regions' attempts to establish protected Me-Too Net industries by cloning. The market just moves too fast.

Pressure to create robust national Internet industries is tremendous. Prosperity, jobs, national prestige, and reputations of politicians and management are all at stake.

Trouble is, the Internet respects neither territorial boundaries nor time. As a consequence, it is very easy for nations to err when it comes to selection, pace, and/or timing of Net initiatives. The result can be whipsaw when regions jump into sectors just as they are changing from Dot-Com darlings to Dot-Com dogs (Figure 8.2).

"Let's Just Borrow Their Business Model"

Companies and countries seek to develop their own potent domestic Net industries. High income, non-polluting, high growth—what's there not to like?

The preferred path is the same that has worked well in the past: copying successful models elsewhere, then adapting them for local conditions. This is how industries from cars to airlines, from communications to computers, have spread worldwide. Culture, language, and if possible, regulations help insulate those countries' baby industries in their most vulnerable years.

But the Net isn't at all like any of those other industries. Time—*Netspeed*—is the critical difference. Net product/service life cycles are a quarter to a third of the duration of many "terrestrial" products. Six months is how long it takes some Old Economy companies just to make a single major capital decision. By contrast, six months may represent an entire product life of a fast-changing part of the Net.[7]

Physical barriers of entry erected by national governments are hilarious in the case of software transmitted online. In interlinked online global financial markets, when New York gets a cold, Hong Kong sneezes.

The Risks of Choice Just Increased

Cloning the winning business model while that formula still works is never easy, even in periods of slow-creep evolution. But in Netspeed markets, that difficulty is multiplied tenfold. Yesterday's stellar business sector (B2C, B2B) becomes today's turk-e—then tomorrow's star again but in a different configuration, for a different market.

Regional/ national pride brings the desire for geography-bound Internet companies. But despite the valid argument of separate cultures, the pace is set by the world leader, which is always a threat to invade that foreign market.

"It's our turn to participate in the Internet boom" is the cry heard often. But non-US tech exchanges tend to be even more volatile than their US counterparts (Figure 5.2) with the result that Japanese and Indian companies have participated fully in Spring Break 2000.

Some Internet companies based in Japan (JPN) and India (IND) with 50% or greater decrease in market capitalization from peak, in Spring 2000*

<-50%

-44.5%	Yasumitsu Shigeta (Wireless Internet, JPN)
-76.7%	Hiroshi Fujiwara (Net Research Institute, JPN
-73.6%	Masatoshi Kumagai (ISP, JPN)
-75.3%	Azim Hasham Premji (Software, IND)

Note: * Based on year 2000 highs in Feb–Mar, 2000 versus late May 2000.

FIGURE 8.2. It's our turn now . . . to be chopped down by the end of netPhase I plunge.

valueOUTPERFORMER
www.vbmresources.com

March 21, 2000

Adapted from
MEEKER ON EMERGENT TWO TIER DOT-COM VALUATION

When the phrase "two tier market" arises, assumption is often made that the subject is Price to Revenue (PTR) or Market Value to Revennue (MVR), the difference between Dot-Com high fliers and so-called Old Economy companies. While Dot-Coms MVRs soar at levels that exceed expectations and sometimes credulity, MVRs for Old Economy stars of the past in fields from insurance to distribution languish. But a MVR valuation gap pattern also emerges within the Dot-Com category, suggests Mary Meeker.

Meeker raises this Dot-Com valuation leadership group point in addressing the controversial issue of VeriSign's recently announced acquisition of Network Solutions. Analysts at this time are roughly divided equally between those who denounce the deal as value-demolishing overpayment versus those who instead see a solid value-building shrewd move. The Morgan Stanley Dean Witter analyst is clearly in the latter camp. She is quoted in a March 21 transmission from *The Industry Standard* (www.thestandard.com) as stating that

> We continue to believe that it is crucial to be the leading company in an Internet sector in order to create long-term value. The large discrepancy in valuation multiples between companies with leading market positions and those that are No. 2, No. 3, or No. 4 in their sectors [illustrate] that the Internet leaders generate more than their share of value, both in revenue and shareholder value. America Online, Yahoo, amazon.com and EBay have been prime Internet examples of companies showing us that "to the victors go the spoils."

Meeker's point underscores our contention that companies commanding a relative valuation advantage in their segment have the advantage in adding external growth to internal growth as Dot-Com consolidation accelerates.

Struggles of Net IPOs such as lastminute.com and World Online during the week of Mar. 13, 2000, suggest that while Dot-Com blue chips (such as the firms Meeker mentioned) have the means to reshape their sectors through prudent but aggressive combinations, the low MVR stragglers probably become lunch.

Yesterday's projected high profit Dot-Com business model (browsers, Internet Service Providers, possibly Web hosting in the future) becomes "future profit-challenged" in spin-doctor speak, just a couple of years later.

The Economist's Frances Cairncross had it half right. Her 1997 book *The Death of Distance* describes a world where instant communications render national boundaries irrelevant. Add Netspeed to that equation, and the potential of difficulties and losses for Net laggards becomes massive.

Sluggish Europe responds to the B2C opportunities a full year-plus behind the scorching pace of the US and is six to nine months behind the pace in many B2B sectors.

Freeserve, an Internet Services Provider, is proclaimed by some analysts in 1999 as Europe's showcase Internet company. But in the US, viability of the dial-up consumer ISP business model began to crash as early as 1997. By 1999, even the most eager Never-Met-an-Internet-I-Didn't-Like venture capitalist shied away from the ISP model for the simple reason that it is profitless today and probably tomorrow as well.

At the time of the Nasdaq's peak on March 10, 2000, Europe's Net portfolio was crowded with out-of-favor, pedestrian B2C companies. The US moved nine months earlier, away from B2C and headlong toward B2B and online infrastructure. Hong Kong's slow clone problem is similar: by the time the Me Too is devised, the global market has already shifted.

Negative Payback

It is wrong to think of these timing gaps as harmless. Hong Kong's very accommodating GEM junior securities exchange permits shares of Internet companies and shells with no business plan at all to be floated, with highly-publicized buying panic mania in the first few months of 2000. Even by loose netPhase I standards of comparison, the Asian Happybang.com's look absolutely frothy. When capital markets contract, the clone Me-Too markets are the bubbles that pop first and loudest.

(NEAR) DEATH OF THE SPINNERS

One of the more conspicuous aspects of Spring Break 2000's aftermath is the changing role of the corporation's communications specialists, those spin doctors who focus on influencing all perceptions, on all matters Dot-Com. You didn't actually think that those CEO interviewees on CNBC learned that they should never answer a question directly all by themselves, did you?

---

valueOUTPERFORMER
www.vbmresources.com

JUNE 16, 2000

THOSE OTHER KINDS OF DOT-COM MERGERS

In the aftermath of Mar. 10-Apr. 14, 2000, Spring Break and end of the netPhase I momentum market (confirmed by volume statistics since), Net M&A news has mostly focused on forced consolidations involving early burn rate victims. CDNow, one of the first on the Willoughby List to admit problems, titillated the Market with deal news that caused the company's now single-digit share price to temporarily surge (CDNow's peak during Dot-Com prehistory, 1999, was $22.70). Finally, CDNow management warns that even if the firm IS acquired, any outsider's offer may well be below present share price. Not exactly what current shareholders want to hear, and a reflection of tough PIPE (Private Investment in Public Equities) terms being extracted these days from cash-challenged smaller Dot-Coms, now effectively excluded from the public financing market.

No, no, no, you've got it all wrong. The real estate magnate who prospers is the one who is expanding while others contract, acquiring all the prime properties right as all the small players around him are collapsing. What we are not seeing (yet) are the Big Dot-Com to Big Dot-Com (Big Net2Net) mergers between segment leaders and cross-segment, with both merger partners having adequate financing for the time being, thank you. Not desperation deals of the news-grabbing small Dot-Com burn rate variety, but rather, bold moves to radically restructure entire Dot-Com segments. Actions to accelerate external growth while setting the stage for a future secondary market for segment-champion blue chip Internets as vibrant as the VC-IPO netPhase I structure will succeed.

The spinner is the one behind the curtains who pushes the button that sends the jolt of electricity at just the right time, preventing the chief executive of troubled e-Bankruptcy2001.com from responding directly to questions about the company's future.

He's also the internal apologist who tries to do the best he can in dealing with questions such as "if the Dot-Com wasn't overvalued three months ago as you adamantly insisted, why then is market value halved now?" Which was the under-, and which was the over- valuation (Prepare yourself for the standard issue-long treatise on volatile markets, assuming that spin sticks to the topic at all.)

Some spoilsports have become so unreasonable that they suggest that in the nanosecond Dot-Com change era, the spinner is an anachronism. With multiple online bulletin boards and print and cyber-columnists all seeking their own distinctive angle on every topic, one thing's for sure: every topic is flooded with instant opinions from every side.

For every exposé declaring (with as few facts as possible) that the Old Economy companies will be taking over all of B2B and will have the independents for breakfast (Chapter 7), there is another spinner who takes the opposite position. Without the spinner to guide perceptions toward the interpretation that favors his client, investor-shareholders might actually (gasp) be forced to think for themselves to look only for hard facts about confirmed performance.

Aha, but with your eagle eye you notice that we speak only of the *near* death of spinners. For as with other simple life forms (primordial ooze comes to mind first), the corporate spin doctors for Dot-Com matters demonstrate remarkable powers of survival.

Some of the more competent ones are even able to rise above the competitive threat of instant, unspun data on the Net by developing their own command of the black science. Heaven forbid that we might ever suspect Spin of taking advantage of the openness of online site chat rooms to plant positive fog about his client, or delicious doubts about his client's enemies. Never.

THE WARNING. THE OPPORTUNITY.

(An accelerated clean-out of weak Dot-Coms is) a natural process of trying to figure out which companies will succeed. . . I don't think that there are any indications that the industry is in anything but a strong upwards growth trend.

Economist Stephen Levy, June 2000 [8]

The opportunity: A new netPhase II order focusing on champion companies rather than raw start-ups, as the Net grows up. But delayed transition to this new order threatens the Net juggernaut.

It is time to clean out the Phase I hubris quickly and deliberately. To clear the market of NIQ companies that should never have come public at all, in order to make room for others that can excel.

We conclude with some observations from Jeff Bronchick, Chief Investment Officer of Reed Conner & Birdwell. In a way, Bronchick presents us with both a warning sign as well as a hint of future opportunity. Figure 8.3 is developed from the same data Bronchick referred to in his May 31, 2000, piece for TheStreet.com. [9]

His point is that the Dot-Com boom and bust cycle seems to exert a direct wealth effect on general prosperity in the US (*Is that a Qualcomm-financed pick-up truck you're buying for Christmas 1999, Bubba?*). The officer of the LA-based money management firm raises the point that Wall Street and Main Street are joined at the hip. At least according to this data, quakes in the tech-heavy Nasdaq mean aftershocks soon afterwards at Tiffany's. Even at Wal-Mart.

Now it may be true that margin debt wiped out Bubba GreaterFool in mid-April 2000, so the connection shown in Figure 8.3 may be moderated somewhat going into the future. But let's assume Bronchick is on to something. That surges and collapses of companies in Silicon Valley and Silicon Alley are not just some economic curiosity, but rather, the American economy's coming main event.

Bronchick sees this type of effect involving more and more companies, as Andrew Grove's mandate of becoming a Net company (or else) is taken seriously. "Let's say I have a company selling online help desk software. In a slowdown that might "just" be 20% revenue reduction directly. But that same firm can easily find itself losing three-quarters of its revenue foundation because of multiple market impacts."

He continues, "Some sales are lost directly—because lower Net activity wipes out budgets. But then there are other, secondary, revenue effects, not because that first account is tapped out, but because ITS customers are suffering from lower Net activity and won't pay or can't. And a third effect. And so on. You get the idea."

Jeff agrees with us on a key point: Dot-Coms slipped into a transition period sometime after the 34% March 10 to April 14, 2000, Nasdaq Composite plunge. Where we seem to differ with Jeff is in how long this transition period between crazy, permissive netPhase I and the somewhat more structured and sedate Phase II might take (some suggestions about how netPhase II could evolve are suggested in Chapter 6).

Jeff suggests that if the Net mentality turns 180 degrees away from the optimism and excess of 1998/1999, it might not be until 2001 that the Dot-Coms make the full transition to the next Internet phase.[10] That's the warning, because it is probable (to us) that such an extended interim period would have serious effects.

But we're not so sure that that's necessary. Thinking of the Wall Street-Main Street linkage Bronchick makes, we wonder if concerted efforts to clear out the e-dross and refinance and revitalize the strong Number One or Number Two candidates in key Dot-Com segments can't help compress the transition period and help bring the beginning of the new Net era sooner.

How? Some of the structural and financial paths are described in Chapters 6 and 7. The real opportunity has to do with acceleration. With how fast financiers and analysts are able to move beyond netPhase I as if it never happened, into the new opportunity ahead.

Accelerating the transition to netPhase II calls for active culling of all the companies that cannot become sector dominants. This includes companies that were placed in the IPO pipeline but that now have little chance of leading their industries, their segments. Active culling means taking the initiative to remove these walking dead Dot-Coms before they collapse, poisoning market sentiment with disaster headlines.

Will those Dot-Coms affected claim that this is a jolting change in the rules of the game, as they were set up back in the halcyon days of Phase I? Of course they will. Are they right? Of course they are. Does it matter? No.

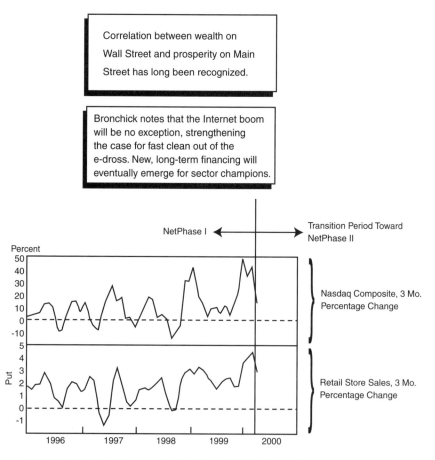

Correlation between wealth on Wall Street and prosperity on Main Street has long been recognized.

Bronchick notes that the Internet boom will be no exception, strengthening the case for fast clean out of the e-dross. New, long-term financing will eventually emerge for sector champions.

*Source: Nasdaq and US Census Bureau as presented in Jeff Bronchick, "The Next, New, New Thing," Commentary: The Buysider, TheStreet.com (www.TheStreet.com), May 31, 2000.

FIGURE 8.3. The case for clean-out, strengthening-up: Bronchick's linkage.

There's no sense at any time in bringing a non-investment quality company public—not a firm whose long-term viability is still highly questionable. Nor is there any provison for initial or post-IPO financing for *any* company that cannot mount a serious challenge for dominance in its sector.

Another key dimension of a deliberate, active agenda to speed successful transition to netPhase II is accelerated development of the Dot-Com sector leaders. A futher key requirement is the creation of a mechanism for post-IPO secondary financing for Dot-Com blue chips, marking a full transition away from netPhase I's VC-IPO financing structure. It means e-cubators within Net champion companies, reducing Dot-Com IPO risk with a built-in customer-supplier link, a customer relationship, and a path to future profitability—far beyond just front-end start-up funding.

NetPhase I was dramatic and erratic. The Dot-Com first phase created billionaires in 1999 and Dot-Com cemeteries one year later. Most important, netPhase I set the stage for the next period of sustained, accelerated growth. It's just the beginning for tomorrow's true Dot-Com champions.

Notes

1. Geoffrey Moore, "Approaching the Chasm," *The Industry Standard*, www.thestandard.com, May 15, 2000, 87.
2. Key point from book's first chapter is that traditional discounted cash flow methods could have performed a greater role in the valuation of netPhase I prospects, but only if such valuations are done without the contortion that comes with trying to use DCF to justify top-heavy temporary valuations. Objective DCF methods and conservative inputs showed many Dot-Coms to be grossly overvalued in January-February 2000, a reality that was soon confirmed.
3. "Portfolio Tracker," May 31, 2000
4. "QXL," "The Lex Column," 24.
5. Source: Yahoo! Finance, June 7, 2000.

6. Noel M. Tichy, Stratford Sherman, *Control Your Destiny or Someone Else Will: How General Electric Is Revolutionizing the Art of Management* (New York: HarperCollins Publishers, 1993), 61-62, 89-90.

7. Chapter 7 of *The Value Mandate* deals with challenges of operating under conditions of continually shrinking product/service life cycles.

8. Quote from Ben Charny, "Dot-bomb Deluge: Is Net Shakedown Only Natural?," *Upside Today* (www.upside.com), June 7, 2000. Levy is the director of the Center for the Continuing Study of the California Economy and took the opportunity to try to look at the Spring Break 2000 collapse and its aftermath in the context of the overall future course of the Dot-Com movement.

9. "The Next New, New Thing," Commentary: The Buysider, TheStreet.com (www.thestreet.com), May 31, 2000 (jbronchick @rcbinvest.com).

10. VBM Consulting, interview with Jeff Bronchick, June 1, 2000.

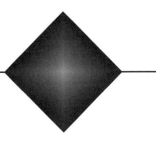

Glossary

Black Hole Start-up company requiring massive front-end and continuing investment but headed down the tube

B2B Business-to-business e-commerce segment

B2C Business-to-consumer e-commerce segment

B2G Business-to-government e-commerce segment

B2B buy side Companies offering business-to-business e-commerce service, primarily to buyers of goods and services (e.g., e-procurement)

B2B sell side

Bubba GreaterFool Companies offering business-to-business e-commerce service, primarily to sellers of goods and services (e.g., e-procurement) industry-defined vertical markets. Individual investors eager to buy anything Dot-Com, who often find themselves being the ultimate holders of shares dumped by others in a market collapse

Dark Model Company with little or no possibility of future profitability or viability

DCF Discounted free cash flow, considered by many as the most reliable method for determining corporate value

ecubator Development-oriented holding company, which seeks to nurture online start-ups and then sells (all or part) in an initial public offering

EPS Earnings per share

etailers Online retailers

Exotics Homespun make-it-up-as-you-go-along guesses about what might change shareholder value—almost always with no solid proof

FMA First move advantage

IPO Initial public offering

ISP Internet services provider

M&A Mergers and acqusitions

Mo Momentum

Modelz Dot-Com business models with no real substance and less credibility. Projections ready to fall (see *vapor*)

Nasdaq Composite peak Refers to the peak of the Nasdaq Composite index on March 10, 2000

netPhase I Initial boom phase of the Commercial Internet as described here, roughly from 1996 through the first quarter of 2000

NIQ Non-investment quality—refers to overvalued companies that should not have gone public

Net-to-Net acquisition Acquisition of one online company by another, e.g., AOL/Netscape

Net-to-terrestrial acquisition Acquisition involving both an online company and a traditional, or "terrestrial" company, e.g., AOL/Time Warner

Nosebleed valuation Excessive, unjustifiable valuation, common during netPhase I

P/E Market share price to earnings ratio

PEG P/E, divided by annual revenue growth rate

PIPE Private Investment in Public Equity

P2P Path to profit

PTR Market share price to revenue ratio (used by necessity when company has no revenues)

Scalability Capacity to support far greater level of service with little or no extra investment or development

Seventy percenters Companies with a 70+% probability of failure or insolvency, probably before January 1, 2002

Spring Break Five-week period of Nasdaq Composite's precipitous decline, March 10 to April 14, 2000

Vapor Elusive value that exists only in the mind of the beholder

VC-IPO Venture capitalist IPO

Willoughby's List Refers to companies singled out in Jack Willoughby's March 20, 2000, "Burning Up," article in *Barron's*.

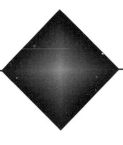

About the Authors

Peter J. Clark and **Stephen Neill** are partners of VBM Consulting, an international organization helping client firms worldwide to maximize shareholder value—through specific strategies and actions aimed at the five principal source areas within the corporation.

Peter J. Clark joined Stephen Neill and VBM Consulting as a partner in the late 1990s and has nearly two decades' experience with major consulting organizations worldwide. His first book, *Beyond the Deal*, set a new direction for the pursuit of corporate maximum value by emphasizing key actions in the principal parts of the business where value is created. An MBA graduate of Southern Methodist, Peter is based in New York and London and can be reached at: peter.clark@vbm-consulting.com.

Clark is the author of *Beyond the Deal* (1991). Steve Neill and Pete Clark are co-authors of *The Value Mandate*, also published by Amacom (Autumn 2000).

Stephen Neill is a founding partner of VBM Consulting, with more than a decade's experience working with management at all levels of client organizations to help those groups achieve their maximum value. Based in London but working on assignments worldwide, Stephen worked with two other shareholder value-oriented consulting groups prior to forming VBM Consulting. A recipient of a Master's of Philosophy in Economics from Cambridge, Stephen can reached at: stephen.neill@vbm-consulting.com.

Index